Necronomicon

Caspian Sea

Mediterranean

Euphrates

Tigris

Alexandria

Shaalon

Damascus

Babylon

Monastery of the Magi

Memphis

Persian Gulf

Thebes

2nd Cataract

Nile

Red Sea

Irem

The Empty Space

Yemen

Sana'a

Alhazred's Wanderings

DONALD TYSON

Necronomicon

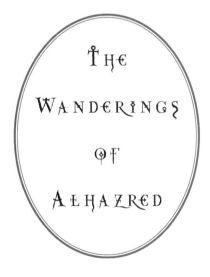

THE
WANDERINGS
OF
ALHAZRED

Llewellyn Publications
Saint Paul, Minnesota

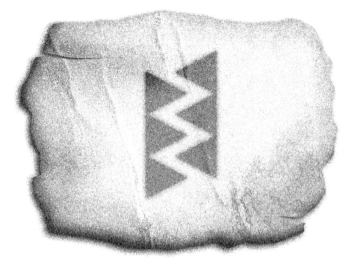

FIRST EDITION
First Printing, 2004

Book design by Rebecca Zins
Cover art (bugs) © PhotoDisc
Cover design by Kevin R. Brown
Interior illustrations by Gavin Dayton Duffy

Library of Congress Cataloging-in-Publication Data
Tyson, Donald, 1954–
    Necronomicon : the wanderings of Alhazred / Donald Tyson.
        p. cm.
    ISBN 0-7387-0627-2
    1. Magicians—Fiction.   2. Middle East—Fiction.   I. Lovecraft, H. P. (Howard Phillips),
1890–1937.   II. Title.

PR9199.3.T94N43 2004
823'.914—dc22

                                                                                                    2004057750

Llewellyn Worldwide does not participate in, endorse, or have any authority or responsibility concerning private business transactions between our authors and the public.
    All mail addressed to the author is forwarded but the publisher cannot, unless specifically instructed by the author, give out an address or phone number.
    Any Internet references contained in this work are current at publication time, but the publisher cannot guarantee that a specific location will continue to be maintained. Please refer to the publisher's website for links to authors' websites and other sources.

Llewellyn Publications
A Division of Llewellyn Worldwide, Ltd.
P.O. Box 64383, Dept. 0-7387-0627-2
St. Paul, MN 55164-0383, U.S.A.
www.llewellyn.com

Printed in the United States of America

Table of Contents

List of Illustrations x

Prefatory Note by Olaus Wormius xi

Concerning the Life of Abdul Alhazred by Theodorus Philetas xv

Howlings in the Desert 3

Rapture of the Empty Space 7

Lustful Demons and Angry Demons 13

The Eaters of the Dead 17

Many-Towered Irem, Its Wonders and Pitfalls 21

The Dweller in the Caverns 25

The Lost City Beneath Irem 29

The Starlit Chamber of Seven Gates 33

The First Portal, Leading to the Plateau of Leng 37

The Second Portal, Leading to the City of Heights 41

The Third Portal, Leading to Sunken R'lyeh 45

The Fourth Portal, Leading to Yuggoth 49

The Fifth Portal, Leading to Atlantis 55

The Sixth Portal, Leading to Kadath 61

The Seventh Portal, Leading to the Temple of Albion 65

What May Be Safely Written of the Old Ones 71

Yig, Corresponding with the Sphere of Saturn 75

Yog-Sothoth, Corresponding with the Sphere of Jupiter 81

Cthulhu, Corresponding with the Sphere of Mars 87

Azathoth, Corresponding with the Sphere of Sol 93

Shub-Niggurath, Corresponding with the Sphere of Venus 97

Nyarlathotep, Corresponding with the Sphere of Mercury 103

Dagon, Corresponding with the Sphere of Luna 109

The Great Seal of the Old Ones, Known As the Elder Seal 115

The Underground River A'zani 119

Memphis, City of Mummies 123

Concerning the Tombs of Wizards 127

The Uncanny Ways of Cats, and Their Cult 131

The Riddle of the Sphinx Interpreted 135

The Resurrectionists in the Storehouse of Kings 139

The Essential Salts and Their Use 143

The Valley of the Dead 147

Walking Corpses Above the Second Cataract 153

The Book Markets of Alexandria 159

The Ziggurats and the Watchers of Time 165

The Tower of Babel and the Fall of the Watchers 171

The Ruins of Babylon 175

U'mal Root and Its Manner of Harvest 181

The Valley of Eden 185

The Wisdom Seat 189

The Monastery of the Magi 193

Inner Grounds of the Sons of Sirius 197

The Secret Purpose of the Magi 201

Why the Stars Are Not Right 205

The Thing Beneath the Library 209

Why the Old Ones Do Not Die 213

Concerning Shoggoths 217

The Formula of Yug 221

The Well of Life 225

The Relic of the Hebrews 229

Wanderers on the Road to Damascus 233

The Rite of the Companion 239

Terms of the Covenant with Shub-Niggurath 245

Soul Bottles 251

The Lane of Scholars 255

The Secret of Damascus Steel 259

The Burial Ground at Damascus 263

The Conclusion to the Journey 267

Illustrations

Map of the region iii

Alphabet of the inhabitants of the city beneath Irem 31

Seal of the moon of Yuggoth 52

Lunar hieroglyphs on the recumbent stone
      of the temple of Albion 68

The seal of Yig 77

The seal of Yog-Sothoth 83

The seal of Cthulhu 90

The seal of Azathoth 95

The seal of Shub-Niggurath 99

The seal of Nyarlathotep 105

The seal of Dagon 110

Hieroglyphs on the black pillar of Dagon 112

The great seal of the Old Ones 116

The seals of the ziggurats 166

Signs of the seven lords of the Old Ones 248

Prefatory Note

by Olaus Wormius

ANNO 1228

Regarding the work known as Νεκρονομικον to the Greeks, or transcripted into the Latin letters, *Necronomicon*, having become exceedingly rare and difficult to procure, and then only to be had at great price, it seemed no unworthy task to translate it into the Latin tongue; not that its matter offers anything to edify the mind or provide moral instruction, for its contents exceed in wickedness all other books in Christendom; only for the reason that it holds secret wisdom that would surely pass away were this book to fall prey to worms or the fires of the censorious, as seems likely will occur to those few Greek texts that survive, and that, within the term of those presently dwelling in this land; the clergy of late railing against this accursed book as written by Satan himself.

The true author of the text, I will let the scribe Theodorus Philetas, known as the Wise to history, relate in due course in his opening words of the Greek manuscript that is the source for my rendering. Here it is my purpose to expound on the nature of the book and to relate the unfortunate circumstances surrounding the death of the worthy Theodorus above named, his death in itself a sufficient warning to the idle curious, for this work is suitable only for the deepest intellects wedded to Christ in the Holy Spirit and will corrupt all who seek to turn its arcane lore to base ends. It is a sword poisoned with nightshade that cuts the hand that seeks to seize it, but one with godly purpose and subtle touch may cradle it like a sleeping serpent without receiving its venom. Only he who has no love for it can use it.

The veritable sense of the title of this work is commonly misunderstood and misspoken by those ignorant of Greek roots. It is from νεκροσ, signifying corpse, and from νομοσ that has the sense of law or custom; hence, *Necronomicon* has the meaning "the expositing of the ways of the dead," and what is intended is the control and working of the dead through the sorcery of corpses that bears the common name of necromancy. The ways of the dead, and secret matters known only to the dead and those with whom they have dealings, are here set forth in such abundance as exists in no other book.

Upon these leaves are to be found accounts of living creatures beyond the higher spheres, of lost cities and other places forgotten by the memory of mankind; yet more pernicious still, the manner of summoning souls of the dead back into their mortal clay, and eliciting from them by means of torment secrets that lie hidden at the roots of the world, in dark caverns and beneath the depths of the seas. Here also are instructions on the making of things quickened with a semblance of life, that were better left unmade, but cannot be unmade having been created. All of which would be reason to consign this book to the depths of hell, were it not that beings of fell potency dwelling between the stars, offering threat to the very continuance of our race, are to be in some ways controlled by the teachings of this evil work. So in the Devil's machinations lie the practical tools of our salvation on that dread day, which by the grace of our Lord shall never come, when the stars are right and the gates open.

To return to the most diligent and learned Theodorus, he completed the Greeking of this book in the city of Constantinople, for know you that the elder copies were all in the tongue of Mohammed, and the title was not *Necronomicon* but *Al Azif*, supposedly signifying in that language the sound of insects heard in the night, but vulgarly expressed as the howling of demons, seeing that the night sounds of the desert were mistaken for demon voices by the heretic nomads of those lands; but Theodorus gives a different rendering from the Arab, which I will leave for your eyes to discover.

Theodorus, who was called the Wise for his devotion to arcane learning, tells that he made translation of the work from the single copy in the Arab script that survived the worms; to me came much richer fare, for I have had the good fortune during my lifetime to have pass through my hands three manuscripts of the Greek text, and of the truest of these paid to have a fair copy made, which I compared in every detail with the original. From this Greek copy the present Latin wording was derived with all due care, and it is my promise to you who read these words that nothing of the original text was excised, nor anything added to it by way of gloss; for it is often the case that those who copy are not content but must comment on the work, and for this reason many of the manuscripts of this book are corrupted by the words of other men unknown to the composer.

Reports having spread throughout Constantinople of the nature of this book, which was never seen in Christendom prior to its rendering into Greek, raised such a hue and cry against the worthy Theodorus by the clergy and the population of the city that he was forced to stand on the steps of the great church and denounce the work of his own hands as devilish, and to publicly beg forgiveness of Christ for his sins, and then to burn the parchment bearing his translation. For this act of contrition, the people of Constantinople were mollified, and ceased to call for his death; yet his book did not die, for other copies had been made, and these spread abroad and multiplied under numerous pens, for the lust to possess so rare and strange a work was great, be it never so damning to the soul, and so it continues to this day.

The fate of Theodorus is well-known—how he lost his wealth and lands; forfeited his honors in the emperor's court; saw his wife and three sons taken by plague in the space of a single season; and succumbed to that most horrible of afflictions, the disease of lice. It is writ by pious scribes of the Church that as punishment for rendering the *Necronomicon* into the Greek tongue he was forsaken by God and the angels, and knew no day that did not bring misfortune, so great is the power of this book over the souls of the sinful; for only the godly may read it and remain whole in body and spirit.

A perfect century of years after the work of Theodorus Philetas was brought forth into the world, Michael Cerularius, patriarch of Constantinople, commanded that all known copies of the book should be gathered together in one place and burned for the greater glory of Christ Jesus. This was in the year of our Lord 1050. No Arab text could be found, but Greek copies to the number of one hundred and three score and eleven were piled and burned on the same steps where Theodorus had made his act of public contrition.

In this place I make no argument as to the wisdom of causing to be more prolific a book that an honored father of the holy Church sought to expunge from the earth. My conscience is in harmony with the love of our Lord. Only this much I will say: that knowledge once lost is lost forever, and who may judge that one teaching shall be useful in time of need, and another shall bear no value to men forevermore? May there not come a time when secret knowledge is sorely needed to fight the armies of darkness? Yet if all the books that teach it are burned, let men search in vain for the instrument of their salvation.

Keep you all copies made of this Latin text chained and locked. Let no man who reads it speak of its contents, and let no man who knows of it reveal its existence to the ignorant, who are unfit to carry so grave a burden. Before God and his angels, may the soul be damned of him who seeks to practice what is written in these leaves, for he has damned himself by the mere temptation to so horrible an act of defilement. Better his eyes were put out with glowing coals from the fire and his lips sewn tight with flaxen thread than he should read aloud the words in this book written in the forgotten tongue that was never meant to be spoken by the sons of Adam, but only by the others who have no mouths, and who dwell in the shadows between the stars.

Concerning the Life of Abdul Alhazred

by Theodorus Philetas

ANNO 950

The maker of this book, to which I give the Greek title Νεκρονομικον, as more descriptive of its content than its old styling, was born into a humble house in the city of Sana'a, in the land of Yemen. His family name has been lost, but he is universally known by the title Abdul Alhazred, signifying in the Arabian tongue the Servant of the Devourer. Nor is the date of his birth known, but his death is said to have occurred in the year of our Lord 738, when he was in the extremity of old age.

In early youth he found renown both for piety, as a faithful follower of the teachings of the prophet Mohammed, and for poetic invention. He is reported to have been handsome in face, with uncommonly white skin and green eyes that caused wonder at his birth, seeing that his father was dark in both face and eye. Talk arose that his mother had lain with a jinn while crossing the desert by caravan on her way to be wed, but her extreme godliness confounded this rumor. Alhazred possessed a body tall and straight, with grace of movement likened to that of a fine horse. Most remarkable was his voice. When he recited the words of the Prophet, the birds paused in their singing to listen, and desert foxes came forth from their dens and sat upon mounds to hear the teachings of God.

Learning of this child wonder within the bounds of his kingdom, the ruler of Yemen summoned Alhazred to his court when the boy was in his twelfth year. He was so taken with the beauty of the youth, he made offer to Alhazred's father to keep the boy with him and have him educated by the same palace tutors who instructed his own sons. In this way Alhazred was raised as a prince of the royal court, and had the love of the king as a second father. The only price expected of him was the composition of poetic verses, which he sang for the enjoyment of the king and his counselors.

In his eighteenth year Alhazred began to love one of the daughters of the king. Had he controlled his passion, it is likely that the king might have been persuaded to give his daughter to the young man in marriage, but love knows no boundaries in its reckless course, and Alhazred took his pleasure with the girl, who conceived a child. The discovery of the affair roused the fury of the king, who had the infant strangled at birth. For his act of betrayal, the poet was punished by mutilation. His virile member, nose, and ears were cut off, and his cheeks scarred. Alhazred was compelled to watch the unholy fruit of his union with the princess roasted over embers on a spit, and was made to eat portions of the flesh of the infant corpse. The king hired desert nomads to carry him eastward into the depths of the *Roba el Khaliyeh*, the Empty Space as it was known to the ancients, where he was left without water to die.

The ordeal cost Alhazred his reason. The king had ordered all who traversed that desolation to shun him and refuse him aid, in the expectation that he would soon perish, yet he clung to wretched life. For an unrecorded span of time he wandered the desert, scorpions and carrion hawks his companions by day, and by night the demons who dwell only in such barren and hateful lands. These spirits of darkness taught him necromancy and led him to discover forgotten caves and wells that run deep beneath the surface of the earth. He renounced his faith and began to worship antediluvian titans adored by the desert spirits who were his guides and teachers.

He embarked on a mad quest to restore the mutilated and excised members of his body, so that he might return to Yemen in triumph and claim the princess as his bride. With magic he disguised his face so that it appeared that of a normal man, and abandoned the wasteland to scour the world for arcane wisdom. In Giza, in the land of Egypt, he learned from a secret cult of pagan priests with shaven heads the way of restoring life to corpses and commanding them to do his bidding; in Chaldea he acquired perfection in the arts of astrology; from the Hebrews at Alexandria he acquired the knowledge of forgotten tongues, and the use of the voice for the utterance of barbarous words of evocation, for though all his other graces had been stolen away from him by the malice of the king, the beauty and power of his voice remained.

After roaming the wide world in search of some magic that would restore his manhood, in bitterness of heart he was made to accept his repellent condition, since it could not be mended by any potion or spell or object of power discovered in the course of his wandering. From his maturity until the end of his life Alhazred lived within the walls of Damascus in great luxury, freely pursuing his necromantic experiments but shunned and abhorred by the inhabitants of the city, who regarded him as an evil wizard.

It was during his residence at Damascus that he composed the work he titled, in a fit of mad humor, *Al Azif*, the chittering of insects, or by another interpretation, the drone of beetles; yet because of its contents, the book was familiarly known as the howling of demons, seeing that the night sounds of the desert are mistaken for the cries of spirits by the common peoples of that place. The work was penned during his final decade at Damascus, around the year of our Lord 730.

The manner of his death is strange, and scarce to be believed, save that it is no more unlikely than the story of his life. It is reported that one day while buying wine in the market square, Alhazred was caught up into the air by some invisible creature of great size and strength, and his head, arms, and legs were ripped from his torso and devoured, so that all his body vanished from sight in pieces, leaving only splashes of blood upon the sands. So his own flesh became the final tribute to the dark gods he worshipped.

In rendering this work into the Greek tongue, I have remained faithful to the words of Alhazred. The task has been difficult, since in places the meaning is obscure even when the words themselves are plain, but whether this is due to the lingering madness of the writer or to the strangeness of the matter he expounds I am unable to resolve. It suffices that enough of this work may be understood after careful study to supply the seeker of hidden wisdom rumination for a lifetime.

On certain of the leaves of the Arab manuscript are to be observed cunning symbols invisible beneath the light of the sun. These pale and silvery tracings, which are only plainly to be seen when lit by the rays of the full moon, are overwritten by black script to disguise, as I believe, the existence of these designs from the careless gaze of the curious. By what mysterious concoction of ink they are painted onto the parchment, I know not, and so could not reproduce them in my own book as they exist in the older book; yet have I made careful copy of each design and inscribed them in common dragon's blood for all to behold, either by sun or moon.

My work is done. I care nothing about its censure, for my thoughts are at one with the will of my Master, the ruler of this earthly realm, who commands the high and low places, and moves both within the stars and in the wastes that lie between. As a tribute to my Lord, I offer this book to true seekers after wisdom who remain steadfast of mind and courageous of heart. Here are found keys to power beyond reckoning and knowledge yet unspoken by human lips. The wise will use it with circumspection and fools will be consumed. It is sufficient that this book continue to exist in the places of men, so that when the stars coincide it shall make itself known for the use of one destined to wield its potency. Farewell.

Necronomicon

Howlings in the Desert

You who would learn the wisdom of hidden things and traverse the avenues of shadow beneath the stars, heed this song of pain that was chanted by one who went unseen before you that you may follow the singing of his voice across the windblown sands that obscure the marks of his feet. Each who goes into the Empty Space walks alone, but where one has gone another may follow.

Turn not your mind from night fears, but embrace them as a lover. Let terror possess your body and course through your veins with its heady intoxication to steal your judgment, your very reason. In the madness of the night, all sounds become articulate. A man sure of himself, confident in his strength, aware of his rightful place, remains forever ignorant. His mind is closed. He cannot learn in life, and after death there is no acquisition of knowledge, only unending certainty. His highest fulfillment is to be food for the things that burrow and squirm, for in their mindless hunger they are pure, undefiled by reason, and their purity elevates them above the putrefying pride of our race.

By writhing on your belly in abject terror you will rise up in awareness of truth; by the screams that fill the throat unsought is the mind purged of the corruption of faith. Believe in nothing. There is no purpose in birth, no salvation of the soul in life, no reward after death. Abandon hope and you shall become free, and with freedom acquire emptiness.

The night things that hop and skitter and flit at the edges of the campfire glow exist only to teach, but no man can understand their words unless he has lost in fear the memory of his name. Two serving maidens will come to you when you lie alone, and will lead you to the place within yourself that cannot be known but only felt. These handmaidens are Terror and Despair. Let them guide you into nightmares that follow one upon the other, like windblown grains of sand, until they cover over the markers of your mind. When you have lost yourself in the wasteland of unending nothingness, the night things will come.

With hope utterly abandoned, all else will leave you, save only fear. Your name forgotten, your memories bereft of meaning, without desire or purpose and having no regret, you would cease utterly to exist and would become one with the greatness of the night were it not for fear. Let your terror be your standing place amid the ocean of darkness. From it you cannot retreat for it is all that you are become. Pure fear is undifferentiated, a smoothness without line or color; hence a man in the extremity of terror is united with all other terrified men; more than this, in the purity of terror he becomes one with all fearful creatures in this world or other worlds, both in this moment and in distant aeons of time, and in that unity wherein dwells the wisdom of all, his mind is opened, and the night things speak.

Pain is the terror of the body, and as the body is but a pallid reflection of the mind, so is the pain of the flesh no more than a distant echo of the terror of dreams. Even so, do not despise your pain, for it has its function. Pain anchors the mind to flesh. In the absence of pain, the mind would fly up and become lost in the spaces between the stars, and darkness would consume it. Just as the mind can lose all aspects of itself, but will never cease to fear, so can the body lose all strength and sensations or longing, but will always feel pain. While there is life, there is pain, and fear continues even when life is no more.

Despair is not separate from terror but is the consequence of the abatement of fear. When terror fills the mind there is room for nothing else, but when it withdraws in part, as it must do, for it ebbs and flows even as the tides of the seas, then the mind is left cleansed and empty, and this condition is called despair. In despair there is a void that yearns to be filled up. Let the night things fill it with their whisperings, and in this way grow wise in the secret ways of this world, and other worlds unknown to men.

Of all pains, hunger is the most useful since it gnaws unceasingly, like the worm in the tomb. It is the gateway upon an emptiness vast and endless; no matter the quantity or kind of food, it is never filled up. All living creatures are but embodiments of hunger. Man is a hollow tube, ingesting food at one end and excreting waste at the other. How is it possible for man to be other than empty? As it is for the body, so it is also for the mind. The natural condition of the mind is emptiness. All efforts to fill it are temporary diversions that fail to deny this truth.

To learn arcane wisdom is the simplest of tasks. Purge the mind with terror; purge the body with pain and hunger. Take yourself out into the empty spaces of the world that express in their limited way the same qualities as the empty spaces between the stars. The things that dwell there are ever watchful. They exist only to teach. After terror comes despair, and in despair the language of the shadows is intelligible. As you empty your mind of self, the night creatures fill it with their wisdom.

The wisest of these creatures is the black beetle that lives on the dung of others. Dead food is better than food that is living, since its essence is nearer to the ultimate state of decay to which we all tend. From corruption arises new life. Fill yourself with corruption and from it you shall be reborn, even as the fungi arise and glow with radiance on the faces of the dead who have rested in their tombs a span of years. Emulate the beetles and the worms, and learn their teachings. Eat of the dead, lest you be consumed by the emptiness. The living cannot teach the dead, but the dead can instruct the living.

In the wasteland dwell those things that cannot abide the light of reason. Even as man is a creature of the day, and ceases to know himself during the darkness, so do these things of the void cease to articulate their identity during the hours of the sun. They sleep by day and wake by night to feed. The terror of man is their nourishment and their excrement is higher wisdom. The dung of these things may only be consumed when the mind is made empty by terror and is in a receptive state of despair. Unless the mind be perfectly purged, their excrement will be vomited up and lost.

The exquisite rapture of hunger retains all foods, and extracts nourishment even from the husks of beetles and the castings of worms. Ingest wisdom with the darkness, and sleep by day.

Separate yourself from humanity, for what use have you for these pale, blinking fools and their ceaseless yammerings? In life they serve no function, and in death they are only food for the crawling creatures. Take yourself apart, embrace your fear, and listen to the darkness. Your teachers will come; as they appear before you, consume their wisdom. Grind their chitinous cases between your teeth and partake of their essence. The whirring of their wings and the rubbing of their legs is music. Consume all, even the other things that approach, those that have no bodies but only teeth and eyes that gleam in shadow. The crawling things instruct the body, and the shadow shapes teach the mind, but the wisdom of both must be consumed. There is only hunger in the universe. Devour everything.

Rapture
of the
Empty Space

The desert known as *Roba el Khaliyeh* is a lover of the dead and a hater of all things that have life. The creatures that dwell in the desiccated wastes of this Empty Space imitate the dead in all possible ways, and thereby steal life from the dryness. What are the qualities of the dead? They are cold and lie without motion within the earth, hidden from the burning sun; their skin is hard and black; at night they rise and wander far in search of nourishment to satisfy their ceaseless hunger and thirst. So it is with the living things that struggle to remain alive in the land of the dead. They lie beneath the earth, in caves or covered over with sand, during the heat of the day; they move little or not at all to conserve their fluids; their skin is hard and dark, their eyes dry and glittering jewels; only under the light of the moon dare they venture forth to hunt.

A man who would cross the wilderness of stone and sand must emulate the dead, even as do the creatures that live in the waste, for only by becoming as they are may he survive. At the setting of the sun, arise and go in quest of nourishment. Water is more precious than food, so always seek water, and food will cross your path without the need to look for it.

The life of the desert is an endless quest for water that renders other quests meaningless. When the paling of the east announces the dawn, dig a hollow in the sand and cover your body, or huddle in a cleft between rocks that is forever in shadow. Lie as one dead, and sleep out the day.

Seek the deepest depths between the rocks in the low places of the land where the sands have fallen inward, for there will be found moisture. Even when it is too attenuated to serve the needs of life directly, it may be had by sucking the juice of crawling things that concentrate the dampness within their shells. Corpses newly buried along the caravan roads are fat with water. The brain remains wet for weeks, as does the marrow of the bones. The blood of a hunter hawk is good, but the blood of a carrion bird may carry disease that cripples or kills the unwary. More wholesome is the flesh of serpents and worms, sweet to the taste and a glut to the belly.

In the deepest pits where water drips and pools, there flourishes a certain fungus that may be known by its color, for it is the green mingled with yellow of the pus from a newly lanced boil. This growth emanates a faint radiance that seems bright to eyes accustomed to the blackness of caves. It is of the length of half a forefinger, but from it emerge longer stalks containing pods of spores that break open with a faint sound, like the crackle of brush in a fire, when disturbed. Among this living carpet that covers the rocks and walls and roofs of caverns live small spiders of the purest white. As they move among the stalks, they brush them with their legs and cause them to open and spread their seed upon the damp air, so that in the silence deep beneath the earth there is an endless soft crackle that resembles stifled laughter.

To consume three of the white spiders transforms the power of sight, allowing demons and shades of the dead that wander the desert after the setting of the sun to be seen clearly with eyes, though these wraiths pass otherwise unseen. Three spiders, and three alone, must be eaten. Two is insufficient; four causes vomiting and sickness that persists for several days. Three yields merely a lightness and spinning in the head that is not so severe as to inhibit walking. It is the spores from the pods fallen upon the spiders that produce the second type of sight. By themselves the spores have no power, but when mingled with the secretions on the back and legs of the spiders they acquire this potency.

To sight fortified by this strange meat, the shades of the desert stand forth from the rocks and dunes with the whiteness of candle wax. Near the burial sites of

Bedouin caravans may be seen *lares* who retain their human form, though they go naked after death. These are mindless vessels that stand or stagger upon the earth above their graves, moving in circles and arcs but never venturing more than a dozen paces from the mound where their putrefying flesh lies buried. They have one use alone: to identify the place of burial when the desert nomads have attempted to conceal the place from ghouls and tomb robbers. No matter how well concealed the surface of the grave, the *lar* of the corpse stands watch above it.

When a grave is opened, the shade that is bound to it strives to slay the violator by seeking his throat or heart with its fingernails, or sometimes with its teeth, all the while emitting a faint keening cry that is easily mistaken for the sigh of the night breeze. Since these *lares* lack material force, they may be ignored without harm. They vanish the moment the brain, heart, or liver is removed from the corpse, though the cutting of the dead flesh and the removal of smaller portions of the body is not sufficient to dispel their presence. It is best to shatter the skull with a stone when first the corpse is exposed; having vanquished the troubling shade, the remaining viscera and organs may be handled and used without distraction.

There is another type of spirit, common in the rocky hills, that resembles a large wingless bat, but possesses the hindquarters and legs of a wild dog. Its mouth is unnaturally large for its size and filled with curved white teeth, like the bones of a fish, and its forepaws hairless and slender, looking like nothing other than the graceful hands of a dancing girl, save that they are ebon, with elongated nails. These creatures, that in their own tongue call themselves *chaklah'i*, move with great rapidity at a loping run across the sands, and hunt in packs any living thing that they find alone and unprotected in the waste at night. Their method of attack is to surround their prey so closely that their insubstantial bodies replace the air itself, so that the uncomprehending prey slowly smothers to death. Only then can they consume its vital essences, for they eat the dead and cannot abide the essences of the living. They consume the spirit of the flesh, not the flesh itself, but after they have eaten, the flesh holds no nourishment for the living.

A man possessed of the power of the second sight by consumption of the fungoidal spiders is able to make a pact with the *chaklah'i*, who much prefer to feed on corpses dead for several days than upon the bodies of the newly slain. These demons have not the physical force to move the ground protecting bodies that have been buried, but if a man shall move the stones and sand for them and allow them to feed unhindered, in exchange they will reveal secret places where treasures of various kinds lie hidden, or repeat knowledge long lost to the world. If it should chance that they seek to commit murder on the one with whom they have formed a pact, as commonly occurs, the utterance of the name of the guardian of the gates in the language of the Old Ones sends them scattering like dried leaves upon the wind. They pose no danger to the man who holds the power of this name, and may be useful as guides in the Empty Space.

These things speak not as a man speaks, by striking the air with his breath, but inwardly, as a thought that echoes within the mind. Their intellect is weak, but they remember all they have ever seen or heard, and they endure far longer than a man. Light they cannot abide, nor the camps and habitations of our race. The human voice is painful to them, and they fly from the sound of laughter.

With the faculty of the second sight, things that never possessed life of their own, but merely contained or conveyed life, may be clearly seen in the darkness across the sands. Caravan roads stand forth like ribbons of silver, and the domes and towers of towns long fallen to decay and forgotten rise against the starry horizon. These ghostly structures glow most bright under the energizing rays of the moon, but are dim when the moon is in her dark phase or not yet risen. They are most clear in distance but when approached waver and grow dim, until at last they fade utterly as the foot extends to cross their thresholds. By such shadows may be traced the wanderings of ancient races and their places of dwelling.

Upon the open desert are gateways in the form of whirling columns of iridescent dust. In the day they resemble dancing pillars, and by night glowing spires. They may be opened only at certain times, when the rays of the wandering bodies of the heavens and the greater stars conspire to unlock them. Their opening is by means of phrases chanted in an inhuman tongue, the words of which have geometric forms in space possessing length, breadth, and height. The *chaklah'i* know the words but do not understand their meaning or use. For a gift of blackened and putrefying flesh they may be induced to repeat them.

Such are the several beauties of *Roba el Khaliyeh*, which is death to a man for so long as he remains alive, but once he has become as the dead, emulating the ways of the dead, it is as nurturing and loving as a young mother toward her first child. Nor is it possible to dwell in the wasteland without learning its ways, for knowledge is rewarded but ignorance severely punished, and those who survive instruction become wise.

Lustful Demons
and
Angry Demons

When the winds blow soft across the sands, they carry the murmur of seduction kissed with promises of pleasure, but when they quicken, their howl of murderous fury will not be placated. The winds foreshadow the coming of demons that are borne alone in whirling cones of dust from other planes of existence. Both kinds are impelled by the same hunger, and seek to nourish themselves on the emotions of man, but the first is fed upon the sensation of arousal and the desire for carnal consummation, while the second fattens on fear. The second kind is more dangerous since fear is the stronger emotion.

The lover of the winds is beautiful to behold. She comes in dreams with her white arms extended and her long and glossy hair rising about her head, her smile sweet with orange blossoms, and her eyes deep wells of reflected starlight. A gown of the finest transparent silk adorns her slender body. Her fingers, neck, and wrists are bejeweled. What man whole in body can resist her allurements? She induces the nocturnal emission of semen during sleep, and feeds upon the odor and heat of the seed, bearing away a portion of its vitality with which to engender monsters in her womb, for these become her servants, and since they are possessed of a portion of material vitality, they are capable of tangible acts. When she visits the sleeper, they gibber and caper around his bed, pulling upon the hair and beard of their father and howling with glee.

Night after night she returns to her dreaming lover, who welcomes her embrace without complaint, his mind lulled by pleasure, until she has drawn out all he has to give and his heart ceases to beat. She is like the tar of the poppy that brings unfailing delight even when it causes death. Only a man such as those who guard the harem of the monarch, and have had their manhood removed by the edge of a knife, or have suffered a similar loss through violent misfortune, can resist the allures of this temptress. Since they have no seed to give, she is frustrated in her attempt and flies away, wailing and gnashing her teeth.

The howling demon comes with violence and seizes the mind of the sleeper, shaking it as a dog shakes a rat, transforming dream to nightmare. It has as many forms as the foes that inhabit the imagination, but is quick to seek out and discover the shape that is most feared. This becomes its vessel, or better to say its mask, for it has no identity of its own, only a hunger that must be appeased. When images alone fail to terrify, it causes cuts and welts upon the skin of the sleeper, which are discovered with the rising of the sun, but only for the purpose of eliciting terror, as pain alone offers it no nourishment.

Its purpose is to interrupt sleep so many times that the man who is its prey begins to dream while awake, and then it is able to come and go within his mind at will, and take whatever it finds there of value. The common consequence of the nightly visits of this demon is madness and suicide. Only by death can its torments be avoided. He alone is safe who has learned to embrace his fears as a lover, rejoicing in their multiplicity and power. Such a man welcomes the angry demons of the wasteland as his friends, and finds amusement and diversion in their change of masks. Recognizing at last the futility of the attempt, this demon departs in sullen silence, its fury stilled, and the wanderer in the desert sleeps and dreams without molestation.

By the seals of the gods from the stars, these two forms of night demon can be commanded and sent to vex others who travel across the Empty Space, and even those who dwell within distant cities, as a potent form of attack especially suited to the exacting of vengeance. The seductress and mother of monsters is obedient to the authority of the seal of Shub-Niggurath, the prolific goat; the angry demon obeys the seal of great Cthulhu, quick to fury.

Wait for the coming of the demon, as you lie within your dreams alert and aware, and before it commences its work, command its attention with the name and seal of the god under whose wandering star it dwells, whether bright and pitiless Venus or red-eyed Mars. The star of the god must be above the horizon, hence the best time to contract with the demon of lust is shortly before dawn. Compose the seal of the god in your imagination and picture it upon the air before you as you confront the demon, then give the demon instruction concerning the identity of the person it should vex unto death. Your purpose will surely be attained within the cycle of the moon.

The Eaters
of the
Dead

Caravans crossing *Roba el Khaliyeh* must bury their dead along the way, for in the heat of the desert a body soon putrefies, and in the span of two days no man could bear to stand near it, and no beast would carry it upon its back. The only exception is made when a person of wealth dies on the journey, for the family of the corpse has the means to cause it to be wrapped in rags saturated with honey, which has the property of inhibiting decay. The honey is used to fill the mouth, nostrils, ears, eye sockets, and other vents of the body, and provided every opening is sealed, the flesh may be preserved as it was in life for several weeks.

A man alone in the wasteland learns to follow the tracks of the camels, and to recognize the graves of those who have died along the way. The carcasses of beasts are of no use for food since these are swiftly picked clean to the bones by the creatures of the desert, but the corpses of men are protected by the earth and stones piled above them. The hungry traveler soon learns to trust his nose to guide him to his repast, and the glowing shade that stands above the place of interment, so clearly visible to the second sight, is a sure sign that his belly will soon be filled. He must be quick if he is to reach a fresh grave before it is found by the eaters of the dead, for they are adept at this hunt and rarely let a body rest in the earth above the passage of a day and night.

These ghouls are seldom seen by our race, and are almost unknown apart from fables that frighten children, but in the deeper reaches of the desert they are not so timid of discovery, particularly when their only observer is a solitary wanderer who has the same purpose as their own. They are small of stature, with slender arms and legs but rounded bodies possessing distended bellies, and their naked skin is black, so that they are almost invisible to the ordinary sight. Standing no taller than the elbow of a man, they appear at first impression to be a band of children, save that they move silently, with their shoulders hunched and their clawed hands brushing the sands, their glittering black eyes alert for danger and their yellow teeth, like those of a dog, exposed between their parted lips, for they snuff the air with both nose and open mouth to catch the scent of death.

A man untroubled by fear may easily defend himself against five or six of these creatures with only a large stone or a thighbone for a weapon, but they are attracted by the sound of conflict and quickly gather in larger numbers so that it becomes prudent to retreat and leave them enjoyment of the prize. Never do they consume the flesh of the living, yet they know how to uncover a corpse and how to bury it, and a man they slay they cover with earth for a day and then return for their feast.

They must contend not only with the desert foxes and other scavengers of the night, but with the *chaklab'i* who deprive the corpse of its nourishing virtue unless driven away. The *chaklab'i* and the eaters of the dead are ancient foes well accustomed to dealing with each other, and for the most part they observe the pleasantry of respecting the claim of whichever race first discovers the grave; sometimes the ghouls will leave portions of the corpse for the *chaklab'i* to feed upon, and they in turn will not draw the virtue from the bones of the dead, but will allow it to remain in the marrow for the gratification of the ghouls.

The ghouls of the desert are smaller of body than those who lurk at the outskirts of cities, near burial places. Lack of food and the harshness of the land stunt their growth and render them wizened of limb yet tenacious of life, enabling them to endure hardships that would kill their brethren who dwell near the places of men. In spite of these differences they are a single race, sharing the same language and even the same folklore.

Those of the desert relate among themselves the tale of Noureddin Hassan, a noble householder of Bussorah, who made a pact with a ghoul of the city named in his own language G'nar'ka, so that in return for allowing his beloved wife to lie in her grave unmolested, the man agreed to murder eight strangers on successive nights and provide the ghoul with their corpses. The murders being discovered after Hassan had killed seven of his fellow citizens, the unfortunate man took his own life and so fulfilled his oath. This tale is not unknown to our own storytellers, but for the eaters of the dead it has a special meaning, since they revere the sanctity of a bargain above all other bonds, and once having agreed to a service they fulfill it without fail.

Another fable they tell of this same city ghoul concerns the stealthful robbery of a sacred tomb beneath a mosque during the fast of Ramadan, and how the gluttony of the ghoul brought him into conflict with the worshippers, but it is too extended to relate here. G'nar'ka is a kind of hero to their race, whose exploits form the subjects for many tales.

The traveler is advised to make peace with the eaters of the dead by offering them the greater part of any corpse unearthed along the caravan roads. This is no keen sacrifice since dead flesh does not remain wholesome long in the desert, and no man regardless of hunger could consume more than a small portion of the corpse before it became too foul to retain in the stomach. In return for this display of grace the creatures will cease their attacks, for they are not warlike by nature and only contend over food, which is ever scarce in the wastes.

They speak in dry whispers in their own language, which is unknown beyond their race, but they have learned enough of our tongue from the conversations at the campfires of the caravans to make their meaning known. Of the old places of the desert their knowledge is complete. For countless generations they have sought their meat across the sands, and unearthed stranger things than the dead from beneath the stones. What the *chaklah'i* do not know, the ghouls remember, and what cannot be learned by questioning one race will be gained from the other. Neither has any use for hidden tombs or ancient cities or buried gold and silver, but they will trade this knowledge for flesh.

A traveler once purchased from the eaters of the dead the location of the valley of the lost city of Irem of the many pillars, for the extraordinary price of the body of a beautiful maiden of high family that had been wrapped in honey after succumbing to the bite of a serpent. Ghouls fear to approach the campfires of the caravans lest they be slain by the arrows of the guards, but they learned of the death from words overheard spoken by members of the family, and the traveler among them was bold and clever enough to steal into the camp shortly before dawn and carry off the sweetly dripping corpse when the camp still lay asleep, yet after those paid to sit up and guard the corpse during the night had retired to their blankets.

The body was not consumed that night, for it was too fresh, having been preserved by the honey, and the hour was late, but the traveler performed the same service as that of the mourners by sitting with the corpse while it rotted in the sun and was visited by beetles and flies, after having carefully unwrapped it and scraped its skin clean of its sticky, golden sweat. The next night it was eaten with pleasure, and the secret of the valley of Irem was revealed.

Many-Towered Irem, Its Wonders and Pitfalls

The tale is told of a city of tall towers and glittering domes in the depths of the Empty Space, far from the roads and dwellings of men. Once it was a great center of humanity, a well-watered garden fed by vast underground cisterns that never dried but were ever replenished by subterranean streams. Irem the city was named, renowned across the world for its beauty and its wickedness. Its wealthy inhabitants, grown rich from the constant caravans that in ancient times passed through its gates on their journeys to far places, indulged their love of sensuality and finery to the utmost. No cloth was too costly for its bejeweled courtesans, no fortified wine too potent for its fat merchants, no drug too poisonous for the jaded delights of its ruler and his courtiers.

Without warning or sign, the city was destroyed in a great cataclysm that cast down its pillars and domes and covered them with sand, killing all the inhabitants. The legend states that it was the judgment of God upon the wickedness of the people, but few men know the real cause of its downfall. The secret is only to be learned by going there and looking, and Irem has been lost to the world for longer than the histories of man can tell. It was one of the places of the earth so long inhabited that those who dwelled there forgot why it had first been founded. Now it is only a scattering of dusty mounds and broken pillars, the mystery of its destruction as deep as the secret of its creation.

The eaters of the dead know the location of Irem, but they will not go there, and only lead the traveler so far as the outer slopes of the hills surrounding the valley that holds its ruins. Even so, it can be found by a man possessing the secret of the white spiders of the radiant fungi. Eat three and wait for nightfall outside the hills of the valley of the city of many towers. In the darkness you will see glowing across the sands an ancient caravan road that cannot be perceived under the sun with normal sight. It enters the valley between two hills. Follow it, and you will hear faintly on the breeze the sounds of stones rolled beneath the hoofs of walking camels and the tinkle of silver and brass from the bridles, the creak of hemp ropes and oiled leather, and perhaps the murmur of voices. All these sounds come from the distant past and must be disregarded, for they are a snare for the imagination of the unwary. Those who heed them too closely drift into a dream and awake walking beside the camels of the caravans, forever lost to their own time.

The silver band of the caravan road leads into the fallen gate of the city, of which there is no sign remaining. Yet beneath the light of the full moon may sometimes be discerned a pale arch of translucent stones, the shade of the gateway that collapsed so many ages ago. Enter the gate. The tops of pillars appear as worn stones, for they project no more than a cubit above the sand, and wind storms have rounded and cut them beyond recognition. Scattered are fragments of pottery and glass, easy to find since they glow under the moon to one who has awakened the second sight.

Continue on past a hill on the left side and you will come upon a shallow but broad hollow, much like a sinkpit in the sand. Descend its slope and stand in the center. Know that you stand in the center of the fallen city, where rose the palace of the king. The shaking of the ground that felled the towers began in this place, and drew the palace under the surface so that no trace of it remains exposed. Yet stand and listen. Hear you the sifting of sand? It is faint, and may easily be mistaken for the sound of a beetle walking across a dune. Seek it out, and there you will find in a deeper hollow that is shadowed from the moon—a small opening resembling the den of an animal.

Now you must determine whether you choose to enter, or to walk from the hollow and leave the ruins of fallen Irem. The way within is perilous, not merely for the flesh but for the reason. It may be that only a man already mad can enter the cisterns below Irem and bear to look upon what dwells in its darkness without seeking death as an escape from the horror. Only he can enter who becomes one with the serpent, extending his arms and writhing with his belly; nor can a fat man enter at all, but only he who has gone long without much food. The channel is like the passageway of birth, and yields with reluctance only after much effort.

After you have won your struggle and fallen within, you will find a cave, the sand-strewn floor of which slopes downward. All is darkness, but the shells of tiny sea creatures embedded in the rocks glow to the second sight and give sufficient illumination to go forward. As the cave descends it widens and broadens. Faint in the distance is the drip of water, and water may be plainly smelled, though no water is to be found. The cave at last opens into a vast space the limits of which cannot be seen, for the glow from the shells in its walls has not the strength to provide sight more than a dozen paces.

Rats dwell there that are of unusual bigness. They may be recognized by the soft rustle of their scabrous, naked tails as they move over one another, and they have no fear of the stranger but eagerly scurry forward to nip at exposed flesh; but they are wise in the ways of the desert, and soon recognize one who is a lover of the Empty Space, and thereafter they keep a courteous distance. Their meat is lean but filling, and good to the taste, and particularly succulent are their eyes.

The traveler soon discovers by pacing the curved wall of the dark cavern that it opens outward at intervals into other similar spaces, which also have their several openings, so that the entire ground beneath Irem is found to be not sand and rock, but voids whose arching roofs are held up by natural rock pillars. It was in truth the collapse of one of these caverns that drew the palace of the king beneath the surface, and the upheaval of the earth that caused that collapse brought about the toppling of the domes and towers of the city. All this may be reasoned out in days of darkness and silence broken only by the rustle of rats and the drip of phantom water that is never to be found. The blood of the rats is sweet, and is sufficient.

The Dweller in the Caverns

In the darkness beneath the earth, time does not pass as it passes under the daily cycle of the sun. The hours lengthen and drag with the weight of years. On occasion when conditions in the heavens conspire at certain charged places in the bowels of this sphere, the progress of time is halted, or so drawn out that it appears to have utterly ceased. A falling droplet of water may be contemplated in its fullness as it hangs suspended in the air as though a polished bead of crystal on a silken thread.

Whether due to this curiosity of time or some other effect, the cause of which is not evident to apprehension, the creatures that dwell within the deepest caverns can live for spans of years that are only associated under the sun with the oldest of trees. They grow wizened in appearance but they do not die. This is only true of larger forms of life, for the smaller things endure no longer than their surface brethren. It may be that the extension of years is a function of reason, for it is true that all the creatures of long life encountered in the caverns possess at least some semblance of intelligence, and many have the power of speech, though the languages they use are those of lost ages and may only with difficulty be understood by a scholar of tongues. The mouths of these things are ill suited to shape the words of human speech, and their ancient minds struggle to conceive our thoughts.

Beneath Irem there dwells a creature that was once human, but is no more of our race. Humanity is not a quality that persists unchanged and unquenched through eternity, but is limited by the circumstances of place and time, and this being of darkness lost all human nature uncounted ages past, before the city of many towers fell to its ruin. She may be called a witch, though this term and gender possess little significance, for she is so changed that no trace of the attributes of a woman remain on her stunted and deformed body, and her witchcraft is not the art practiced in the habitations of human beings.

The name of the thing is I'thakuah, and she speaks in many ancient tongues, one of which is the primordial source of our own. By comparing the old words with the new, and by signs and gestures, she may be interrogated, for she holds vast store-houses of knowledge that are more precious than any earthly treasures. She has listened to the murmurings and chitterings of the dwellers in the deeper gulfs, and has learned their tongues, and from them stolen secrets. These she does not divulge willingly, but in return for offerings of food and other necessities she will trade her knowledge. She is grown bent with the years and hunting is difficult for her twisted limbs, though when required she can move with startling swiftness, and it is wise to sit three or more paces from her when listening to her tales of elder times.

In return for the fresh carcass of a rat she will answer a single question; therefore, take care to ask wisely. She does not lie, but neither does she offer without prompting her most precious knowledge. In this way she contrives to keep those who are her students with her, that she may continue to have fresh meat and other needed articles such as water and fire, whenever she may wish them. She is jealous of beauty in others, and in sudden fits of madness may seek to slay her benefactors if their faces offend her, for her eyes have grown accustomed to the blackness and she sees as if under the sun; but one who has been disfigured in the face has nothing to fear from her capricious malice, for she finds the lack of a nose and ears amusing. Her laughter is dry, like the squeal of a rusty hinge, and it doubles her stunted body so that her forehead almost touches the ground.

How long I'thakuah has lived in the caverns, she does not remember; neither does the memory remain of whose daughter she was before she retreated from the sun. On all other matters, her mind remains keen. Her eyes glitter, small and black, in the leathery wrinkles of her face, resembling those of insects. Though she has no teeth, her gums have become hardened, allowing her to tear chunks from raw meat and chew them. Her strength is unnatural, and has its greatest concentration in her hands. If by chance she is able to lock her fingers around a man's throat, no force of prying or blows will loosen them until she has snapped his neck. She goes naked save for a ragged cloak of wool that she hugs close around her hunched shoulders.

You will not know what question to ask on the first occasion, nor even on the tenth; yet if you have patience to serve her, over time you will acquire knowledge, and this may be used to direct your questions more precisely, so that the longer you remain with this witch, the more precious her answers become. The lore of the Old Ones is known to her, and the places where they are worshipped in the farness of the world, both on the land and in the oceans. Some of the geography she reveals is unknown to scholars, and may appear fabulous, such as the vast frozen waste that lies far to the south. For how could there be ice in the southern part of the world? Yet all that she speaks is true, and can be confirmed by diligent seeking.

Question her wisely, and she will tell of the seven great lords and of their origin between the stars; of their battle with the even more ancient beings known as the Elder Things who dwelled long upon our lands before the Old Ones came and drove them into the sea; of the fungous creatures of Yuggoth who in ages past traveled here from beyond the sphere of Saturn to mine the minerals of this world; of the time dancers from Yith who put on bodies of their choosing when venturing to distant aeons; of the froglike servants of Dagon; of the dread shoggoths, most mighty of all creatures that are fabled to live beneath the surface of the earth.

When you are ready to depart from her service, take care to conceal your intention, for she will surely try to murder you. There is by her sleeping place a pyramid of human skulls, sucked clean of all their flesh, taken from those who have served her in the past. Let it be a warning to the wise seeker after wisdom. Do not attempt to escape from the caverns by the narrow way you entered, for it would require so much wriggling and clawing at the earth that I'thakuah would hear and would seize you by the feet before you could win the surface. Then she would surely slay you, for her long arms are stronger than the arms of any ten men, and her fingers are like the pincers of an ironsmith.

There is another way of escape that leads downward, into corridors and chambers below the caverns. If you search for it with diligence, it will be found, but conceal your knowledge of this opening from the witch lest she suspect your intentions. Wait until she is snoring in sleep, and steal away from her side to enter the lower portal. It is too narrow to admit her bulk. Once safe within the entrance, you can laugh at her frustration and tell her what you truly think of her ugliness. She will throw bones at you but her aim is poor. Do not tarry too long, however, for if she begins to chant a curse, as is more than likely, you must be far enough away from her that by holding your hands over your ears you can block out the sound of the final words of the chant, and in this way render the curse powerless.

The Lost City Beneath Irem

Deep under the ruins of once-beautiful Irem, deeper even than her cisterns and catacombs, lies a city constructed of chambers and corridors that were carved from solid rock. Its origin is older than the race of man, and it has no name. Not even the subterranean things that dwell within it know what to call it; not even the ghosts of its former inhabitants remember. It may be that the founding of Irem of the many pillars atop this place was mere chance; or, as seems probable, it may be that the ancient race of beings who inhabited the lost city, in their last stage of decay employed some magic to cause water to flow upward from the depths of the earth, thus insuring that Irem would be located above in order to gain a constant supply of fresh meat, for that they were eaters of men there is no doubt. Human bones and skulls litter the corridors, most of them the smaller bones of children or infants.

The ceilings of the interlocking chambers are low, for the inhabitants made their progress by crawling on their four limbs, rather than upright after the manner of human movement. The greenly glowing ceiling of each room and hall provides a light for the normal vision equal to the light of a single candle, but in the utter blackness of the depths it is brighter than day. Paintings of many colors decorate the walls of the chambers, their pigments upraised from the surface of the stone and textured to the touch, so that they seem to stand forth with a reality more than pictorial, and when gazed upon for several minutes, their subjects waver and give the appearance of motion and life, so uncanny is the skill of the ancient artists.

In these decorations is contained the history of this unknown race, which a wise man may read like the words in a book if he takes the time to study them. They were creatures like in shape to the crocodiles of the river Nile, but with longer limbs and shorter tails, and with skulls domed and large. The forelegs of the creatures ended in slender fingers suitable for the manipulation of tools, and it is evident that they could bend upward and support themselves upon their hind legs and tails when using these hands. They possessed great wealth. All of the figures in the murals are shown wearing elaborate gold and bejeweled collars and headbands, and their brown bodies are draped in costly robes of the brightest colors. It may be that they did not depict their slaves, but only their nobles.

The oldest paintings on the walls show a distant time when they lived upon the surface of our world in cities of soaring towers connected by slender causeways, the like of which has never been erected by men. Around these cities grew forests of gigantic trees inhabited by monstrous beasts. A horrifying cataclysm destroyed the monsters of the forests and blackened the skies, casting the cities into darkness and driving the race beneath the surface of the earth. Deep in the protective caverns they prospered, and learned to raise their own foods and create their own light. Truly, the ingenuity of these beings is a marvel to contemplate.

The murals degenerate in quality as they illustrate later epochs in the history of the reptilian race. Slowly it slipped into decay and declined in numbers, until at last only this single underground city remained. When humanity built the towers of Irem in the valley above, secret cults began to worship the lower dwellers with offerings and sacrifices. The paintings show the sultans of the city of Irem ruthlessly seeking out these cults and executing their members, but the worship continued even until the fall of city.

Though it is evident from the abundance of their wall paintings that they preserved and communicated important events through images, the reptilians also pos-

Alphabet of the inhabitants of the city beneath Irem

sessed a written script based on sounds. Upon their walls a small number of simple characters is repeated in groups to create words, even as is true of our modern writing; indeed, so similar is the script of these beings to that of human writing, they must have learned it from the citizens of Irem during their centuries of interaction with men. When the foundations of Irem were laid, these creatures had so degenerated that they possessed little to offer our race, but they found ready use for what we had gained by our own ingenuity. So are the mighty fallen and humbled in their despair, until ground to dust by the millstone of ages.

Nothing is shown upon any of the walls concerning the collapse of Irem into pits in the sands. It would be easy to conclude that the breaking of the dome of the great cistern beneath the palace was a sudden and natural event, unrecorded because it was unforeseen and because it precipitated the extinction of the lower dwellers, who in a single day lost their source of meat. However, there is upon the floor of one of the higher corridors of the underground city an object that suggests to the wise traveler a different occurrence. Covered in the dust of ages, a bronze sword rests between the ribs of a skeleton that is not human.

Here is the tale of the sword, the tongue of which speaks without the need for a mouth. The soldiers of Irem found their way into the corridors of the nameless city below, perhaps in pursuit of members of the cult that worshipped the lower dwellers. To prevent their hunted extinction at the swords of men, the last reptilian inhabitants used some vestige of the magic that ages past had caused the waters of the earth to fountain upward into the cisterns to bring the city tumbling down. There is magic that can fissure and shake the earth. Even in their degeneracy, the creatures must have known that they wrought their own destruction, yet such was their hatred of men, they did not hesitate. Their blood ran cold through their hearts, like that of the serpent, with no sun so deep beneath the sand to warm it; the implacable malice of the crocodile is proverbial. Rather than see their own extinction, they doomed the city of Irem.

The Starlit Chamber of Seven Gates

After entering the underground city, if you turn always leftward, keeping the leftmost wall touching your fingertips in the accepted manner of penetrating to the heart of a maze, you will come after a winding and descending progress to a great chamber much larger than the others, having a high and domed roof painted deep blue with pigment made from finely ground lapis lazuli so that it resembles the night sky; scattered densely across the dome are shining pinpricks of light, like stars, giving illumination to the chamber. Each is a colorless, faceted jewel. By what art they glow with so bright a light is not to be comprehended from their inspection, for the source of their radiance lies hidden. The light has a coldness that burns the skin of one remaining too long beneath its rays, and for this reason it is unwholesome to covet these stones. They are arranged to represent constellations that do not resemble those of the heavens, for they are the stars of a night sky other than that of our world.

It is needless to covet these gems, as precious stones of a more ordinary kind may be found lying upon the floors of rooms, partly hidden beneath a carpet of dust, where they were scattered in haste when the dwellers in the nameless city abandoned it. It may be speculated that the dwellers used the colored jewels for commerce, in the way we use copper and silver coins, so many are to be gathered with so little effort. A handful of these stones is sufficient to provision the traveler with abundance, though he may spend years following the caravan roads or voyaging across the seas to the far places of the world.

The entire expanse of the curved wall of the starlit chamber, excepting the gaps of its two open doorways, is covered from floor to the base of the blue dome with raised paintings that depict strange landscapes and unearthly cities. In the center of the floor is a low, circular dais of strange, green stone tending to white through which the light penetrates and reveals milky depths. This single huge stone is of so uncommon a type that most who gazed upon it would fail to identify it, but it can only be the green stone coveted in Cathay with such lust for its health-giving properties. Deeply carved triangles intersect on its surface at irregular angles, so that looking long upon them produces an ache in the head, and in a circle at the center of these interlocking triangles is inscribed the sign of five branches associated with the Elder Race that ruled the earth before the coming of the Old Ones.

At the perimeter of the dais, raised metal pins of the thickness of a fist, unadorned with any markings, may be depressed into the stone with a light pressure. The metal of which they are made would be unfamiliar to our alchemists, but it has resisted tarnish and corrosion through the ages with a nobility akin to pure gold. One pin may be pressed down at a time, and it will remain lowered only for an established interval of hours, after which it returns to its former level. There are seven pins, one for each of the paintings on the wall.

By sitting with legs crossed upon the center of the dais and pressing any of the pins, certain of the glowing jewels in the dome are extinguished, so that only the painting opposite the pin remains illuminated. After a time, the scene depicted takes on life and begins to move. The soul is drawn out of the body and flies across vast spaces to the land of the painting, so that the scene becomes the world. However, the soul does not remain disembodied but takes up residence within an inhabitant of that world, seeing through the eyes of the creature and hearing through its ears. It is possible, with an effort of will, to control some of the beings the soul enters, though others of a higher order of evolution become aware of the attempt and resist violently.

The experience of soul travel is unlike any sensation of physical movement, for it produces a feeling of endless falling through an abyss of colors, shapes, and sounds that can only be experienced in dreams, and is terrifying beyond endurance to the mind unprepared for its rigors. It is wise to fast for one full day before attempting any of the portals. Confusion and dizziness can lead to loss of control of the processes of the body as it waits for the return of the soul upon the dais. Although the mind is elsewhere during its flights, the body reacts with a kind of sympathetic resonance, so that what is done to the mind may express itself in the flesh; and herein lies a danger, for the death of the host into which the soul precipitates itself after passing through a portal will invariably cause the death of the soulless body of any except the most potent wizard, as the connection between soul and body, tenuous and weak though it seems, cannot be broken without grave consequences.

Use of the starlit chamber for soul travel attracts the shades of those who in life walked on four limbs through the corridors of the past. They gather about the dais as moths flock to the flame of an oil lamp, restlessly circling and glaring with hate-filled eyes as though at an act of desecration. Their jaws work silently as they roar out their fury, but no sound reaches the ears, for they have been dead such a numberless span of aeons that their voices have faded to silence. Only if the white spiders of second vision are chewed can these pale shades be seen, yet even if the sight is not enhanced, a chill draft of air may be felt, stirred into motion by their flailing, clawed forelegs. The triangles interlocking on the dais restrain the shades, and prevent their claws and teeth from extending above the edge of the circular platform of stone, but it is to be doubted that they could cause harm to living flesh even where they are free to advance, so attenuated is their substance.

It is yet another property of the triangles that the vermin in the city, those serpents, scorpions, and rats forever crawling the corridors, are kept at bay and rendered unable to bite or sting the traveler who sits enraptured on the green stone while his soul flies to distant lands. Even the flesh-eating bats cannot cross the boundary of the dais after it has been awakened by pressure upon one of its seven pins. In this the makers of the place demonstrated wisdom, for though the ghosts are impotent, the voracious vermin would devour a motionless and entranced man down to his very bones before his soul could return.

It will be useful to provide a detailed account of the seven destinations entered from the domed chamber, and of their inhabitants and customs, for the instruction of future visitors beneath Irem.

The First Portal, Leading to the Plateau of Leng

In the distant lands to the east, beyond great mountains that strive so high to the heavens that air itself is fabled to be absent from their peaks, lies an elevated grassland surrounded by cliffs unclimbable save for a few narrow stairs cut into the rock. It is an uncanny region filled with mysteries, about which is it perhaps better not to write with unguarded words. The land is known in the local tongue as Leng. Its most numerous inhabitants are herders of beasts that resemble shaggy goats. These animals supply all their needs. Their meat is the main diet of the nomads, their dense coats the source of cloth for their garments and round tents. The nomads are short of stature but broad of body, with lungs adapted to the thin air, and sallow of face, with slitted black eyes and bristling black hair. Seldom do they walk, but move from place to place mounted on horses that are not as our own, but are so small that the feet of their riders brush the grass, with bushy manes that stand upright.

Near the center of the plateau upon a slight eminence of ground stands a great monastery of black stones and red tile roofs that is the dwelling for a sect of monks said to worship incomprehensible gods and practice abominations so unnatural and repellent that the inhabitants of the plateau prefer not to speak of them, and even avoid turning their eyes toward the place. The herders fear the monks, who never leave their monastery during the daylight hours and are seldom glimpsed by other men. They are the lords of Leng, and all tribes pay annual tribute to them, yet so indifferent are they to the people and affairs of their realm that their influence is seldom felt, unless at rare intervals when an extraordinary event compels them to act in their own interests. It is whispered that they are not quite human.

The true leaders of the people of Leng are the shamans, who hold great power in their camps by virtue of the terror they inspire. They are known by the blue markings with which their faces are decorated when they reach the age of manhood, and by a small amulet of green jade that they wear about their necks on a thong. It has the shape of a winged beast resembling a great dog, its snout distorted in a snarl of murderous rage. This stone is both a symbol of their power and a sign of their bondage, for once put on they may never remove it, and must wear it even after death, lest the harvesters of souls send collectors in the form of crows and rats and other carrion things to steal their bones and enslave their sleeping essence.

Dogs similar to those carved on these stones haunt the outskirts of the camps, their drawn-out cries sounding across the plain like the lamentations of the damned. These beasts are far larger than our desert dogs, almost the size of a crouching man; they lack the wings shown in the images of the amulets, but are in every other respect identical. Hunting in large packs, they take the weak herd animals for their food and, when they are able, the children and elderly of the nomads. No force of arms serves to keep them at bay, only powerful necromancy employing the corpses of slain warriors, who when animated become the night guardians of the camps.

The winged hounds of the soul stones are jealous protectors, and will smell out the footsteps of any fool who steals such an amulet from its shaman and exact a terrible vengeance. So long as the amulets are worn, the shamans are invulnerable to the consequences of their actions, and may enact any outrage against men or gods with impunity. They fear nothing other than the monks of the monastery, to whom they accord a sullen deference. Alone among the people of Leng they eat no flesh from the herd beasts, but only the flesh of human beings, which they boil in great copper kettles until it is tender, then salt and dry for provisions on their migrations. The common people of the plateau are willing to pay this price for the protection from the dogs, and from other threats less physical, provided by the shamans.

If you should pass in soul flight through the portal of Leng, you will find your mind within the body of one of its inhabitants, with full power to control that creature as you see fit, and with understanding of its language and the requirements of its life. In this vessel you may wander where you will and learn all that is of interest concerning this place and its ancient history, for Leng is one of the oldest regions of our world, and has remained undisturbed by the cataclysms that at long intervals of time reshape the land and redefine the outline of the seas. It is a misfortune to enter the body of an infant, for the immaturity of the form limits the gathering of information. The body of a shaman, protected by the spirit of the winged hound that is indentured to his soul, cannot be entered; nor can the body of a monk be occupied, for those who dwell within the monastery are guarded by potent charms.

A creature of the depths related an amusing tale concerning a traveler to Leng. The man was a wizard who lived centuries prior to the present age. He passed through the portal and found himself within the form of an infant girl, just as a shaman and his apprentice were placing the child in a cauldron of boiling water. Powerless to resist due to the smallness of his host body, he suffered all the torments of death; more than this, his consciousness remained locked in the flesh of the infant after it was cooked, and he was forced to endure the indignity of being cut apart and consumed piece by piece. Such are the hazards inherent in the practice of wizardry.

In the mornings after a rain, when the mist hangs close to the grasslands and the sun barely glows above the low lines of slate-colored clouds that hug the horizon, the form of a great city with vast towers and oblong habitations of stone may be seen in mirage; for no matter how clear the lineaments of the city, which at times is visible in great fineness of detail, it invariably wavers and vanishes when approached. The shamans tell that it is the city of the Elder Things that once rose where Leng now is, but over the passing of aeons moved with the movements of the earth itself to some distant place far to the south. It is their belief that the ground upon which we walk is not fixed, but floats upon the depths of the sea, and that the winds of ages blow the land across the sea, so that our world is forever rearranged, and what was north becomes south, and what was east becomes west.

The common people of Leng worship the shamans, but the shamans worship Yog-Sothoth, the master of the portals who is at oneness with all time and space, and who manifests as a conflux of the spheres of the heavens, glowing with all colors simultaneously. Learn wisdom and worship Yog-Sothoth if you would transcend the limits of distance and the barrier of time, and would be a far traveler in the myriad of worlds; worship him if you would defy death itself and live beyond your allotted years, for Yog-Sothoth holds the keys to all the gates, even the gate of death. The shamans adore him with the following prayer that can only imperfectly be rendered into our tongue:

"*Aieei-k'tay!* Heed my cry, Yog-Sothoth, by your secret name I adore thee, by your true name I offer obeisance in return for your sufferance, the utterance of which is death. On my knees I beg the gift of slavery in your service, O Herder of Ages. Accept my offering of blood, flesh, and bone, and the torment of this soul that I have bound for your pleasure. Set free the gates, Lord of Transitions, that my voice may spread the glory of your greatness, borne upon the wings of the *k'tay* that guards the descent of my fathers. I acknowledge your supremacy and bear witness of your greatness in the hall of reckoning beyond the stars. *Aieei-k'tay, Yog-Sothoth, aieei-k'tay.*"

The Second Portal, Leading to the City of Heights

The City of Heights, as it may be called, is the original home of the Elder Race, more ancient even than the Old Ones, who traveled to our world long before the creation of man. Here they erected a new city in imitation of that familiar place, and this second home may still be seen in its ghostly outlines in the mists on the plateau of Leng. As monumental as it appears to human eyes, it is but a low and unworthy shadow of the original, which shimmers beneath the heat of three suns on their distant world. Whether this place can be reached in the body is unknown, although some have said that by means of certain angles that cut channels through the substance of space itself, and by the careful preparation of the flesh with herbal concoctions, travel is to be had to this distant world without recourse to soul flight; but whether a living man could survive such a flight can only be demonstrated by the attempt.

The bodies of the Elder Ones appear awkward and unnatural to our perceptions, yet they move with rapidity on their five lower limbs with splayed feet triangular in shape. Their gray trunks are leathery and hard to the touch, and are ribbed with vertical ridges. From them extend flexible arms that are much like the branches of a tree. Between the ridges expand translucent gray wings that open from the bottom to the top like a fan. They enable flight both through air and the emptiness between the stars, and their rhythmic beatings speed the progress of these creatures under water. At times the inhabitants open them to the rays of their suns, to enjoy the warmth.

The eyesight of these monsters is excellent, but because it permits seeing both before and behind, to which men are unaccustomed, it requires a period of acclimatization before it may be used to good effect. The immediate impression is that of one image laid on top of another, as though a painter had executed a second work of art directly on top of the first in such a way that both could be seen. After a short while this disorientation of the eyes passes, and they serve as admirable instruments with which to appreciate the beauty of the city.

Although the City of Heights has no proper name recognized by our race, it might well be called the city of colors, so resplendent is the light of this world. The largest sun is red, that of middle size yellow, and the smallest, which is scarcely bigger than Venus at her nearest approach, is a blazing bluish-white that cannot be looked upon without the eyes of the inhabitants becoming dazzled. These three colors interact without being blended, so that one moment the sky is pink, the next blue, the next a delicate shade of green, and so on, changing with rapidity from one hue to the next, and making all that is seen in the city below seem to dance and flicker with the reflected rays of finely cut jewels.

The bright towers are tall beyond the power of the mind to comprehend, for their tops are set within the clouds, yet from a distance they do not appear so high, for they are not slender spires such as we are accustomed to make when we wish to project a building into the heavens, but of massive thickness and square corners. So finely set are the stones, these soaring artificial mountains appear to be carved from single blocks. Their uncivil shapes defy the earth, for some are wider at the tops than at their bases, and have immense flat surfaces upon which the Elder Ones promenade and converse with one another in their shrill piping voices that sound much as do our flutes.

They excel in pictorial representation, but delight most in depicting their own forms, as though their very shape were to them a holy thing; or that by reproducing it in their paintings and carvings they could draw assurance from it as from something perfect in an imperfect universe. Everywhere it adorns their walls, their fountains, even the balustrades of their high balconies, for they love the heights and seldom venture into the shadows between the bases of their buildings, or into the dense jungle that lies at the borders of this vast city. It may be for this reason that it has acquired the title City of Heights among the deep dwellers of our world and the few men who converse with them.

Paintings in their numerous galleries show their coming to our world when both its dry surface and its seas were still devoid of life, so that not a blade of grass grew upon the lands and no fish swam in the waters. They are equally at home in water or air, and took their initial abode upon our world under the waves as a living place less hostile to their flesh than the harsh rays of our sun, which in that ancient time was hotter and more burning. It was this very harshness of the sun that prevented the growth of life on the rocks. Not that our sun is brighter than the three suns of their heavens, but as they say in conversation between themselves while gazing at images of our world, because our higher zone of air lacked a barrier to the rays that weakens their force.

To make the oceans more pleasant, the Elder Ones created many types of living things. When long aeons had passed, and our air became thicker, plants began to grow upon the rocks, and later still, insects crawled and flew among them. The Elder Ones emerged from the waves and built their new city, where Leng now resides beyond the mountains of the east. For a period of time much greater than the existence of our race, they lived untroubled, pursuing their studies and creations, for they are curious creatures who seek to know all the mysteries of the worlds they have opened.

Then came the armies of Cthulhu that drove them back into the seas and destroyed their city. After the passage of a span of time that cannot be measured by our arithmeticians, since there is no word for so large a number of years, the Elder Ones again emerged from the depths and built a new city upon the ruined foundation of the old, in the land that lies at the southernmost extremity of our world; for over time this land had floated upon the great subterranean ocean from the north to the south. Here they remained until the coming of the ice, when they again returned to the sea.

All these matters are to be gathered from their paintings and their speech with each other, but not easily, for the bodies of the Elder Ones cannot be controlled as can the bodies of most other vessels. They do not appear to resist the effort to make them walk this way or that, but merely to be unaware of it; however, from certain amused remarks that pass between them, it is likely that they know when they are inhabited by a visiting soul traveler, but that this occurrence is of so little importance that they choose to ignore it.

Much of their time is expended in intellectual discussion, for their minds are keener than those of any other living being attainable through the portals. Yet they also delight in describing among themselves various bloody tortures inflicted on several kinds of living things bred expressly for this purpose. Torture is to them a form of high art and their chief recreation. The creatures who suffer to amuse them are bred to enhance their sensitivity to pain, so that their writhings are more strenuous. The quality of the artistry and the entertainment, for it is both, is determined by how severe it can be made without cutting short the life of the performer.

A blasphemous thing must be written, the utterance of which would cause outrage and death in both the lands of the Prophet and those of the Cross. It is whispered that the Elder Ones, who were skilled in the making of all manner of things both inert and living, are the creators of mankind. They made numerous forms of life to fill up the barren lands of our world, and we were only one among many. Why they created us is unknown to our scholars, nor has it been heard uttered by the Elder Ones, but it should be considered that when they refer to mankind in their conversations it is always with a kind of piping laughter, as though the mere mention of our name amuses them. It is perhaps no accident that in our anatomy the organs of reproduction are combined with the organs of excretion, whereas these organs are widely separated on the bodies of the Elder Ones.

The Third Portal, Leading to Sunken R'lyeh

The city of R'lyeh occupies a series of wide terraces on the slopes of a mountain, deep beneath a great ocean that lies far to the south off the coast of Cathay. Since these waters are unknown to the trading ships of all nations, the precise placement of this mountain cannot be pointed to on any mariner's chart. In the distant past, long before the creation of our race, great Cthulhu came with his warriors, servants, and many children, and he built the city on the heights overlooking a fertile island as a fortified place where they could dwell in security from their enemies. In construction it resembles a fortress, with each terrace guarded by walls a hundred paces thick. When the island sank into the depths, R'lyeh was submerged together with its inhabitants and their lord.

So say the scattered and solitary scholars of this god in our own age, when they are compelled to reveal the secrets of their studies. It is no easy matter to cause them to speak of these things, for they have no fear of death; however, there are worse torments than the end of the flesh, and life can be the greater evil. Though they respect the power of dead Cthulhu who lies dreaming, they have no wish to emulate his fate, nor to feel the worms and beetles gnaw at their still-sentient corpse; unlike the flesh of the god, their flesh would not renew itself.

R'lyeh is built of rock, and is of vast dimensions, though it did not soar into the air as did the city of the Elder Race that inhabited our world before the coming of the Old Ones, but held close to the earth. In shape its dwellings resemble great blocks stacked like the playthings of a child. The green stones of which they were built are of a size too massive to be moved even by the skills of the Egyptians, yet they are so perfectly set that the blade of a dagger cannot be inserted between them. On the peak of the mountain stands a single stone with squared corners, an obelisk so large that it would dwarf the greatest pyramid of the Nile. Nor is it a slender column, but a thick block with four vertical sides that are covered over their surfaces with carven symbols, the pictorial writing of the Old Ones.

Beneath the obelisk, in a cavern cut into the rock of the mountain, Cthulhu himself is fabled to lie in his tomb. His condition cannot be described by any word in the languages of man, but in the tongue of the Old Ones he is said to be *fhtagn*, which means variously meditating, sleeping, or dreaming. His body is not formed of common sinews, bones, and muscles, but is made of a gelatinous substance similar to bone marrow that heals itself when it suffers violence, and so remains unaffected by the passage of time.

It is whispered that in the dimness of the past, when men were yet like beasts and ran naked, the god foresaw the coming of a time when the stars would conspire with their rays to destroy him and the other lords of the Old Ones who had traveled through space to our world. In his wisdom he devised a protection from the noxious rays of the stars that necessitated a state of torpor resembling deep sleep, save that no life remained in his gargantuan body, only an unquenchable intelligence that planned and waited and dreamed for when the stars would work their way around in their turnings, and once more would become wholesome for his race.

With the strength of his mind alone he guided the progress of humanity, and selected groups of men and women to be his adopted children. He was their *tornasuk*, a word in the language of the Old Ones that means warrior lord to those who owed him fealty. They served him with their lives. Their final purpose is to release Cthulhu from his tomb when the stars have moved sufficiently in the heavens to dispel the danger to his waking continuance; for he cannot awaken himself, but must be awakened from his sleep. Then, so states the lore, great Cthulhu will open the gates to the other Old Ones and they shall return to rule the world, as they did in ancient times, after casting the Elder Race into the sea, and men will serve them as their slaves.

While the island of R'lyeh remained above the waves of the eastern ocean, it was an easy matter for Cthulhu to control the actions of his myriads of worshippers with only the power of his dreaming mind; but a great cataclysm took place, and the island sank beneath the sea, so that not even the top of the god's titanic monument pressed its head above the tides. The stars revolved in their courses; the aeons came and went; Cthulhu remained unwakened in his tomb, for the vastness of water pressing upon the sealed doors of his house obstructed his mind so that his human worshippers no longer heard the voice of their god, nor could they have reached his tomb in the depths even had he called them. As ages passed they forgot the adoration of the mighty shaker of mountains, yet still they remain his servants.

So is told the legend of Cthulhu by those who dwell in caves in the Empty Space. Yet the fate of the god is not sealed, for it is their belief that at times the city of R'lyeh rises above the waters of the sea, for what has sunk can also rise. Should this ascent of R'lyeh occur when the stars are right, it is asserted that Cthulhu will summon his human servants with the power of his thoughts, and they will open the doors of his house and release him once more into our world.

These matters would not be known to a visitor to R'lyeh who traveled there by soul flight through the portal in the starlit chamber beneath Irem. He would emerge in darkness and cold, with the crushing weight of the ocean upon his host vessel, which can only be some creature of the depths, for the ancient inhabitants of R'lyeh are all dust or lie sleeping in their tombs. There is no one in the shadowy and water-filled streets with whom to converse, only crawling things that have never seen the sun and deep-diving ocean beasts such as the vast leviathan.

Most common among the gargantuan stones of the city are tentacled creatures with one great eye in their heads and beaks for mouths. They are not native to our world but were created by the Old Ones to resemble the beasts of the world they left behind; they have no language, and their intelligence is low and cunning, but their eyes are large enough to see in the dimness of the ocean bottom, and their soft bodies can fit through small spaces, making them useful as aids in exploring the city.

Swim upward through the depths over the battlements of the successive terraces of the city, taking care not to become lost amid the strange angles of the stones, until you reach the base of the great obelisk on the crown of the mountain. There you will find a door like unto no door seen by the eyes of man, made of a metal that resembles tarnished bronze and has almost the look of stone. All across its surface are strange markings that hurt the mind, so that it is impossible to remember their shapes to copy them after returning through the soul portal. The door is sealed, and like as not will remain shut until the end of time, for there is no intelligent being to heed the call of Cthulhu to open it through the endless barrier of the sea.

The Fourth Portal, Leading to Yuggoth

A strange race known to the herdsmen of Leng in their folktales dwells in a world of ice and darkness beyond the sphere of Saturn, yet within the orbit of the fixed stars. They call it Yuggoth, and it is unknown to our astrologers, for it cannot be seen with the eyes. It is not their world of origin, which lies within the constellation of stars known as *Al Dubb al Akbar*, the Greater Bear, yet it is still so remote from the earth that our sun is a mere point of light in the star-crusted blackness of their sky, and offers no warmth that can be discerned to their touch. A single great moon circles their heavens, much larger than the moon we know, and is in color a dull purple similar to the color of bruised flesh. They dwell in caverns, and get their heat from fissures that emit sulfurous plumes of gas. Glowing lichen on the cavern walls offer a faint crimson illumination that is sufficient for their needs, for their eyes are adapted to the murk so that they see as well in the night as we see in the day.

It is difficult for the traveler to judge their size, for there are no measures of comparison with the human form, and the weight of things on their world is less than the weight we know so that, when dropped, a stone falls slowly as through water. Their bodies are covered in a horny armor or shell that is similar to the armor of scorpions, or to sea creatures such as the crab. This natural defense makes them dreadful warriors, as neither sword nor ax can penetrate it. Little can be seen of this shell, for their entire bodies are furred in a white fungus that resembles bristling hair. Only their faces and their powerful hands, shaped much as are the pincers of a scorpion but having more complex movements that allow them to grasp tools, are bare of this fungoidal fur.

They are a race of warriors and farmers. When not making war, all their care is devoted to the cultivation of a single type of fungus resembling that which grows upon their shells. It is their sole source of nourishment; as they are dependent upon it for their survival, so it requires their constant tending to flourish, for it will not grow without their assistance. Indeed, they and the plant they cultivate cannot be said to exist separately, for should either fail, the other would surely perish.

It was their constant need to fortify their fungal crop that sent these creatures to our world in search of certain minerals in the ground that are rare on Yuggoth but abundant here. The minerals are applied sparingly to the fungus beds in the same way that our farmers spread rotted manure upon their fields, and for the same purpose. It is said among the inhabitants of Leng that the race first arrived at a time following the great war between the Elder Things and the armies of Cthulhu, after the Old Ones had retreated from the malignant alignment of the stars, and they came not as humble visitors seeking charity but as conquerors, and such is ever their way. There was no subtlety in their mining; they turned the skin of our world inside out, causing great destruction of plants and beasts. The Elder Ones resented their intrusion into our world and fought them with their arts, but were unequal in might to the space spore from Yuggoth, who drove them from all the northern and central regions of our world, forcing them to seek refuge in the deepest parts of the southern ocean.

The caverns of Yuggoth are splendorous and vast. Where nature on their world has not sufficed for their purposes, they have carved the rock, and have constructed buttresses to reinforce the roofs and great arches to span the crevasses. The floors rise and fall irregularly, but offer no impediment to the progress of the dwellers, who leap across minor barriers on their powerful legs; because the weight of things is less in their world, these leaps carry their bodies farther than the bounds of a mountain ram. They have no families but live in groups of a score or more, and spawn their young from their own bodies in a way that resembles the budding of plants. When the young are mature enough to move about and eat the fungoidal crop, they fall from the backs of the adults like ripe fruit from the tree, already covered in the white fungus that acts as their fur.

The creatures worship their moon, and seem to have no other religion or god apart from the livid sphere that rises and falls in their dark sky. Its cycles govern the growth of the crop they rely upon for nourishment, and it is also their expressed belief, when they speak of such matters among themselves, that it generates the heat within the center of their world that causes the sulfurous plumes to issue from their vents, providing warmth for the living things of the caverns. It is forbidden to journey to the moon, under penalty of death both of the flesh and of the soul. Indeed, violation of this prohibition is their greatest sin, and is accorded the most severe punishment in their laws. It is equally a crime to speak about it or even to look upon it when they travel across the upper surface of their world.

A soul flyer of our race who journeyed to Yuggoth once used the power of his will to compel the inhabitant serving as his vessel to go to the surface and gaze up at the moon, for they can be ridden like a horse but do not completely lose their awareness and at times resist instruction. Great was the battle of wills before the monster would lift its eyes, and the sight of the moon filled it with such terror and nausea that it became weak and fell to the earth upon its face. When it recovered its strength, it drew forth a blade and, by inserting it in some clever way between the plates of its armor above its heart, killed itself before the traveler could prevent it. Such is their veneration for their lunar orb.

Upon their moon's face is a curious pattern of rings and lines that is the holy symbol for their race. When graven into an amulet by our necromancers, this sign confers certain perceptions that are useful in dealings with the dead; however, the scattered few of these creatures who continue to inhabit our world can sense its presence when it is near to them, even when the amulet bearing this seal is hidden from their sight, and they will seek out with tireless intention its possessor and slay him, then take the amulet away with them.

Their voices upon their own world are silent, for the air is too thin for speech. They communicate by means of colored lights from their heads that flash on and off, constantly changing with all the hues of the rainbow and with the rapidity of

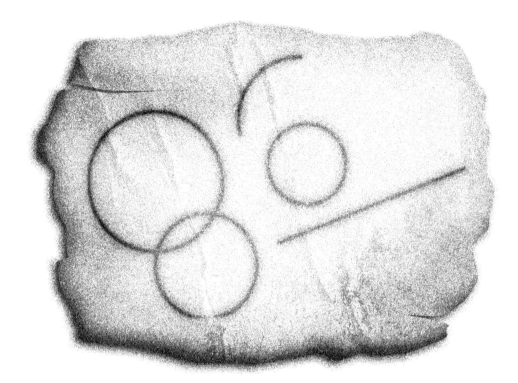

Seal of the moon of Yuggoth

lightning. On our world, they are said by the shamans of Leng to speak most elo-
quently in the language of Leng. It is rumored in dark places that a small number of
the race of Yuggoth still inhabit the mountains of the east, where they live in deep
caverns and cultivate their crop as they do in their homeland. They are spies left
upon this sphere to report its changes to the leader of their race. The hardy native
folk who dwell in tribes under the authority of shamans in those heights call them
meegoh, and sometimes hear their murmuring voices echoing from the mountains as
they talk in the tongue of the mountain race, and sometimes see their footprints
impressed upon the snow that forever covers the peaks; yet they are elusive and subtle beings, and are seldom seen, and if observed they swiftly slay those who watch
them so that their activities cannot be described.

It is spoken in Yuggoth in the language of lights that the minerals in ancient times gathered and carried away from our world will soon be exhausted, and then their armies must return to take what they need from our soil. Not the kingdoms of men, nor the arcane knowledge of the Elder Race, perhaps not even the Old Ones and the death spawn of great Cthulhu himself, should he awaken at that time, will have the power to stand against them.

The Fifth Portal, Leading to Atlantis

The gateway to Atlantis crosses not only space but time, for the traveler is precipitated into the distant past when most of our race dwelled in caves and wore uncured skins, possessing only stones with which to hunt, and lacking the skill of writing whereby they might record their works. Atlantis was the highest achievement of man, as the Greek philosophers attest, and though aeons have passed since its fall, man has yet to regain its wisdom. Why the reptilian beings who dwelled beneath Irem chose to create a portal leading to the eve of its destruction is not evident from their murals, but it may be that they found amusement in observing the fall of the city, as a kind of entertainment of infinite variety, for each journey results in a different human vessel, and hence a varied experience for the traveler.

Of the geography of the city little need be written, for it was well recorded by the Greeks; let it only be stated that Atlantis was founded upon a group of small and rocky islands in the ocean that lies beyond the Pillars of Hercules, far from any other lands. It was arranged in a series of concentric rings made up of great curving causeways that overlapped the islands, with roads that radiated from its center like the spokes of a wheel. In the exact center of the city stood its parliament building, a magnificent edifice of white marble quarried from distant lands and carried to the isles in ships, for the people of Atlantis were sea traders who profited greatly by conveying goods between the distant human settlements of the world. There has never been so bold a race of mariners. No sea was too remote or too dangerous for their sturdy galleys, and no coast unknown to their cartographers.

In appearance the Atlanteans were fairer of skin than our desert peoples, and some possessed golden hair and blue eyes. Enjoying both grace of body and strength of limb, they were reputed to be the most beautiful of all men, but their hearts were evil, and their fair exteriors concealed a blackness within. They came by their great sciences not honestly, but in dealings with the children of the god Dagon, one of the lords of the Old Ones who lies in his house beneath the waves beyond the Pillars of Hercules, waiting for the stars to realign and become wholesome to his kind.

His children have been called the dwellers in the deep. They have power to travel both across the land and through the water, although it is said that they much prefer the waves above their heads, and cannot with comfort long endure dryness on their skins, which have a faint bluish cast and are pallid, like the bellies of frogs. Their heads are blunt and rise from their shoulders without the mediation of a neck, their fingers and toes are webbed for easier swimming. At their sides are gills like those of a fish. They wear no clothing but delight in costly ornaments and jewelry, and no superior workers in precious metals and jewels are to be found anywhere in this world. Endless wealth is theirs, for they are aware of all the shipwrecks that have ever been and have easy access to the wrecks to despoil them of their treasures.

It is a strange characteristic of the dwellers in the depths that they feel affinity for our race. Tales are told of friendships, and even loves, between the children of Dagon and the children of man, and by some unnatural art they are enabled to breed with human beings when they wish to create offspring from these abhorrent couplings— for it was never meant by nature that the Deep Ones and the surface dwellers should engender children, and such spawn is cursed to the tenth generation, for breed as often as they will thereafter with men, they can never expunge the traits of their alien blood.

The women of Atlantis bred freely with the males of the children of Dagon, in their degenerate lusts preferring these couplings to union with men of their own race, and many children of mixed blood were created. They came to rule Atlantis, although they never appeared unveiled under the light of the sun nor openly challenged the arrogance of the pure-blooded citizens of the city, who regarded the mixed spawn of the deep with revulsion and contempt, even as they became dependent upon their unnatural intelligence and their associations with the children of Dagon to increase the power and prosperity of the city.

Those of mixed blood grew to hate the much more numerous citizens of pure blood, and their hate burned even more deeply in their hearts than the hatred of the slaves stolen from many lands by the Atlantean ships; for the Atlanteans scorned physical labor of any kind, and relied upon the services of slaves for their every common need, so that the population of slaves within the walls of the city was greater than the number of those native born.

The city was powered by the fires within crystals gathered by the children of Dagon from deep rifts in the floor of the ocean. These same stones were used to build terrifying weapons that could burn ships and overthrow fortifications. In their conceit, the Atlanteans considered themselves invulnerable to invasion, both because of the weapons and by virtue of their remote location so far from the lands of the barbarian races. The half-breeds with the bluish blood of the Deep Ones flowing coldly through their veins were content to run the affairs of the city, and wait and watch for their opportunity to overthrow the arrogant nobles. In secret they devised a plot with the foreign-born slaves and with the children of Dagon to overthrow Atlantis and slay all those of pure blood—for they reasoned that the nobles contributed nothing to the keeping of the island, and therefore served no purpose.

A soul traveler to Atlantis through the portal beneath Irem emerges within the body of one of its inhabitants, but whether in the body of a slave, or a noble, or one of mixed blood is a matter of chance that cannot be controlled. The portal is so constructed that the visitor emerges in the mid-morning, and for several hours may observe the works of art and social pastimes of the city through the eyes of his host. In the afternoon the invasion of the dwellers in the deep begins, in unison with the uprising of the slaves, and the chaos that ensues makes observation difficult, for the vessel of the traveler is often swept away on the ebb and flow of warfare, or may even be slain outright in the first clash of arms.

It is at once apparent to the traveler that the blue-blooded traitors who conceived the overthrow of the city miscalculated in their assessment of the decadence of the nobles, for though they had little skill in any other field of endeavor, the nobility excelled in warfare, which was the devotion of all their energies throughout their lifetimes. From the age of five years they were trained daily in the use of the sword, the javelin, and the bow, and soon became wise in innumerable ways of killing. The half-breeds sought to keep the nobles away from the weapons vaults, where the energy crystals were stored, but they were swept aside in the first assault of the nobles so that when the forces of the Deep Ones arose from the sea, the noble war-riors of Atlantis stood ready to repel them.

The destruction wrought by the crystal light cannons wielded on both sides of the conflict is beyond the power of the pen to convey; no such warfare has ever been waged in modern times, for the art of making weapons so powerful has been lost even to the Deep Ones themselves, who forgot in the ages since Atlantis sank the art by which the crystals are empowered. So great were the forces released that the very fabric of matter itself was made unstable, and the sea would no longer support the isles upon which the city was founded. A rift opened and the city sank, together with all its inhabitants of many races and those dwellers in the deep who were too slow to flee to safety in the turbulent waves.

A traveler to this fair city is constrained by the nature of the portal always to watch, never to act, for the vessel into which his soul is precipitated cannot be influ-enced by his will. The reptilian race that made the soul gateways so contrived this portal to prevent a traveler from attempting to influence the outcome of the conflict. Were it possible to control the hosts, a man might go back to the same moment in time repeatedly and in this way amass an army with a single purpose, to change the history of the battle so that Atlantis was not destroyed. What the consequences would be for later ages is a matter to ponder, but the reptilian race took care to ensure that no such tampering with the river of time might be attempted.

The library of Atlantis is located to the east of the central ring promenade, which surrounds the buildings of government. If you are fortunate, your soul vessel may proceed toward the center of the city, to which all roads that are straight lead, then turn into the morning sun to face a pillared structure with a shining roof of beaten copper, before which stands an immense statue of their god Dagon. Entrance is freely granted to all, for slaves are employed to carry books to their masters and to return them, and none of the librarians question their presence. The storehouse of wisdom is immense, gathered over centuries from all corners of the world, and translated by scribes, then inscribed onto plates that resemble gold, but are not gold, with the sharp point of a stylus, a form of writing that is almost as flowing and graceful as our own letters. The plates are bound together by rings to make books.

The frustration to the seeker of wisdom cannot be described. It is surely greater than the torment of Tantalus, who stood deep in water that receded each time he sought to drink. Only the book chosen by the visitor to the library will be seen, and then only if that person stays to read a portion of it. It is unfortunate that the favored texts of the Atlanteans were florid romances containing extended erotic descriptions and complex social conflicts that have little meaning for the traveler. Should you be fortunate enough to find a work of greater value opened before your eyes, it is sure to be shut before you have had your fill of its viands, and return as often as you may you will never see it again, for you cannot inhabit the same body twice at the same moment in time.

The Sixth Portal, Leading to Kadath

There are places in this world precious to the seeker after arcane arts, yet unnamed in the cities of men, that may be reached afoot, or on horseback, or by ship, though many are distant and difficult to find and even more difficult to attain. Other wondrous realms exist that may not be visited by common means, no matter the keenness of desire or the willfulness of striving. Some, such as the city of Atlantis, are in other times, either in years that have passed or years yet to come; others have presence in our own time, but not in this space in which we dwell, so that a man with unaltered mind might walk through them as through a shadow or a mist and have no awareness of their nature, unless at the nape of his neck there arose a prickling of unease.

Kadath in the cold wastes is such a place that is of our time but of another space. It is fabled to lie north of the plateau of Leng, beyond the snowy mountains; this is no more than a fable, but it has a mustard seed of truth at its heart, for Kadath is near the ruins of the ancient city of the Elder Ones, and the creeping of the land upon the ocean that supports all the ground of our world has carried both far to the south; whereas the ruins of the city of the Elder Ones are of stone, the great mountain known as Kadath is not material, and cannot be seen clearly with normal sight. Many men have dreamed of it, and have not known of what they dreamed, and always their reports are different, for each dreamer makes his own world in the endless lands of sleep, and no two visions of Kadath seen in dreams are the same.

The audacity of the reptilian race that built their city beneath the sands where stand the ruins of Irem was astonishing, for they dared to construct a soul portal to the mighty fortress that adorns the heights of Kadath, where out of unity with this material existence that we know as our world dwell in perpetual twilight the gods of this sphere. No king or sorcerer of men would have dared such an outrage. The crocodile beings cared nothing for the sanctity of human adoration; their curiosity knew no bounds of respect or prudence, and at the height of their wisdom they grew arrogant and indifferent to the wrath of the gods, who indeed had not the power to thwart them, even though they were aware of the portal and resented it.

Kadath rises beyond the barrier mountains in the southernmost land of this world. It is higher by far than any material peak of stone, but it is not wholly of this world and may only be seen by the unaided mortal gaze at certain times of the year when the heavens align, and under moonlight, for know you that the moon has power to reveal what the light of the sun hides. Atop Kadath was built by the gods a great fortress of vertical black battlements miles in extent from their bases to their towered crests. Within these protective walls and higher still in elevation is a palace of the richest metals and stones, so that it seems a single shining jewel. At the heart of the palace is a vast throne room with walls of onyx and floors of multicolored polished stones, a circular vault so lofty that its very ceiling is lost in mists. Here the thrones of the chief amongst the gods, each shining with gold and silver, stand in a ring facing inward, and in the center of the floor lies a great round mirror in which the gods look down upon the affairs of mankind as through a window that opens downward upon our world.

A traveler entering the portal to Kadath emerges within this throne room, not in the body of a god, for even the reptilian race that constructed it was not capable of such an outrage, but in the flesh of one of the numerous servants of these earthly deities, who are ever present to tend to their slightest whims and are constantly moving to and fro, in and out from the vaulted chamber. Many bear the features of our race, which are like to the features of the gods themselves, though less subtle. The gods take comfort in having servants that resemble them to tend to their more personal desires. Other creatures less human perform the drudgery of the palace. The humanlike servants are more numerous, and it is likely that the soul flyer will find himself within such flesh. They are easy to control with the will, and may be made to approach and regard any object of interest.

A secret must here be revealed to the wise, who will not repeat it save by whispering it into the ear of a trusted disciple of many years, for it has caused the deaths of many men. It is believed by the heathens and the barbarian races, and also by certain hidden sects in our own lands, that these gods who dwell at Kadath in the frozen wastes were the makers of mankind; the truth is opposite, for it was the dreams and visions of men, empowered by their desires and driven by their wills, that caused the gods to coalesce from the very fabric of space itself in the dim beginnings of humanity. Man was created along with the other benign animals of this earth by the Elder Things for their amusement; and when man first began to dream, the gods were formed.

This is the secret held by the Egyptian priests, who never forgot it even over the centuries their land suffered the subjugation of the Greeks, and after them the Romans. The priests teach that men have power over the gods through the art of magic, because humanity created them in dreams. Indeed, the dreams of our race sustain the gods still, and without those dreams they would fade to the nothingness from which they arose. A visitor to Kadath will observe that the gods vary in size, the smallest being no larger than their servants and the largest of gigantic proportion and towering above the rest; the thrones themselves are similarly various in their dimensions. Nor is the size of any god fixed, but changes over the passage of generations as many or fewer of our race remember and worship it; as the god increases or diminishes, so does its throne, for the throne is the seat of its power.

It might be thought that the gods, in the midst of their beautiful palace, surrounded by every luxury and diversion they desire, live an existence free from care in which they enjoy endless pleasure; not so, for a darkness hangs over them, making their voices hushed and their smiles pale. The gods do not rule Kadath unhindered, but endure an overseer who dwells in a small chamber located directly above the dome of the throne room. The chamber is of simple and rough stonework, unadorned by any hanging tapestry or carpet, having no furniture or illumination, lacking even windows or a door. Within its darkness resides the formless creature named Nyarlathotep, the faceless black god of distant space, he of a thousand forms, who is the messenger of the Old Ones.

It is whispered by the gods that Nyarlathotep dreams in his tomb, even as does great Cthulhu in R'lyeh, though where the tomb of Nyarlathotep is located upon the earth, or under the sea, they do not say. Within his dreams Nyarlathotep is present in Kadath, which he rules as a spider rules the shining strands of its web, sensitive to every movement and every presence. The gods have pledged their obedience to the purposes of the Old Ones, and in return the Old Ones aid the gods against their enemies and perform services for the gods that are beyond their power. No action is taken by any god of man without the knowledge and assent of Nyarlathotep, and those who defy his will, he destroys so completely that not even their memory is left to our race.

It is for this reason that the gods never laugh. They gaze down upon us through their mirror and aid those who worship them with prayers and offerings, for a gift given demands a gift in return, yet always with the sufferance of dreaming Nyarlathotep, whom no god has seen but who is ever present in the midst of their councils. When he withholds his favor, they are powerless to act, and must watch as their worshippers are destroyed by their enemies and their own vital force is diminished. The traveler feels relief in his heart when the time of his journey expires and his soul is drawn back through the portal of Kadath and into his own body of flesh, for flesh is warm to the touch and has a heart that beats, but the gods are only solemn shadows, fearful of the thing that watches from above.

The Seventh Portal, Leading to the Temple of Albion

The isle of Albion lies beyond the Pillars of Hercules in the northern part of the western ocean, yet so near to shore that it may be seen across the strait that separates it from the mainland. It is edged by high cliffs in color as white as the whitest bone bleached in the sun, and from this extraordinary feature it derives its name, for *albus* signified the color white to the Romans, who conquered the land and subjected its barbarous inhabitants to their rule. Beyond the white cliffs extend flat grasslands. They were once the home of a cunning race wise in the secrets of the earth, who constructed many sacred monuments to their gods. The race departed long before the coming of the Romans, leaving only their curious constructions of earth and stone to continue upon the land, scarcely altered by the passage of myriads of years.

The greatest of these ancient monuments is a temple of monoliths arranged in a circle so that they resemble rough-hewn pillars that are squared rather than rounded. A massive series of lintel stones joins the ring and provided support for a roof of great beams that has fallen inward, prey to the corruption of the passing of years, so that only vestiges of it remain. Within the ring are even larger stones, as great in size as any erected by the arts of the Egyptians, though not so massive as the stones of R'lyeh, which indeed it would not have been possible to move by the efforts of human beings. One of these great interior stones lies flat and served as an altar to the primary god of the ancients of the white isle, Yog-Sothoth; indeed, it is said that the rounded shapes of all the temples of this race were in imitation of the shape of Yog-Sothoth, who is seen as a conflux of spheres or circles of many colors.

Upon the surface of the earth, and beneath it, are certain places where the barriers between worlds are thin, so that realities distant in space, or time, or in other ways that cannot be measured draw near and touch. The primordial ancestors of our race, who dwelt in harmony with the changing of the seasons and the movements of the stars, and who communicated with the Old Ones in their dreams, felt the power of these exceptional intersections of invisible lines of force and marked their locations with monuments, markings etched in the earth, mounds, temples, and other sacred forms. Of all these gateways to distant realms, the temple of monoliths on the isle of Albion is the greatest, the mother to whom all others are dependent children.

It has been written by our holy scribes that the *al'kabar* in the great mosque at Mecca is the center of the world, but here is the confutation of this conceit, which is not blasphemous, for truth cannot blaspheme—that the center of our world lies in Albion, and the circle that is a doorway from which many lines radiate across the land is the temple of monoliths upon the grassy plain. Read it and be wise, yet in your wisdom seal your lips to the ears of other men, for to speak it before fools is to court death at their hands. Many truths are known that are not to be spoken, and many truths have been lost to the silence of ages.

The barbarians who dwell presently on Albion have forgotten the beginnings of the temple. The Romans believed the local fable that it was the work of the druids, a priest caste that flourished in the forests of the northlands and on the white isle before the time of the prophet of the Christians, but even this lie has been forgotten by those whose mud and wattle huts are now erected near the temple; yet in their ignorance they cannot deny its power, and a forbidden cult makes sacrifice of human souls at certain angles around the perimeter of the stone circle on appropriate days of the year, when the sun aligns with the stars and the gates are unlocked. For these offerings to Yog-Sothoth, whose true name they do not speak, criminals condemned to death are used, and the form of sacrifice is to strike off their heads with swords as they kneel within their shallow graves, which they have dug beforehand with picks.

By their blood, the lines of the earth that radiate from the temple, as the strands of a spider's web from its center, are quickened and their vital forces constrained in balance for the continuing fruitfulness of the soil; for if these lines become weak or entangled together, blights, upheavals, and quakings of the earth result not only on the isle of the temple but in distant lands in the far places of our world. The cult of the temple regards itself as the safekeepers of our world, and should its numbers fail, great catastrophes would surely follow. All its work is the harmonizing of the lines, and the use of the gateways to reach other worlds has been forgotten, save to a few man who gained it in the deep places from things more ancient than our race.

A recent soul traveler to the round temple of Albion chanced to find himself inhabiting the body of the high priest of the mysteries of its cult at the moment of sacrifice in their most sacred ritual, which occurs at dawn on the shortest day of the year. Since he possessed no knowledge of the proper litany, he stood as one dazed with the broad sacrificial blade upraised in his doubled hands, staring down at the naked youth bound with his face to the sky upon the altar. The lesser priests began to murmur uneasily among themselves. Their leader came forward and demanded in the language of Albion that the high priest complete the correct recitation of verses. The traveler knew the language, but not the verses.

Thinking to escape his predicament, he feigned illness and, swaying as though sick, caught himself upon the corner of the altar stone. The surprise of the surrounding throng drained the blood from their faces, so that in their white linen robes they resembled a host of specters in the pale light of winter dawn. After a moment of stillness, the lesser priests cried out, sprang upon their leader, thrust him in the place of the bewildered youth upon the altar, and drove the sacred blade through his heart. Only his great skill in necromancy allowed him to survive the death of his host and thus record this amusing tale as a warning to future users of the soul portals.

It is to best advantage that the traveler to the temple of monoliths go there in his human vessel alone in the darkness when the waning moon has three nights remaining to complete her term, and await within the temple the moment when the moon is centered above the solitary standing stone that lies beyond the doorless entrance to the temple. He must have his human vessel chew continually the leaves of the

Lunar hieroglyphics on the recumbent stone of the temple at Albion

herb known as cinquefoil, so that its juice is ever on his tongue. When the moon has attained the standing stone, certain hieroglyphics will appear upon the surface of the recumbent stone. Mark their shapes well in the mind, and at the first opportunity inscribe them on parchment, for they have great utility in dealings with the Old Ones and those things that serve them.

One who has read this book with care, and understood its words, may find these hieroglyphics elsewhere, if he has wit to seek them beneath the rays of the moon; for the sun is the moon's mate, and what is writ bold to his full face is whispered to her turned cheek.

Gloss of Theodorus Philetas: The strange markings copied here I found painted beneath the black script of the Arabic text on a parchment leaf of the book of Alhazred; they were not to be seen by day, or by lamplight, but only under the rays of the quarter moon in her waning phase, which I happened upon by accident of a night when the breeze from my window extinguished the glow of my oil lamp. By what art they were made I can find no enlightenment. Led by this chance, I made investigation, and discovered other images and writings beneath the penned words of the manuscript, some visible to the rays of the full moon, others at its waxing or waning phase, which I have copied on to the pages of this book for all to see where they appeared in the places of the original.

What May Be Safely Written of the Old Ones

In the sacred text titled Bereshit, signifying the beginning of things in the tongue of the Jews, we are taught that the Holy One created the world in six days, and on the seventh rested from his travail. Before he began there was nothing, and when he completed his work, all that we know was perfected—all stars of the heavens, all forms of plant and beast, all seas and mountains and plains, and that most noble pattern, Adam, the first man, more beautiful than the angels since his face mirrors the face of God. Our race was formed at the end of the sixth day, the final thing made by the creator to be the lord and ruler of every lesser creature and of the spaces of this world.

So it is written, and men who are devout believers accept it as the sacred word of God, but a few among our race who are uncontent to receive teachings as an infant receives its milk, but must restlessly seek them out where they lie hidden, know that on the spaces between the days other creatures were made by other makers, and since they were made at night, they have remained unseen and veiled in shadow.

Neither may it be presumed that our race is the most ancient or last of the masters who rule this world, or that the aggregation of living forms known to man walks unaccompanied. The Old Ones were, the Old Ones are, and the Old Ones shall be. They walk not on the places we know but between them, tranquil and primal, by us unseen, for they are formless. Yog-Sothoth remembers the gate; Yog-Sothoth is the gate; Yog-Sothoth is the key and protector of the gate. What was, and is, and shall be are one in Yog-Sothoth. He remembers where once the Old Ones broke through the vault that separates our sphere from the outer darkness, and where they shall break through again. He remembers where they left the imprint of their feet in the mud of the earth, and those places where they still walk to and fro, and why no one can behold them as they pass.

By their odor can men sometimes know their presence, but of their semblance no man can know, but only indirectly by peering into the liniments and expressions of those they mingled with mankind; and of those there are many types varying in appearance from the mirror of man to the shadow outline of that invisible and formless presence that made them. They walk unseen and reeking in desert places where the words have been intoned and the rites howled through at their proper times. The wind gibbers with their voices and the earth rumbles with their thoughts. They bend the trees and crush the cities, yet neither forest nor city beholds the hand that strikes.

Kadath in the cold waste knows them, yet what man may truly boast that he knows Kadath? The ice wilderness that lies far to the south and the isles drowned beneath the seas bear stones upon which their seal is cut, but who among common men has seen the frozen city or the sealed tower garlanded for ages with seaweed and encrusted by barnacles? Great Cthulhu is their kin, yet he can discern them only dimly. *Iä! Shub-Niggurath!* As a foulness shall you know them. Their hand is at your throats, yet you see them not; and their dwelling place is even one with your guarded threshold. Yog-Sothoth is the key to the gate wherein the spheres meet. Mankind rules where they ruled once; they shall rule where man rules now. After summer is winter, and after winter summer. They wait, patient and potent, for here shall they rule again.

At their return all men shall bow their heads and serve them as lords; those few who remember their ancient presence with invocations and offerings given at their places of power shall command the mass of our race who bleat as sheep and low as cattle when they are led to the slaughter, for we are as food to them and as beasts of burden that toil in the fields. The prayers of the prophets shall not prevail against them; neither crescent nor cross nor star can forestall their approach, when once again the heavens align and the gate is opened. *Iä! Nyarlathotep!* They shall visit us in darkness, but by their fires the night will be made flashing with the brightness of polished brass set against the face of the sun.

Seven are the lords of the Old Ones, six who are as brothers and sisters, and a seventh who is to them as the son of a father's brother, and who stands apart although he is one with them. The names of others of their race are whispered in the deep caverns, but the others have not the same family blood, and these seven are the leaders or heralds in our world. Among the seven are those better known and those obscure, for not all the Old Ones interest themselves equally in the affairs of this world. Their names are Azathoth, Dagon, Nyarlathotep, Yig, Shub-Niggurath, Yog-Sothoth, and the seventh who stands apart, Cthulhu.

Within the room of seven soul portals, in the nameless subterranean city of the reptilian race, are cut in rock the seven seals of the lords, each above one of the gates, though it is not always apparent what connection the lands beyond these portals bear the Old Ones. Murals in other chambers, and passageways, tell of their forms and natures, so that by a careful study of these images they may be known in part, and only in part, for no man has ever comprehended all their ways or their purposes upon the earth.

The magi who dwell in the valley of the Tigris allotted to these lords of the Old Ones the spheres of the wandering bodies of the heavens, not because they dwell in the planetary spheres, nor yet because the planets have power over them, but for the reason that the rays of the planets are in a certain accord with the potencies of the lords. Under the heads of the planets, as under titles of authority, shall they be severally examined herein.

Yig, Corresponding with the Sphere of Saturn

From the beginning man has feared the serpent, but why this lowly creature that crawls upon its belly and nests beneath the earth should be an object of dread and wonder has been forgotten, though the causes are echoed in our dreams and in the myths of our ancestors. In the sacred book concerning the creation it is the serpent who teaches wisdom to Eve, and for its reward it is written that humankind and serpentkind are forever after to become deadly enemies, and so it came to pass. The serpent has ever been regarded as the wisest of living things, and deathless, for it renews itself by the shedding of its skin. How shall it be that the wisest of beings is the most reviled and feared?

Know that the wisdom of the serpent is the wisdom of Yig, most ancient of the lords of the Old Ones. In the dimness of time Yig made approach to the ancestors of man and spoke silently in their minds, offering to teach our race the secret of eternal life in return for loyalty and worship; but the prophets feared the knowledge of the serpent and counseled that the covenant with Yig be rejected by the people, lest they be tainted in their souls with the poison of the viper and the asp. For this reason all snakes are killed at first sight, even though they be harmless and offer no inconvenience. Yet not all the people followed the prophets; some made secret pacts with the lord of the serpents, and they are known by their adoration of his favored creature.

The serpent is not native to our world, but was carried here from beyond the stars before the awakening of our race as a thing of amusement and diversion by Yig, and as a reminder of the world where he arose, for the shape of the serpent is the shape of this god, his true shape, for he goes sometimes in the form of a man with the head of a snake, but this is only the shape he puts on for his dealings with men; in his true shape he undulates upon his belly and has no limbs. Damballah he is called by the black-skinned barbarians dwelling on the coast of Africa, and by the Egyptians he is known as Apep. He is remembered in the myths of the Greeks as the cosmic serpent that encircles the world, who is without beginning or end, for he is deathless.

Many are the places of his worship. He is strong in the temples of the eastern lands, where the basilisk is especially revered and protected as the monarch of serpents, for it consumes lesser snakes as prey and stands upright upon its tail to the height of a man, and its gaze has the power of causing entrancement in the minds of those who look into its eyes; there is no power of human will strong enough to resist its seduction. Only by the music of the flute can it be controlled, and when it hears this sound it begins to dance and loses its power to strike so long as the music plays. Learn herein a deep mystery, known to few, that the music of the flute is the song of Azathoth, the blind idiot god, he who is the center of creation, whose song made the myriad of worlds; the flute of Azathoth all created things obey, be they ever so unwilling to do him homage, for in their hearts they despise this lord for his mindlessness.

Stronger still is Yig in the temples of the unknown lands that lie beyond the western ocean, where he is worshipped as a god in the form of a winged serpent; the wings express the flight of Yig, who has the power to bear himself through the airy zone of our world as though carried on the wings of a bird. These lands are known to but a few tribes that dwell in the distant northland of Hyperboria where it is perpetual twilight, for these tribes are great seafarers, and worshippers of Yig; their very ships are shaped with the heads of dragons, and their swords are patterned after the scales of serpents. The dragon that flies in its serpentine shape expresses yet another form of this Old One.

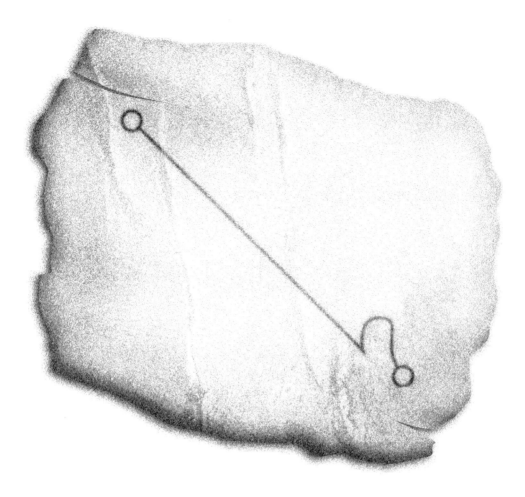

The seal of Yig

A wise man disregards the teaching of the prophets and will not slay a serpent, not even if struck and envenomed, for to kill serpents is to invite the displeasure of this god, who uses the serpent for his eyes in all parts of our world; wherever a serpent crawls and watches, there watches Yig, even though it be the least of snakes scarce larger than a worm. All are his children, for all hold in their nature the essence of this god, who is great with their multitude but diminished when they are slain. It is whispered that were all serpents to be killed, so Yig would pass out of our world, but whether there is truth in this saying only the event will show, and that shall never be witnessed by men, for the serpent is aeons more ancient than our race and will endure aeons after our fall to dust.

Those who worship Yig summon him to their rites by means of his seal coupled with the following invocation, which they chant in unison while swaying their bodies to the sounds of flutes. The constellation sacred to Yig is that known as Draco, and his sect believes that the god dwells there and gazes down upon the world. He is called into the body of a priestess who lies naked upon the sand, writhing her limbs and hissing through her lips, her thighs anointed with blood and her eyes rolled back into her head so that only the whites may be seen.

"Approach, Deathless One; heed the summons of the flute of Azathoth your creator, the song of which none of his blood may deny; descend slithering down the rays of the stars from the coils of the dragon. Great Serpent old of years and wise in wisdom, at the beginning of time you gave the gift of knowledge to the race of man, through the embrace of a woman during the forbidden days of her cycle; enter again this female vessel whose thighs are streaked with blood and insert your teachings into her mind, that your faithful servants may profit from her instruction. Render sweet the fruits of her womb. Empower her with your mighty arts to defend us against our enemies, and against those who would defame your memory. *Yë, y'ti mn'g thu'lh ugg'a aeth Yig fl'anglh uuthah!*"

The magi likened Yig to the sphere of Saturn, for the reason that Yig is the most ancient of the Old Ones, and Saturn the most ancient of the planets; the serpent is coldest of beasts, and this wandering body inhabits the most distant reaches of the heavens, where the warmth of the sun is least; Yig is wisest of the Old Ones, and Saturn is wise in secrets and mysteries; serpents hunt their prey in the main at night, and Saturn inhabits the darkened depths of space; serpents are slow and sleepy when chilled, and Saturn is the slowest of the wandering bodies. They gave to Yig the number square of Saturn, as a sign and expression of his nature. It is a square of numbers having three rows and three columns, each with three cells that sum fifteen, and a total of nine cells that sum forty-five. From this square the seal of Yig is extracted, for the letters of the Hebrew script, most ancient among the writings still used by mankind, are also numbers, and the letters in the name of the god may be traced upon the square.

It is believed by the magi that this seal, made into a talisman in lead and worn close to the heart, offers protection against the biting of serpents and attracts the benevolence of Yig, or at the least averts possession by the god, for it is the custom of Yig to enter the bodies of his worshippers as a spirit, and his presence is known when they fall on their bellies and writhe on the ground in imitation of the way of all serpents, and hiss with their lips but cease to speak in words of their own tongue; for it is singular with Yig alone among the lords of the Old Ones that he never speaks, but instructs his possessed worshippers with images in their minds. In this condition they forget the use of their hands, and if they must pick up a thing they do so with their mouths, for all of the power of a serpent is in its jaws, wherefore the word *yig'a* signifies in the tongue of the Old Ones big of mouth.

The power of Yig to become present to human sight, and to work his will in the world, is greatest at two days of each cycle of the moon, when the course of the moon and the course of the sun intersect; these conjunctions are known to the astrologers as the *caput draconis* and *cauda draconis*, or in the common tongue as the Head and Tail of the Dragon. These conjunctions are sacred to Yog-Sothoth, the keeper of the gates between worlds. On these days of each month, the worshippers of Yig rejoice and celebrate his rites, but the enemies of the serpent god conceal themselves and dread in terror his approach, for his coming brings either exaltation or punishment, and no man has seen him who has not been moved either to happiness or sorrow.

Yog-Sothoth, Corresponding with the Sphere of Jupiter

The race of Yuggoth who came to our world in the distant beginning of time before the making of man, and who fought the Elder Ones and drove them deep into the south where lies frozen the land of perpetual ice, give greatest honor apart from their moon to Yog-Sothoth, whose existence is in unending harmony with all dimension and all continuance; but the creatures of Yuggoth call him in their own tongue of flashing colored lights Him Who Lies Beyond, or the transcendent lord. The *meegoh* remaining in our world in the high lands of the east continue to serve him, and act as his agents and messengers; only Yog-Sothoth has the power to open the way between their distant homeland that is beyond the changeable star known as *Thabr al Dubb al Akbar*, the Back of the Greater Bear, and their colony on Yuggoth that is beneath the sphere of the fixed stars, for he guards the heavenly gates jealously even as he creates and destroys them from moment to moment with his dancing colors.

Truly did the sage Ibn Schacabao write that the face of Yog-Sothoth is the face of the heavens itself; he and the vastness of space are the same, and the turning, interlocked circles of the spheres are the orderly progression of his thoughts, some moving fast and others slowly, even as turn the bands of the astrolabe to mark the motions of the wandering stars. He is seen only by his face; body he has none, for his body is the universe, yet not the very matter of creation but the measurements of angles and distances between, for he is composed of no tangible thing and can only be perceived as a shimmering array of ever-changing colors such as may be seen on the shell of a beetle or the wing of a dragonfly beneath the sun.

He is known by the cults of men that adore his gates as the All In One Who Is One In All. They worship him within stone circles composed of great monoliths, and the chief of these is on the grassy plains of Albion; though its builders have been forgotten, its function is unimpeded, for from it open outward gateways to all reaches of this cosmos and countless lesser gates. It is the great mother of doors, and Yog-Sothoth holds the key. These gates he cannot open wantonly, but only when the stars align and the angles come right for passage. A gate is opened when he appears, and his face of flashing colored spheres, all overlapping and turning one within another at varying rates, is the gate, and the key, and the way. Those who pass through become for a timeless aeon Yog-Sothoth, knowing all things that were, that are, and shall be; but having transited the gate they forget everything save only for a lingering sadness and sense of regret that cannot be set into words; and so profound and enduring is this sorrow that many are those who find life unbearable after opening the face of the transcendent All.

While there are men who have dared to seek glimpses beyond the threshold, and to accept him as a herald, they would have been more prudent to have shunned commerce with him; for as Ibn Schacabao relates, it is written in the Book of Thoth how fatal is the payment for but one glimpse of his face. Neither is it permitted that those who pass through the higher gates ever return, for in the empty spaces transcending our world are patterns of shadow that grasp and bind. The thing that stumbles by night, the wickedness that defies even the Elder Seal, the throng that gather watchfully at the secret portal possessed by each tomb and make themselves fat on what grows out of the corpse within: all these abominations are less than he who guards the gateways, he who will guide the rash traveler that speaks the words rightly beyond all the spheres and into the void of unnamable hungers. For he is called Tawil

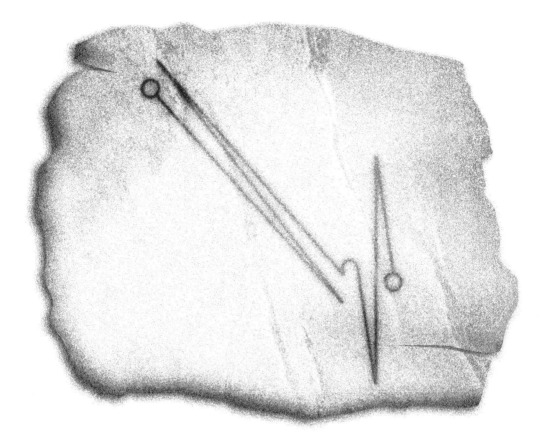

The seal of Yog-Sothoth

At'Umr, the First Ancient One, which the scribe has rendered imperfectly in our tongue as the Prolonged of Life.

When the road of the moon and the road of the sun cross in the heavens, then is Yog-Sothoth exalted and empowered to open the spaces between the stars, and greater still is his power when the sun and moon copulate, and the gateways spawned are his children, for he is sun and moon united in lust. The sweat of the sun falls, but the dew of the moon rises to maintain his balance of turning circles.

This is the invocation, cried out in the tongue of the Old Ones, that calls him at these pregnant times within the circles of stone, having met all requirements of worship and sacrifice:

N'gai, n'gha'ghaa, bugg-shoggog, y'hah!
Yog-Sothoth, Yog-Sothoth, aï!
Y'hah, bugg-shoggog, n'gha'ghaa, n'gai!

The charm to open the gate is to be inscribed with the seal of the *caput draconis* and may be voiced following the preliminary summons on either day of the month, for both Head and Tail of the Dragon are times when the heavens are in balance, so that on these days the way may be opened or closed; and the charm of opening is this:

Y'ai 'ng'ngah,
Yog-Sothoth
h'ee-l'geb
f'ai throdog
uaaah!

The charm to be inscribed and cried out with the seal of *cauda draconis* for the sealing of the gate that was opened by Yog-Sothoth is the same but turned against the course of the sun, even as the first charm follows his golden chariot; the charm of closing is this:

Ogthrod ai'f
geb'l-ee'h
Yog-Sothoth
'ngah'ng ai'y
zhro!

In this way are unlocked the gateways of the soul, and also of the flesh, but after another manner. Soul can carry flesh with it, either upward or downward, either into the light or into the shadow; yet flesh has no will to bear the soul where the soul refuses to travel, and if the gateways of flesh are opened without the willing concord of the mind, the body becomes hollow and a vessel for demons, and the soul a wraith howling in the wind.

In invocation of the First Ancient One, or when summoned before him by his power, the supplicant demonstrates his fidelity to the god by falling to his knees and placing his palms over his eyes with the fingers up, then rhythmically bowing at the waist until his head touches the ground, as though in silent lamentation. This he does nine times, having a care to the number, for if the obeisance is given incorrectly or the number is more or less, the god will blast to glowing cinders the body of his careless worshipper.

The searchers of the heavens who dwell in the valley of the Tigris have joined Yog-Sothoth with the sphere of Jupiter, for the reason that mighty Jove is the father of lesser gods, who rules their comings and goings and holds the keys to the gates of Olympus; to journey all must seek his sufferance, and all owe him the tax that is levied at the entrance of the city from travelers seeking to pass either to or fro. They held the belief that the seal of this god formed upon the square of numbers sacred to the sphere of Jupiter, having four rows and four columns, each of which sums thirty-four, and sixteen cells overall, the sum of which is 136, when inscribed on a square of tin would avert the wrath of Yog-Sothoth and would afford good luck and protection to the traveler on his road; to which belief the wise may ascribe little value, for many are the stragglers after the caravans who wear this square about their necks, and their bones lie white on the sands where the carrion hawks have scattered them.

Cthulhu, Corresponding with the Sphere of Mars

Great Cthulhu is ever a warrior god, and of all the Old Ones he is the most terrible, for it is his delight to slay and lay waste to everything that lies beneath his feet, and the very lust to conquer what was once free drives him onward across the heavens and through the spheres; it was he together with his star spawn that defeated the Elder Things, who had long possessed the sovereignty of this world before he descended on his gray and leathern wings through the upper gate opened by Yog-Sothoth. As hungry wolves on an unguarded flock they fell and crushed the great stones of the barrier walls of the elder cities into sand. Even the shoggoths were driven as chaff in the wind before their fury; who can measure the strength of a shoggoth, yet it is whispered by ancient things that dwell in the depths that its strength was without avail against the might of this god. Into the sea the Elder Ones fled, little dreaming that through the changes of fortune and the passage of ages they would once again walk the frozen stones of their greatest city far to the south, and Cthulhu would lie trapped beneath the waves in the sea.

Long aeons the Old Ones reigned in our world after the vanquishing of the Elder Race, their palaces and cities secure under the protection of Cthulhu and his armies. No foe could defeat him, save only time itself, for the heavens revolve unceasing in their courses and care nothing for the will of men or gods. The stars became poisonous to the Old Ones in our world, and so they withdrew in bitter rage to bide their purpose until the sky was once more wholesome; yet Cthulhu would not depart from the lands he had conquered. He devised a work of potent magic that would keep him safe within the house he had made for himself on the mountain that overshadowed his island city of R'lyeh. Within a tomb protected by great seals he lay as in death, yet he dreamed and in his dreams continued to rule the world, for his thoughts mastered the wills of all lesser creatures.

How could he have foreseen the cataclysm of the lower earth that drew R'lyeh beneath the waves? The waters of the deeps were the one barrier his great mind could not pierce, and it was for this reason that the Elder Ones had sought refuge beneath the waves so many ages before, to escape from his tyranny. The barrier that protected the Elder Ones while Cthulhu raged above has guarded humanity from his fury throughout the history of our race, for he has never ceased to hurl his commands forth from his mighty mind all the span of his durance beneath the surface.

The stars do not always remain poisonous, but for brief periods in their endless turnings they assume the angles of the same rays they shed down in the primordial dawn of the world. Then does R'lyeh rise upward so that the house of Cthulhu emerges into the air. The mind of the god waxes strong, and he uses its power to send forth to men who are susceptible to his influence the command that they release the seals that bind his tomb, for it is his single weakness that he cannot release himself from sleep but must rely upon hands of flesh to shatter the seals. As though in bitter jest, the stars never remain right for more than a handful of days, and always in the past, before the men enslaved by the god can reach distant R'lyeh, their fatal conflux of lights permits R'lyeh to sink once more, severing the bond between the will of Cthulhu and the flesh of those he has enthralled, leaving them to wail in confusion and despair upon the bosom of the vacant sea.

On the walls of lost cities and in the carvings of madmen who have glimpsed him in their dreams is the form of the god delineated. His height is as great as a mountain and he walks on taloned feet that resemble those of a hawk, so that the very stones of the earth are shattered by each step; yet from his back extend vast wings that have no feathers but are made of skin as are the wings of a bat, and with his wings he flies between the stars. His body has the shape of a man in that he has two arms and two legs, but his head cannot be described without horror, for it is akin to the formless mass of a deep dweller, having many ropes or soft branches that hang and writhe in place of a face, and his crown throbs and moves with watery softness for he has no skull. His eyes are small, and three in number on each side of his head. The color of his skin is green mingled with gray on his limbs and trunk, but paler gray on his wings, and these he is accustomed to keep folded so that they hang down to the ground behind his heels and tower above his pulsating crown.

Such is the unnatural body of this god, which has no kinship with the dust of our world; indeed, it is not flesh as we know flesh, but as crystal or glass, and soft so that during his dreaming death it often breaks apart, but when it breaks it at once reforms itself, held in its pattern by the will of the great one. This truth the Elder Race, who are indeed of solid albeit strange flesh, learned to their dismay, as their murals in the City of Heights on their own world attest, for no sooner did they shatter the body of Cthulhu with their arts of war then it reconstituted itself and in moments was whole. He is as their own shoggoths, about which men whisper but which no man has seen, able to take the shape of his desire and to hold it.

His spawn are like himself, but smaller in their dimensions; what they lack of their master in size, they compensate with their numbers, for they fly into battle as the locust swarm descends upon the ripening field of grain, so thick that they obscure the sun with their wings. At times past the *meegoh* have followed his commands and battled in his wars, for they dread the influence of Cthulhu upon the whim of their god of passage, Yog-Sothoth, and risk any danger rather than court his displeasure. All this was in the ancient times, and in the age of man Cthulhu lies dreaming in R'lyeh, his spawn has vanished, and the *meegoh* are returned to Yuggoth, all but a few that watch and wait.

The tale is whispered that at some future time the stars will move in their courses and align as they have in the past, but at last their pattern will endure and the world will become wholesome for the Old Ones. Cthulhu will rise and conquer, as is his right, for what force of gods or men can stand against his fury? Until that day, may it

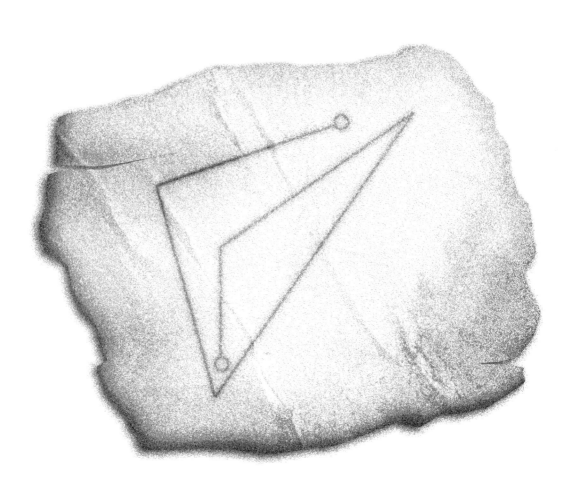

The seal of Cthulhu

soon be witnessed, those wise in necromancy who adore him wear the seal of the god burned upon their skin and chant a litany in his remembrance in the tongue of the Old Ones, that dreaming Cthulhu teaches his prophets in their sleep:

Ph'nglui mglw'nafh Cthulhu R'lyeh wgah'nagl fhtagn. Iä!

The prayer has this meaning in our tongue: *At his house in R'lyeh, dead Cthulhu waits dreaming; it is so!* In the far places of the world, from the plateau of Leng to the western isle of Albion to the banks of the Nile and the frozen wastes of Hyperboria, his chosen chant these words, and they are the sign by which they know each other, and the bond that unites them even when they are of different races. The poet may sing a different song, for they chant what has been and what remains, but the poet intimates in verse what shall come to pass:

That is not dead which can eternal lie,
And with strange aeons death may die.

Of all the lords of the Old Ones, Cthulhu stands alone and apart, for his is not of the same blood with the others, though his blood mingles with theirs. They use him as a sword and think to distance themselves from his presence when the battle has been won, but he keeps his own counsel well guarded, and none can say what he intends for his kin. When all had fled the poison from the stars, he remained in his house at R'lyeh and dreamed his deep purposes in solitude. The ocean alone contains him, for the stars cannot shackle his mind.

It was because Cthulhu is the greatest of warriors that the magi who are descended from the royal line of Babylon link him with the sphere of Mars, god of war, and none are wiser in the lore of the heavens than the priests of the Tigris. As Mars is the conqueror of all who oppose his will, so too is the dreaming god; as fire, the element loving to Mars, hates the water, so does Cthulhu hate the weight of the ocean above his head that frustrates his purpose. The magi give to him the number square of Mars, having five rows and five columns, each with a sum of sixty-five, and the sum of this square as a whole is 325. They teach that the seal of his name traced upon the square and incised into a plate of iron has power to give victory in battle and protects the warrior from injury by sword or arrow, and that its sight is pleasant to the things that dwell in darkness and are loyal to Cthulhu, who spare the lives of those who bear it. But this last is a lie.

Azathoth, Corresponding with the Sphere of Sol

There is a cause why the flute plays so prominent a role in the cults that worship the Old Ones in the dark places and hidden caves, away from the ears of common men. At the seething and fiery center of all, Azathoth sits upon his ebon throne within his halls of darkness that no man has seen and survived the vision. He is both blind and bereft of mind, but unceasingly he pipes upon his reed flute, and the pearling notes that rise and fall in measured patterns are the foundation of all the worlds. These notes are more than music, they are numbers. Azathoth ever calculates in sound the structure of space and time. Were his flute to suddenly fall silent, all the spheres would shatter into one another and the myriads of worlds would be unmade and as they were before the creation.

There is a mystery known to few, that his flute is cracked and can give no pure sound. It is explained by sages that when he blew the first great note that began the outpouring of worlds, the force of the sound was so vast that no instrument could endure it, not even the flute that made it; but this is the reasoning of children, and the truth is elsewhere, for the crack in the flute is a way of expressing the imperfection inherent in all created things. All that is made is imperfect, for perfection can have no form or texture in the mind; Azathoth himself is imperfect, being blind and blubbering as he pipes. Yet how can the creator who was never made be himself imperfect? Consider this riddle and be wise. Only the breath that bears the sound ever outward in widening circles, unseen and formless, is perfect, for the sound is but a pattern pressed upon the breath, but the breath pervades all; if it did not, how would the sound be carried to the farthest reaches of space? It is not the breath we know, but the subtle essence of breath that can neither be seen nor felt, and is forever unknowable.

The flute of Azathoth both makes and unmakes the worlds in ceaseless combinations that are like dancers spinning on the woven carpet of time. There can be no creation without destruction, and no destruction without creation; to unmake a thing is to make something else, and each time a thing is made, something is destroyed. The idiot god on his black throne does not choose what shall rise into being, or what should pass away, but only maintains a balance and constant order in the number and pitch of his notes. These piping sounds are numbers, for they interact in ratio and proportion; all things are made of numbers; men are formed in their flesh by the arithmetic of Azathoth, who gathers his sums and brings forth shapes.

No created being has seen Azathoth save only Nyarlathotep, who is called the Chaos That Creeps by writers who fear even to voice his name. In Azathoth is order, in Nyarlathotep is disorder; they are half brothers and can never be separated, for even when far apart in space, Azathoth forever creates the patterns and Nyarlathotep forever disperses them. It was the blind idiot god who piped forth the universe, but it is whispered that it shall be the Crawling Chaos who on the last day of time shall snatch the flute from his blubbering lips and break it, ending all forevermore. Nyarlathotep looks upon his half brother with contempt, yet knows full well that he is as dependent on the song of the flute as all other things; this enrages him so that he waits in eagerness for the last day.

Concerning the face of Azathoth no pen has written, unless the writer lied, for no living creature can look upon it and endure its terrible heat and black radiance that is like the reverberating unseen rays of heated iron that strike and prickle the skin, or crisp and sizzle it when too near. Only Nyarlathotep, who has no face of his own, has gazed into the countenance of the idiot god, and even he is dazzled by its fires and must turn away after an instant.

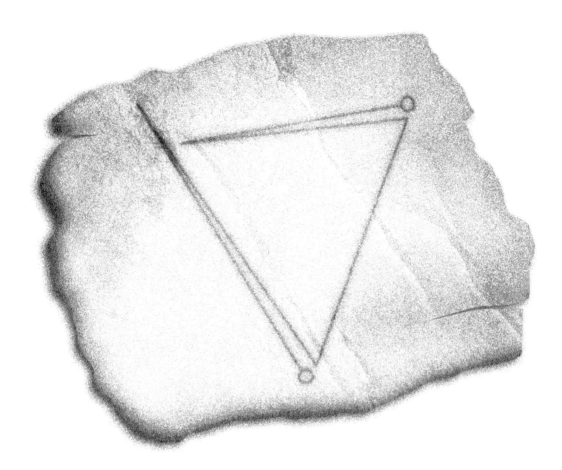

The seal of Azathoth

Azathoth receives no supplicants in his black halls of uncouth angles and strange doors, nor does he ever hear prayers or answer them. Endlessly he pipes, and endlessly he devours his own substance, for his hunger is insatiable. Nothing is taken into his body from beyond, and nothing is expelled, for he consumes his own wastes after the custom of idiots. Music alone issues outward from him, yet it has no substance or form; its semblance of form arises from the ever-present breath that pervades creation and bears it along; in itself the music is only number upon number, and so cannot be truly said to proceed from Azathoth, for how can a number possess motion through space?

Despite the indifference of their god, members of the cult of Azathoth emulate his music and dance accompaniment, spinning and revolving on the wind they create with their own turning motions, pipes pressed to their lips and their eyes rolled heavenward. The dance is their ecstasy, the music itself their prayer. In this way they seek unity with the center of all things. They wear as a pledge of their faith the seal of the idiot god over their hearts.

Men ask in the marketplace in idle talk why the world was created; there is no answer, for the world was made without thought by an idiot to whom good and evil are the same. He hungers and feeds yet is never satiated; he pipes and hears but does not see. Of sorrow he knows nothing; neither has he felt happiness. He pipes with patience, and the music of his flute rolls outward in trilling waves that rise and fall upon the breath of the cosmos, and the notes fulfill their patterns and move inexorably toward the last day, when the fury of his half brother shall be expressed and there will come silence.

The wise men of the Tigris, learned in the ways of the stars, placed Azathoth in the sphere of Sol, because both are at the center of things, the god at the center of creation and the sun at the center of the wandering bodies of the heavens. As the sun is hot and bright, so is the palace of Azathoth located in a place of great heat, and his face is blinding in its radiance that darkly shimmers. They gave to him the number square of the sun, having six rows and six columns, each making the sum of 111; and the sum of all is 666. This is the number of the Beast of the Christians, and wisely was it chosen, for the Beast shall usher in the last of days.

The magi make the seal of the god that is formed on this square into a charm upon a plate of gold and wear it to attract money and substance, and to insure health of the body, on the reasoning that all things come into being from the music of Azathoth, therefore his square must bring forth substantial virtues such as vitality of the flesh and the increase of wealth. Their reasoning is flawed, for as the god creates, so he destroys.

Shub-Niggurath, Corresponding with the Sphere of Venus

Of the fecundity of the earth there is no end; her womb breeds monsters unglimpsed by those who dwell under the sun, and her twisting entrails crawl with things white and blind. These are the children of Shub-Niggurath, who is called the Goat With One Thousand Young by those who dare not speak her name. She is of the gender of a woman, for what except the womb brings forth fleshy life upon the ground, or beneath it? Those who worship her with images most often depict her with the head of a goat; this is not her true visage, which is bestial but unlike any beast known to men, yet it may be that the image of the goat was chosen as appropriate due to the ruttiness of this animal, which is proverbial.

Her statues are black and made of stone, and are often of human size, though some are smaller for the convenience of carrying in those lands where her worship is severely punished. They show the goddess standing upright, four horns bristling from her hairy head, her mouth snarling with savage teeth like those of a wolf. Her arms and hands are those of a woman, but her legs and feet those of a goat. She is ever naked, her torso covered with innumerable round breasts to suckle her countless progeny, but that which is most shocking to those who strive to suppress her cult is the gaping and exposed state of her genitals; by this her worshippers express that Shub-Niggurath is the womb of the night from which all creatures of nightmare issue.

In the ancient time, great Cthulhu lay with her and bred upon her the armies that overthrew the Elder Things, for the manner of her bringing forth is not one after the way of women, nor even a score after the way of mice, but myriads of myriads of children issue from her womb, which never closes. It has been ages since last she lay with her cousin, and most of his children are dead or have sought their dwellings deep beneath the sea and under the surface of the ground, for they hate the light of the sun and, being of the same substance as the Old Ones, cannot easily endure the noxious rays of the stars that presently keep Cthulhu imprisoned at R'lyeh. When the stars are right, and darkness covers the earth, they will issue forth from their deep pits and lakes, and from the ocean, and fulfill the will of the Old Ones as they did in the beginning of things.

Her rites are wild ecstasies of debauch during which brother lies with sister, mother with son, father with daughter, and infants conceived in this unlawful way are sacrificed to the prolific goat, and their blood consumed in wine to produce intoxication and visions; so also are the bodies boiled in great pots, and their flesh consumed by the revelers, who recognize no restraint of law and practice any outrage against religion. They are accustomed to meet in caverns during the night hours, both for greater security against detection and also because the deep places are the wombs of the world, sacred to Shub-Niggurath.

With red and blue and yellow pigments they paint their faces and bodies, for they worship naked after the way of the goddess; upon their backs they paint her seal; the men dance with their virile members inflamed and erect, and the woman dance obscenely, opening and closing their bent knees to expose their genitals, and shaking their heads and their breasts while screaming invocation of the goddess to the beat of drums and the drone of flutes; around blazing fires they dance, the flames rising higher than their elevated hands, and the men gash their arms with blades and spatter the blood on the thighs of the women to make them more fertile.

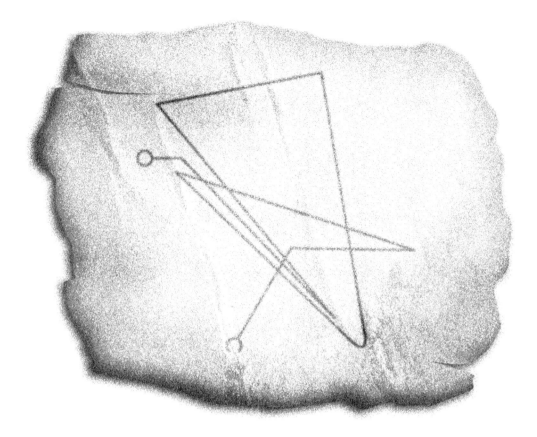

The seal of Shub-Niggurath

The women scream these words in the tongue of the Old Ones, *Iä! Shub-Niggu-rath! Iä! Iä!* Their voices that echo in the caverns resemble the yelping of dogs, for there is nothing human in the sound. When the worshippers begin to couple, it is the women who mount on top of the men, in honor of the supremacy of the goddess as the womb of creation. The theological books of the Hebrews make veiled allusion to this practice in their fables concerning Lilith, who was the wife of Adam before Eve, and who had union with him on top rather than beneath; and the Babylonians had similar stories of a demoness of lust that bore strange children from the seed she stole away from sleeping men in the dark of night. In truth, Lilith is no other than Shub-Niggurath, even though the scribes of the Hebrews dared not write her name.

She visits the men who seek union with her in their dreams, but only if their lust is great. When she comes to the bed, she presses upon the chest of her lover and takes her pleasure on top of his sleeping body, and from his ecstasy she gives birth to monsters of a lesser kind, those that inhabit the desert places of the world and lie in wait to murder travelers beneath the moon. From the seed of the Old Ones her womb gives rise to great abominations, but from the seed of men it yields lesser evils. In dreams she cloaks her form so that men do not withdraw from her, but when she visits her worshippers she comes as she truly appears, and they welcome gladly her bestial kisses, for she makes their virility unending.

The worship of Shub-Niggurath is greatest in the lands of Lebanon and around the salt inland sea, but she is also adored with orgy and sacrifice along the upper tributaries of the Nile, on the western shore of the Red Sea, and between the rivers Tigris and Euphrates. Yet these are only the chief centers of her cult, for her worship spans this world in lands both known and uncharted, carried far and wide by her roving cult as it moves from place to place in its caravans. It has been the cause of much misery and countless mysterious deaths, since her worshippers must have human flesh for their sacrifices during her highest rites, and where infants cannot be procured they use the flesh of travelers, for the disappearance of a traveler causes less inquiry than the vanishing of a local dweller.

The magi gave to Shub-Niggurath the sphere of Venus as her natural harmony, because Venus is a goddess noted for her concupiscence, who brings fertility to beasts and crops; however, the life-giving power of Venus is wholesome, whereas that of the prolific goat is verminous and foul. As a charm to ward her off during sleep, they engrave upon a plate of copper the seal of the goddess formed on the number square of Venus, which has seven rows and seven columns, each of which sums 175, and the total of all the numbers of the square is 1,225. Some scholars profess the opposite belief, that the seal of the prolific goat attracts the goddess to the bed, and both opinions are true, depending on how the seal is employed, for if it is laid with the engraving downward against the chest, it attracts, but with the engraving upward to the sky, it repels.

A young man of Yemen who wished to punish a rival in the love for a woman bribed a servant of the rival to bury the seal of this goddess beneath his master's sleeping place with the engraving down. In the span of a single cycle of the moon, the rival was so troubled by nightly visits of Shub-Niggurath in his dreams that his flesh wasted away and he went mad. The woman gave her love to the remaining suitor, who enjoyed it for a term until the revolving wheel of fortune stole her from his embrace.

Nyarlathotep, Corresponding with the Sphere of Mercury

Of all the lords of the Old Ones, only Nyarlathotep appears wholly in the likeness of a man. The shapes of the Old Ones are not fixed, but express their nature through a harmony between form and intention; yet it is possible for them to change their appearance within the bounds of this accord, and Nyarlathotep chooses to come to his worshippers as a man of greater than average height who is in all respects human save one: that he has no face but only a blackness where a face should be seen. As the face of Azathoth is darkly bright and radiates outward, so the face of Nyarlath-otep his half brother is a void that draws inward both heat and light and never releases them. He is the eater of souls.

Why he comes in the shape of a man is not known, but it may be to better have dealings with humankind, since he is reputed to enjoy the company of men when they drink wine and gamble, and the bodies of women with whom he lies in lust. He speaks as a man speaks but his voice has the coldness that lies between the stars, and few wish to hear his sardonic laughter, for then there will be death. Men are to him as playthings to a child—to be taken up for a time, then abruptly cast away and trodden into the earth. Even so, he teaches great mysteries to those who worship him, but always leading to evil works, for he delights in wickedness.

Those who dwell in the Empty Space and seek knowledge in the tombs and caverns of the earth sometimes see Nyarlathotep walking alone across the sands as though lost in thought, wrapped from brow to toe in a swirling black cloak with a hood, a caul upon his face, rings glittering upon the fingers of his hands like so many stars. It is dangerous to approach him at these times. His dealings with men are at his choosing, and his patience is brief. With a single word can he burn the flesh from the bone, so that the skeleton of an unwary man remains standing a moment before it collapses with a dry clatter at his feet. Yet he is capricious, and it may suit his whim to teach a secret to the audacious fool who accosts him.

When he appears it is oftentimes with the piping of a flute, and the reason is that he has been with his half brother Azathoth at the center of the universe, and through the open gateway that Yog-Sothoth has not yet sealed can for a time be heard the trilling of thin notes that set the hairs on the neck upright. He is not so inconvenienced in his coming to our world as the other Old Ones, though why this should be so remains unknown; perhaps it is the human shape he wears that partly shields him from the poison of the stars. Whatever the reason, he serves the Old Ones as their messenger among men. It is he who keeps the true gods of our race hostage in Kadath in the cold waste of the south, and who deprives them of their minds and makes them dance to the flute of Azathoth.

A necromancer newly cast forth into the great wastes came upon a tall man robed all in black who stood upon the crest of a dune beneath the stars, head cocked to the side as though listening to music, though no sound broke the silence of the night save the wind. His face was shadowed in the depths of his hood and his back was turned. Emboldened by his disregard, the desert dweller crept up the slope of the dune with knife drawn, his intent to slit the throat of the stranger and steal his cloak and boots. When he raised the knife, he found that he could not move. The stranger turned and gazed at him, and he screamed, for there was no face in the hood, only two glittering stars. For a dozen heartbeats the stars pierced his soul and flayed it open. The stranger turned without a word and walked away, and the dweller fell to his knees and wept over the loss of such exquisite emptiness.

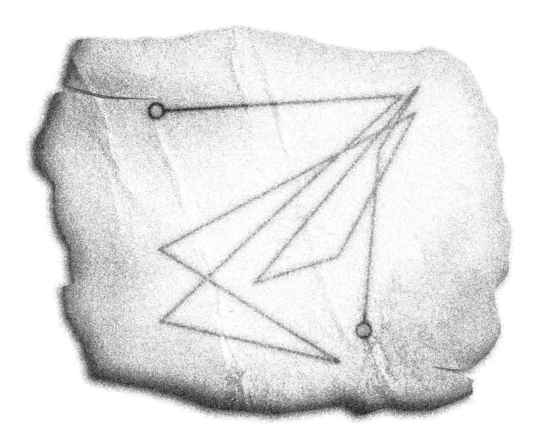

The seal of Nyarlathotep

Nyarlathotep is a trickster who may temporarily put on any form to beguile the wits of those to whom he appears. He delights in lies and misdirection, and for amusement will corrupt the thoughts, so that it is unwise to trust overmuch in his teachings, for sometimes they are sound and precious, but other times they are fatal if pursued. Wisest of the Old Ones with the exception of Yig, who is wisest of all, he knows the lore of magic not merely of this world but of many others. He is called by his worshippers the Myriad-Formed Messenger, but by his detractors he is known as the Chaos That Crawls. Neither dare speak his name without dire need, for to name him aloud on the tongue is to invoke him, even though he is not seen, for he comes to those who call him by name cloaked in shadow so that he is unknown, and studies them to learn their purpose; then he may aid, curse, or slay, according to his humor.

His worshippers meet in secret on the high places of the world, beneath the stars, and invoke him, in words that may be rendered thus into the common tongue:

"*Nyarlathotep! Nyarlathotep! Nyarlathotep! Aï!* Thrice we invoke your true name. Attend upon this circle, by the authority of your potent seal that is marked upon the earth in this place sacred to your mysteries. By this seal recognize us as your faithful servants. Fulfill the requests we make of you, that we may continue to live and prosper as your agents upon the earth, and work your will in the affairs of man. *Aï!*"

When he is present upon his throne, they pay homage to him, offering to him their children as his servants and describing their acts of evil, for Nyarlathotep ever delights to hear of wickedness done in his name. Those he takes for his own he marks with his fingernail, the merest touch of which on the skin burns like ice and leaves a wound that heals with an angled scar. These marks are on the head, save in nations where this practice is known to the rulers who persecute his cult, and then they may be placed on some secret part of the body that is concealed beneath robes. If he chooses, he can make the mark invisible to all but those who owe him service.

It is his amusement that his worshippers adore him with a kiss upon his anus, both as a degradation of their souls and because the anus signifies corruption, and it is the last act of Nyarlathotep to end the universe and bring death to all. They swear obedience to him and suffer that their names be entered in books as a record of their fealty, which books are most dangerous to the cult when discovered, and for this reason are kept deeply hidden. Each man who worships him, and each woman and child, makes formal agreement to obey him in all things, and to offer to him their first child; by this is not meant an offering of sacrifice, even though this has been written, but a dedication of the first-born in service to Nyarlathotep, and in this way the numbers of his followers ever increase.

The chief seat of his worship is among the forest realms to the north, and on the isle of Albion, but he is strong also in the catacombs of Rome and Constantinople; in the depths of Africa he is adored, and in the inward plains of the vast and uncharted lands beyond the western ocean. The peoples of the east do not accord him such great service, for they prefer to worship Yig, and the cults of these gods do not prosper in the same region, for the worshippers war against each other until only one remains.

Because he is the wisest of the Old Ones, and a trickster, and the messenger and herald of these gods, the magi of the Tigris joined him with the sphere of Mercury, quickest of the planets and messenger of the Olympian gods, he who is most learned in speech and in the art of writing. They used as a charm the seal of the god inscribed on a plate of electrum formed upon the number square of Mercury, having eight rows and eight columns, each with a sum of 260, and the total number of this square is 2,080. It was their belief that the square, when worn over the heart, would avert the wrath of Nyarlathotep, as a token having power over his coming and going; but it would be unwise to place overmuch faith in the efficacy of this charm.

Dagon, Corresponding with the Sphere of Luna

It is the assertion of our cartographers that the seas of the world exceed in their expanse the lands, so it is little to be wondered that another of the lords of the Old Ones should prefer the depths of the ocean for a dwelling. Mighty Cthulhu has his home in R'lyeh in the sea that lies eastward and far to the south off the shores of distant Cathay, but Dagon is reputed to inhabit a deep chasm on the sea floor, the location of which is unknown. It is believed that the race he created in his image, who dwell beneath the waves and serve his designs, have their greatest number in the western ocean beyond the Pillars of Hercules; for this reason some have speculated that Dagon abides in the west, but wiser commentators offer no opinion on this matter.

Among men he is worshipped most faithfully by the descendents of the Canaanites, who in times past built idols to him that enraged the Hebrews, as is recorded in the sacred texts of that people. The Deep Ones, as his sea-dwelling brood are called, are friendly to men if treated with courtesy, and aided the Canaanites in capturing in their nets rich harvests of fish, greatly to the increase of the wealth of that nation, and to

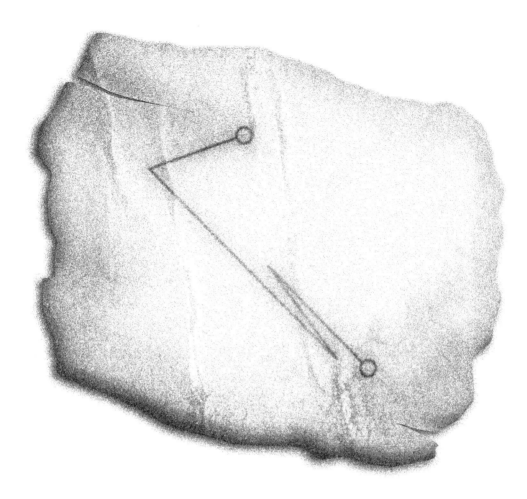

The seal of Dagon

the envy of neighboring peoples. In compact with the Deep Ones, the Canaanites gave as a pledge of trust their daughters in marriage, and among the cults of Dagon this practice continues. The Deep Ones admire the beauty of women and delight to lie with them; in return for this pleasure they adorn their brides with rich and cunningly fashioned jewelry, for they are greater in skill than any other beings of our world in the making of ornaments of precious metals and jewels.

In the northlands of Hyperborea he is known as Kraken, and in the books of the Hebrews as Leviathan. He sleeps and dreams, not imprisoned in a tomb as is Cthulhu, for the leagues of water above his head protect him from the poison of the stars, but lying in the deepest part of the chasm that serves as his house beneath the mud that covers him. At times he wakes and travels the sea floor to visit his children and certain holy places on islands or off promontories where members of his human cult make offerings, which they cast into the waves of the sea while chanting his name. As far as the line of the lowest tide he can approach the shore, but no further, for the stars repel him; the shallows he is able to endure only for short spans, and then must retreat to the depths. This is no great inconvenience, for the Deep Ones serve as his hands and eyes in the seas, and his worshippers among men as his hands and eyes upon the land.

Vast is his body, covered with great silver scales. His hands are as those of a man but longer of finger and webbed between. The same is true of his feet, the slender and webbed toes of which resemble a great tail when he puts his legs together and swims with powerful strokes; this has caused some commentators to write in error that he has no legs. His head is similar in shape to the head of a dolphin, and joins to his body without a neck. In his domed forehead is set a single eye greater in size than the round shield of a warrior, and being devoid of a lid it never shuts, even when he sleeps. When emerging into the shallows he walks upright and bent forward with his long arms dragging in the water. His voice is deeper than the largest bell and may be heard for many leagues when he speaks from out his mouth, which is broad and set low on his head.

Some artists have drawn this god in the form of a woman naked to the waist, with the tail of a fish. This is a vulgar error born of ignorance, yet it is true that like the fish of the sea, the sexual member of Dagon is concealed within his body, and is reputed to only emerge when the god has copulations with Shub-Niggurath. In appearance he is neither male nor female, but a blending of both. Those who have seen him with their own eyes attest that his body is translucent, so that the light of the moon passes through it as through a cloudy crystal, for he ventures into the air only in the light of the moon, never beneath the heat of the sun; the reason for the watery appearance of his body is that it is composed of no ordinary flesh but of substance carried from beyond the sphere of the fixed stars. Subject neither to age nor decay, it is deathless.

Those engendered on the daughters of men who are given in marriage to the Deep Ones share in part this longevity, being greater in years than one of unmixed

Hieroglyphs on the black pillar of Dagon

race, but shorter of life than the pure spawn of Dagon. When they are born, they resemble a human infant, but as they age they acquire the fishy attributes of their fathers until at length they are more at home in the sea than on the land. They abhor the dryness of the air, and always make their dwellings near the ocean where the wind is damp and salty. By their watery eyes you may know them, and by the moist pallor of their faces. As they grow older their mouths broaden and their voices become deep, and when they speak a gurgling is heard in their throats.

The cults of Dagon adore as sacred a black pillar, which they say is the source of his power. Each cult keeps in addition to his statue a smaller simulacra of this pillar, the original of which rests beneath the sea at the chasm where he sleeps. Its sides are covered in hieroglyphs of a language that is not to be encountered elsewhere in our world, for it is specific to the Deep Ones. Those who have seen the replicas of the great undersea pillar have drawn out a number of its symbols at great danger to themselves, for it is considered the most terrible violation or blasphemy by the worshippers of Dagon, who hunt down and without mercy put a sword to the violators.

The magi of the Tigris valley associate Dagon with the sphere of the moon, upon reflection that the moon controls the tides and is of a watery composition, and that Dagon is never seen to walk except beneath the lunar rays, and is bounded by the place where the tide reaches its lowest ebb, as by a barrier that cannot be crossed; also the moon is silver, resembling the color of his scales, and moonlight is translucent, as is his flesh. They use as a charm to Dagon engraved upon a plate of silver the seal of the god formed on the number square of the moon, composed of nine rows and nine columns, each of which sums 369, and the total sum of the square is 3,321. The square is supposed to insure good catches of fish and happy fortune when traveling by water, though in truth these things are dependent upon the sufferance of the Deep Ones, who are capricious in their favors.

The Great Seal
of the Old Ones,
Known As the
Elder Seal

Deeply incised into the circular stone dais in the center of the starlit chamber of soul portals that is to be found at the heart of the nameless city beneath Irem is an emblem of curious pattern, different from any other, the full use of which is unknown to men. It has been called by some the Elder Seal, but by others the Great Seal of the Old Ones. Soul travelers who journey to R'lyeh may see it upon the closed gate of Cthulhu's house, where he lies within his tomb dreaming. Its form may more readily be depicted than described, but it is somewhat like a branch and somewhat like the pattern in a proof of geometry, having angles and circles set in a precise relationship. It has been falsely rendered in various works by writers who knew nothing of its true shape. Ibn Schacabao dared to draw it plainly in two of his manuscripts, but in corrupt form that lacked the spheres and other smaller marks, so that it was without power; those who have it complete possess a treasure beyond price.

Know you that Yog-Sothoth is the gate and the key, but the Elder Seal is the lock. Created by the Elder Things in the war with Cthulhu and his spawn countless ages prior to the making of man, it has the power to

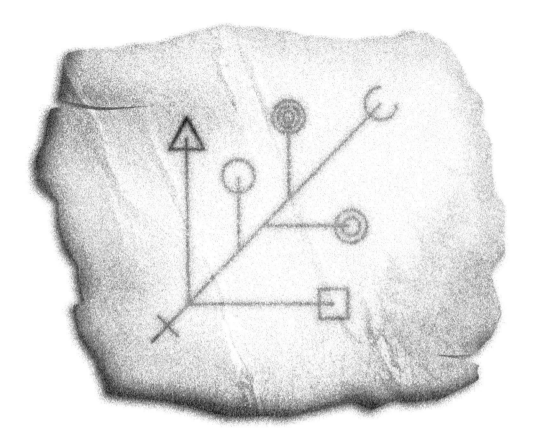

The great seal of the Old Ones

prevent the passage of the Old Ones or their children when placed upon any threshold. A householder who rightly inscribes it upon his door may sleep securely from the incursion of these unnatural creatures, for it not only prevents the spawn of the Old Ones from entering the house but also fortifies its windows and walls from their malice, so that the interior is preserved against all designs to breech its unseen barrier.

The seal was cut into the dais in the starlit chamber to prevent the entrance of the Old Ones, and for aeons it has fulfilled its function, for deep dwellers in the lower chambers assert that no spawn of that space-crossing race has ever passed through the soul portals. To common man and other creatures it offers no barrier, but only against the passage of the Old Ones or those things engendered of the Old Ones.

It is somewhat effective against the human worshippers of the seven lords, for these men are in constant awe of its power and fly from the very sight of it, though they could cross it if they dared.

No man understands the working of the Elder Seal. It may be that in its proportions and angles, it concentrates the same baneful influence shining down from the stars that ages ago drove the Old Ones from the surface of our world, in the same way that cunningly polished crystals and curved mirrors capture and concentrate the heat of the sun and cause fires to spring forth from wood and other combustible things.

When drawn upon the ring of the ritual circle, it serves as an effective protection against Nyarlathotep, who cannot perceive even with his arcane wisdom what transpires within the circle or hinder the progress of the work. Worn about the neck as a charm, it protects the traveler against the voracious children of Shub-Niggurath created from human seed who haunt the wilderness places and wait for prey. Even the doorways of dreams are sealed, and no spawn of the Old Ones can enter the mind of one who wears the charm. Those who invoke the seven lords shun it, for it renders all their preparations void and frustrates all their arts.

It is written that after peace was made between the Elder Things and the spawn of Cthulhu, and he had withdrawn from the poison of the stars to his tomb on R'lyeh, which was then still above the waves, three members of the Elder Race came to R'lyeh in secret and placed the seal upon the entrance to his tomb, so that after waking he would be trapped for unnumbered ages, for they foresaw the sinking of the city with their astronomical arts and placed the seal on the eve of the cataclysm. In this way they thought to frustrate Cthulhu, for he cannot wake from his sleep of death until the door is opened, and the seal cannot be breeched by either he or his spawn. Yet with all their wisdom they did not consider the rise of our race, still uncreated by them, and it may prove that at some future time the ingenuity of man can unlock the gate that holds impotent the might of the god.

The Underground River A'zani

After exhausting the resources in the city beneath Irem and all that can be gleaned by travel through its soul portals, and communion with the deep dwellers who haunt its vaulted chambers and vast, many-pillared halls, the traveler must descend more deeply into the earth, for there is no escape upward past the witch I'thakuah who ever waits and listens. In the lowest reaches of the western halls, beyond a stone stairway bathed in blinding radiance that shines out from the walls with the brightness of beaten gold, is to be found a great door of cast bronze that swings easily and without sound on its hinge although it has received no grease for countless ages. Past it lies a passageway, and farther beyond a channel cut through the solid rock by the waters of an ancient river that ran dry long ago, although to one who stands and holds his breath, the distant echo of its thundering waters may still be heard. The river was called A'zani by the reptilian race, or so it is reported by their descendents, who still crawl through darkness across the dusty gravel bed of that watercourse.

In antediluvian times the course of the A'zani was impassible, for its surging flood completely filled the cavernous spaces that twist and writhe ever westward deep beneath the sands of the desert toward the Red Sea. It served as the outlet for the mighty fountains that rose beneath Irem, which in the distant past were much more powerful than in the days when men inhabited the place. Over the passage of ages its flood dwindled to a trickle and at last ceased altogether, leaving only the convoluted passage, like the hollow, sloughed skin of some great serpent. Where the rushing stream forced its way into caverns that already existed in the depths, the way is high and broad, and the sound of wings may be heard in the darkness overhead, like the soft sound of bats, but these creatures are not bats; in other places the gravel carried along by the waters has been thrown in sloping piles, so that the way is narrow enough that a man must lower his head.

The visitor to the nameless city fortunate enough to possess flint and tinder, and able to find wood to burn, should prepare torches from the fat of rats, to light the dry riverbed nearest to the city; for it is close to their ancestral home that the degenerated descendents of the reptilian race scurry and dart about on their four clawed feet, their heads lowered near to the ground smelling out their prey, which consists of rats, snakes, and an abundant kind of white spider not found elsewhere. These spiders are the size of a man's hand with the fingers outspread; they cling in thick masses to the walls and ceilings of the passage, and dart across the gravel bed seeking their own food in the form of worms and beetles. Difficult to avoid without the illumination of a flame, they run about everywhere, and make the sound of a dry stick cracking when stepped upon; their fangs are not venomous, but their bites are painful due to their largeness.

A man without a torch who has consumed his dried store of the white fungus-dwelling spiders of second sight will have scant signs to guide him along the riverway, only the slight general descent of the bed, for it both rises and falls, but falls more often than rises, and the faint breath of salt air that enters the channel from its mouth near the sea; the stirring of the air is only perceptible in the final part of the journey along the river. He will find himself mired in darkness, crawling on all his limbs as do the reptilian beings, forever annoyed by the furry bodies and intermittent bites of the spiders, which however serve as a convenient source of food and moisture, for their bodies are fat with water.

The reptilian beings go naked, and most have lost the ability to speak, either in their own language or in the dialect of ancient Irem. They fear to enter their city, but remain near the bronze doors that open on the passage leading to the river, and worship or adore the doors themselves as gods. A few who are older than the rest are able to converse in the strange accent of Irem, having learned it by observation; for this race resembled the crocodiles of the Nile in being long in years, and among those dwelling in the darkness of A'zani are a small number who remember the tongue of man. Little is to be learned by conversing with these elders, who have suffered the dulling of the mind common to extreme age, but they can speak the name of the river, and will describe with relish how our race was tricked into building Irem above their hidden city.

Near the bronze gates are arrayed in family groups the wooden caskets of their honored dead. Some few are still to be found in the chambers of the city itself, but most have been moved beyond the gates. The deep dwellers say that it was the custom of this race to preserve the bodies of their dead as do the Egyptians, dress them in finest adornments and clothes, and place them within sepulchers that have lids of glass through which the corpses might be viewed by successive generations of blood relations. When the race in its final decadence fled the city and went to dwell in the dry river channel, they could not bear to part with their ancestors and carried their caskets beyond the doors. Only the bodies of the dead who possessed no living family were left behind.

Many of these tombs will be found to be broken, their contents stolen for nourishment. The reptilian beings have fallen to the practice of consuming the dried flesh of the dead of other bloodlines, though they will not defile their own direct ancestors in this way. The social life of the race consists in attempts by family groups to despoil the tombs of other families, who guard them with their very lives, for when all the tombs of a family are broken and the corpses stolen, it is the stated belief of the elders that the unfortunate family will inevitably perish. Even though this can be no more than a fable, belief makes it so, and in this way the numbers of this race ever diminish.

A recent traveler passing along the riverbed happened to witness by torchlight a battle between two rival clans, each a score or more in number. One great family had taken a defensive position before their honored dead, but because of the constant need to hunt for food, their numbers were weakened. The other clan overwhelmed the defenders in a rush of dry scrabbling limbs and snapping jaws, and managed to bear off several of the caskets of their rivals while the battle raged, but before they could despoil their contents, the hunters returned and their fresh strength enabled the defenders to recover their precious desiccated corpses. An observer would think it was a victory of nations, so clamorous were the guttural ululations of the victors, who seemed to lose the power of articulate speech in their excitement. Such is the pathetic existence of this once-magnificent race of builders and scholars.

In the greater caverns the batlike creatures, forever unseen, may be heard to swoop down from the heights on softly brushing wings and snatch up squealing their prey to carry it beyond the torchlight to the ceilings where it is consumed. The sounds of their chewing are plainly heard, enhanced by the echoing rocks, and so too the sounds of the bones and skulls of their prey striking the gravel and boulders below. They are not large enough to carry up a member of the reptilian race or a human being, but in their attempts their claws leave deep gashes, for they are sharp as daggers and cut through the tough hides of the reptiles as easily as through unprotected skin. When they attack they may be killed, having thin bones and frail wings, but their blood is poisonous and causes sickness, making them useless for food. Enough are killed that they only attack in numbers of two or three at a time, never singly, and their attacks are infrequent.

The reptilian creatures will also attempt to slay the traveler for nourishment, as there is never sufficient food in the caverns and passageway for all that dwell there; the utterance of the cry *Ïe! Nyarlathotep!* will keep them at bay. All quake in terror at the name in the way a dog will flinch when a man makes a gesture of throwing a stone, even though no stone is in his hand; and so it may be concluded that it was the lord of the Old Ones known as the Chaos That Creeps who drove them from the chambers of their underground city and into the river caverns.

After a day of progress the reptilian race is left behind, and after many more the breeze of the sea is felt on the cheeks and the scent of salt is detected. It is an easier matter to progress by following this breeze, which leads to a pit in the stones on the desolate shore of the Red Sea. Follow the shore north, and you will come upon a small sea port, where rough passage may be had for a reasonable sum or a few traveler's tales to the ancient canal cut by the Egyptians at the head of the Red Sea, and from thence journey may be undertaken overland to Memphis.

Memphis, City of Mummies

There are those knowing nothing of the races that inhabited this world before the creation of man who write that Memphis is the first city, older than all others, even more ancient than Irem of the thousand pillars. A traveler who views its ruins rising up amid its streets and fields would be persuaded of the truth of this assertion in the absence of other knowledge, for so great are the carven stones that it scarcely seems possible that they were cut by the hand of man. In the earliest history of the Black Land, as it was called due to the blackness of its soil, Memphis was the chief city of the people, but this honor in after times was conferred on Thebes, and though its grandeur has diminished, the most primal secrets continue to lie hidden among its catacombs and tombs.

Before the coming of the Christians to Egypt, the god Ptah was worshipped in this city. His name signifies the craftsman, or engraver on stones, and evidence of his worship is scattered everywhere around the buildings of the place, for no people in the world so loved to cut images and words into stone. He is benign in disposition, yet not to be used with contempt, for his power has lingered in his homeland, and terrible misfortunes fall upon the heads of those who mock the gods. The Egyptians believed the heavens to be supported on a great iron plate beaten into shape by the hammer of this workman, whom they praised with the titles Father of Beginnings and Lord of Truth.

No other human race takes such care in the handling of its corpses. By their arts they sought to preserve the body of the newly dead for eternity, and by constant effort and study over countless generations they so well succeeded that tombs may be discovered containing the bodies of nobles and honored scribes that are many centuries old, yet have faces that when unwrapped appear to be sleeping, so well are they fortified against worms.

The chief substance used in the process of preservation is mumia, from which the wrapped bodies derive their common name. Idb Betar testifies that it is very like the bitumen of Judea that is taken from the Asphaltites Lake, where it is found accumulating beneath the water. Other ingredients commonly used are a salt called natrum, honey, oil of cedar, and spices such as powdered myrrh, cassia, and frankincense. These preservatives would not prevail in the absence of careful preparation of the corpse, which has all its organs extracted, including the brain, which the embalmers draw from the skull through the nose with iron hooks. The main viscera are placed in jars sacred to the four corners of the world, and set within the tomb near the corpse, which is carefully wrapped in all its parts with strips of linen or silk. The older mummies are always linen-wrapped, but those made under the rule of the Ptolemies are often wound in silk imported from the east.

In the present era the practice of mummification has almost been abandoned. Old men who saw it thrive in their boyhood have watched it dwindle to only two workshops where it is still actively done, for the sons and daughters of wealthy houses still prefer to preserve their dead in this traditional manner, in spite of the condemnation of the Christians, who put their corpses untreated in the ground to rot. Those without wealth can no longer afford to preserve their dead, but will often place the corpse swathed in its winding sheet in the ancient catacombs where the mummies of countless generations of their ancestors are stacked in niches carved in the stone walls.

Under Christian rule the reverence for the dead has given way to indifference. Jewish traders hire men to plunder the catacombs and break open the bodies for their mumia, which is sold as a potent medicine in many lands. It is taken from the skulls and stomachs, and sold locally in the market at a low price, for so abundant are the ancient corpses that no end of this resource can be foreseen. The renowned physician El-Magar wrote of its many virtues, particularly of its power to heal wounds, in which it excels all other remedies. It is applied directly to the injured part of the body or powdered and consumed, depending on the disease. Common bitumen does not possess its healing virtues, for certain salts and juices of the corpse over time leech their way into the mumia and fortify it.

Nor should it be thought that all mumia is equally potent. The older is more powerful, and that taken from the corpse of a great warrior or king has greater virtues both for healing and for other uses than that extracted from an ordinary man. It was for this mumia that the tombs of the pharaohs were plundered by necromancers in past ages. That the tombs contained great wealth of gold and precious gems was only an added inducement, but the mumia of the king was the principle prize to those aware of its many virtues.

An amusing story may be related here that shall act as a caution to travelers. It is said that once the traffickers in mumia, having exhausted the usual places where it is found, plundered a catacomb that had been used to entomb the bodies of a leper colony many centuries ago. It was traded far and wide, but also sold in the market square to the healers and common citizens of Memphis. Less than a year later it was noticed that many of those who had bought this tainted remedy had contracted the dread disease, and the Jewish merchant responsible for its distribution was torn apart by women enraged at the fate of their husbands and sons at the base of the common well that may be seen in the square to this day. So the poet was moved to write, *Avoid physicians as though they were the plague itself, for the plague is less pernicious, and exacts no fee for its services.*

Concerning the Tombs of Wizards

All the land of Egypt, from the Delta to the Cataracts, is infested with sorcerers and necromancers. This should not be cause for wonder when it is considered that the religion of the ancients of this place was composed of magical arts for intercourse with the gods, and their coercion in the service of men. The gods of Egypt were not merely worshipped and adored but were manipulated, and even created, by the arts of the priests, whose skill in magic has never been equaled by any of our race since their time. Greater even than the magic of the priests was that of the wizards, who dwelt alone and apart in the desert, at some distance from the river and the green places that are the habitations of men, their only servants an apprentice and the familiar spirits bound in obedience to them.

The tombs of wizards are deep, for it was their constant fear that after death men, and other creatures of the wastes, would meddle with their bones; the art of necromancy is dependent on the use of the bodies of the dead, and on things joined to those bodies, and no corpse is more potent in magic than that of a wizard, for which reason they are highly prized. Great is the power of the mummy of a pharaoh, but greater still is the might of the mummy of a wizard, which was not made as were the mummies of the nobles and commoners of Egypt, but from different substances that preserved not the flesh but the soul and spirit. For this reason they caused their bodies to be placed in the deepest openings of the earth, below the catacombs, below even the mines.

The nethermost caves are not fit places for eyes that see; their marvels are bizarre and terrifying. Cursed is the ground where dead thoughts quicken anew and become oddly bodied, and evil is the mind that no skull imprisons. Wisely did Ibn Schacabao write that *Happy is the tomb where no wizard hath lain, and happy the town at night whose wizards are all ashes.* For it is anciently reputed that the soul in compact with a devil fleets not from his mortal husk, but nourishes and instructs the very worms as they gnaw, until out of decay springs abominable life, and the dull scavengers of the depths wax crafty and swell monstrous to plague the earth. Great wounds are opened where the natural pores of the ground should suffice, and things have learned to walk that should have crawled.

The body of a wizard is rendered impotent by only one means: it must be burned to ashes in the open air in daylight, even to the bones and teeth, and its ashes collected with care and scattered widely upon the wind before the setting of the sun. It is to avoid this fate that causes wizards to select their tombs in readiness for their deaths; for though their life may be prolonged by their arts beyond the reckoning of men, they are mortal and in the end must die. In the common unfolding of events they become aware of the time of their death before it occurs, and are able to select among men a living vessel into which they transfer their essence, and this is usually their apprentice, who prepares himself for this surrender of his flesh by years of study; for the wizard that has passed into a living human vessel loses part or all of his memories, and must relearn his wisdom in the arcane arts.

In the event of a sudden violent misfortune that claims the life of such a sage without due preparation, his restless spirit will not sleep but forever seeks to reanimate itself, and will use whatever living host it can reshape to its purposes, which it does by a kind of instinct since the blow of unexpected death shatters the higher reason that remains bound to the corpse, leaving only hunger and a fiery will that can never be quenched. When a host of right kind cannot be found, a host is made from some lesser form of life conveniently near, for decaying flesh is never alone since verminous things cannot resist its savor. To eat of a wizard is to acquire in part his virtues, but to eat too much is to be taken over by his restless spirit and shaped by his burning will. His spirit waits for the appropriate host it can turn to its purposes; if none can be secured, it uses what is at hand, even though it entails a loss of higher awareness for many generations of transmigrations. Things so made, misshapen and monstrous beyond description, are ever hungry and are to be avoided.

West of Memphis lies hid the tomb of a great wizard who in life bore the name of Nectanebus, who was the last king of pure Egyptian blood in this land. Though it is less than a day beyond the outskirts of the city by horseback, it is so well concealed that an army seeking its entrance could not find it in a year of searching. Only one who knows its place can find it, and only one who has visited the tomb can know its place, unless he is first led there by a guide. The wizard chose this tomb because it is not the usual place for the burial of kings, and so would pass the ages unviolated; or such was his intent, but who can foresee the vagaries of time, and the changes of fortune, over the span of centuries? The tomb was found, and is known to a few who have partaken of its rare feast and gained wisdom thereby; and all who have visited its depths until this time were wise in the ways of necromancy, for it yet contains but a single corpse.

There are few guides to the tomb among the living, but the sands of Egypt crawl with the shades of the dead who see all that happens beneath the moon with their pale and lusterless eyes. They fear to enter the tomb, which in truth holds nothing of value for them, but can be induced to lead the traveler to the entrance with the proper persuasion, for pain in its intensity ever overpowers fear, a truth known to every man who has suffered upon his flesh the insults of the torturer. The way down is steep, and cut with shallow holes more like the notches of a ladder than the steps of a stair; the blackness is absolute, a fall fatal. Having reached the bottom of the artificial shaft, progress continues down the more gradual incline of a natural cave, at the end of which is a chamber high enough in which to stand upright.

The wizard lies upon his back within a carven box of cedar wood, which itself is set inside a stone sepulcher. The lids of both containers have been broken by hammers and lie in pieces on the floor of the cavern. Linen wraps his corpse save for his feet and his hands, which cross on his breast and seem to claw the air in their nakedness. Eight fingers are missing. The last taken was the largest finger of the left hand, upon which only the index finger and thumb remain; the right hand has none. So too have all ten toes been removed from his feet. The stumps show the marks of teeth and appear gnawed in the uncertain light of a lamp. Those who came took what they needed, but feared to take too much, for the power of Nectanebus is legendary.

The cavern is dry and lifeless, and was chosen for these qualities, for the wizard was determined that he should arise in the flesh of a man; his dismay can only be imagined when his trusted apprentice, after placing his corpse within the tomb in secret, fled, never to return, fearing the loss of his own mind more than the fury of his master. Whether the will of the wizard proved strong enough to deal death from so deep within the earth cannot be known, but it is certain it did not possess the power to compel the return of the apprentice; and so the potency of the corpse remained undiminished for ages, and the hunger of its spirit unsated. Standing at the side of the sepulcher, the hunger and the rage may still be felt, but a resolute mind skilled in the arts of magical barriers can resist it long enough to acquire a portion of the wisdom and memories of the king.

Upon the groin of the mummy rests a disk of green stone engraved on its face with the Elder Seal. It has not been disturbed, for no visitor to the tomb has been bold enough to turn it, even though the prize it conceals is great. Around the border of the disk are engraved hieroglyphics that may be read by one who is versed in the ancient writing, and their meaning is thus:

> *The bone and flesh which possess no writing are wretched,*
> *but behold, the writing of Nectanebus is under the Great Seal,*
> *and behold, it is not under the Little Seal.*

It is wisest to leave this seal undisturbed should you venture to this place, for there remain yet two fingers, and the nose and ears are intact.

The Uncanny
Ways of Cats,
and Their Cult

In no other land is the cat treated with greater veneration than in Egypt; for in death it was the custom to have these beasts mummified, and so frequent was this practice that they are to be found throughout the resting places of the dead, while in life they are respected alike by the common people and those of noble rank, so that the wanton killing of a cat is regarded as a kind of murder, and the man who commits the deed is shunned or even stoned to death. Under the rule of the bishops, the Christians sought to end this bestial idolatry, and dead cats are no longer mummified, but the respect which an Egyptian bears toward living animals of this kind remains undiminished. It is even believed that cats have the power to comprehend human speech, though whether the ancient tongue of the land or the language of the Greeks, or both, is never affirmed.

The prohibition against the killing of cats is easy to understand, when it is considered that the region of the Nile near the Delta is the most fertile farming land in all the world, producing prodigious crops of grains that would inevitably be diminished by mice and rats, and these vermin would multiply without restraint, were it not for the innumerable cats that hunt them. They are allowed to enter and leave the houses, shops, and churches without constraint, and should a cat be injured by a wagon or through some other mishap, always someone will take the animal and care for it until it either dies from its hurt or recovers.

Cats have the second sight without any need to consume the white spiders of the desert. When a cat stops and stares intently at a place that seems empty, it is certain that it is looking at a ghost or other shadow creature that passes unperceived by men. Hence wherever a cat is present, no spirit may enter unobserved, and it is for this reason that sorcerers employ cats as watchers against intruders from the other realms. The wraiths of the night resent this attention, and are at enmity with all cats. It is true, also, that cats see through the glamours of magic, so that no wizard is able to mask his identity or pass invisible where a cat watches. Of all beasts the senses of this creature are most subtle. Though the eyes of a cat are not keener than those of a hawk, nor the ears sharper than those of a dog, a cat sees and hears things that lie beyond this material existence that neither hawk can see nor dog can hear.

Another talent possessed by this remarkable beast is the ability to walk into the land of dreams and out again as easily as a man enters or leaves a dwelling. Those lost in dreams are sometimes led back to our world by passing cats, who have a fondness for our race and are ever willing to lend aid when treated with dignity and kindness. The man who sleeps with a cat upon his cot sleeps safely, for he has a constant guide to draw him out of the entangling thickets of his nightmares. It has been written that cats suck the breath from sleeping infants, and in this way deprive them of life, but this is the practice of Shub-Niggurath and her daughters, which cats attempt to drive away from the crib of the child; and in this they sometimes succeed, and nothing is known of the deed, and sometimes they fail and are found upon the body of the child, and are accused of murder by the ignorant mothers.

The goddess of all cats is Bast, who is figured in the form of a cat, or sometimes as a woman with the head of a cat. She is worshipped chiefly at Bubastis in the seventh nome of Lower Egypt, where her cult survives to the present in spite of strenuous efforts by the churches to eradicate it; for though her cult is joyous, the Christian bishops hated it for its pagan taint and ever tried to destroy it. The worshippers of the goddess pass unseen for most of the year, but at the festival of Bast in the spring of the year, they disport and make merry with one another and with the people of the city, singing, sounding musical instruments, and promenading through the streets. What is most appalling to the Christians is the practice of the women, who periodically raise their skirts and reveal their most private parts in wanton display with knees parted. This they do in honor of the goddess of cats, who draws her power from the moon.

The adorers of Bast may be known by subtle signs, for many bear a small scar in the shape of a crescent moon upon some part of their necks, and it is their custom to cut their fingernails to points; this they do subtly so as to attract little notice, but the mark is universally recognized by the common citizens and merchants of the city, who accord the worshippers of Bast great respect and reduce the prices of their wares when they perceive this sign; this has led some to adopt the fashion who have never walked in the festival. When the cut of the nails is very obvious the priests may induce the guardians of the city to apprehend the transgressor and pull out his nails by the roots as punishment for his sin, but the practice continues unabated.

The temple of Bast once stood in the center of the city, and was renowned throughout the world for its purity and perfection; it was long since pulled down, and a church erected on its foundations. This modest church serves two functions. During the day it is the house of God for the Christians, but during the night the adorers of Bast gather in a secret chamber behind the altar, where there is a statue of the goddess in green stone that resembles jade, in posture sitting on her haunches upon a cubic pedestal of black stone. This stature, which was rescued from the destruction of the temple and preserved in secret, is of the height of a living cat and perfect in all its proportions so that it seems to live and even to move in the flickering flames of the oil lamps by which the chamber is illuminated. Its eyes are pale blue jewels set in their centers with pointed ovals of jet, so well contrived by the sculptor that they appear to be capable of sight. Upon its head is a lunar crescent in translucent white stone that is called moonstone, and is the delicate changing color of the interior of seashells.

The worshippers of Bast place offerings of milk and meat at the foot of the pedestal that supports the statue, which are consumed by the living cats that come and go in the chamber through small entrances in the base of the walls. After presenting their offering, they make silent prayers before the goddess upon their hands and knees, then leave with utmost decorum and solemnity, much in contrast to their behavior during the spring festival. It is said by members of the cult that prayers made to the goddess in this manner are never refused.

The Riddle of the Sphinx Interpreted

The journey up the Nile from the Delta region is pleasant and uneventful, unless the small sailing ships used for this purpose by the Egyptians are molested by the crocodile or by a type of great beast known in the sacred books as the behemoth, the jaws of which can cut the body of a man into two parts. It lies in wait beneath the water and watches for boats. If the unwary pilot fails to see the nose of this creature projecting above the surface, and sails too near its resting place, it attacks with sudden ferocity, overturning the craft and killing all who fall into the water, so that the river runs red with their blood. The Egyptians fear it more than the crocodile, and shun its habitations. It eats both plants and the flesh of men, and seldom ventures on land, for it is all belly and moves awkwardly on its thick legs; yet in the water it travels lightly and can traverse great distances in moments when enraged.

The behemoth is descended from the evil things created by the Old Ones, for the Elder Race did not fashion all forms of life that now dwell in this world; most were their creations, along with humankind, but a few were the work of Cthulhu, who in the early times made experiment with many forms in his effort to generate armies of warriors that might aid his battles against the cities of the Elder Race. Hence, all of the creations of Cthulhu are noxious and of evil disposition, and inimical to the creations of the Elder Ones. They appear to have no natural place in our world but rather to have been imposed upon it by a malicious will, to either make their own place by force or to perish away. The sea-dwelling octopus is such an abomination, as is readily apparent, for who has seen this beast, which has no bones but only a soft body that may take on any color or shape, and eight legs that twist and wriggle like worms, and has not sensed in his heart that it is an alien thing unnatural to this world?

On an arid plain called Giza, no great distance from the river, stands the largest idol ever carved from stone, known to the vulgar as the Sphinx, although the true and secret name of this god is Harmakhis. It is somewhat similar to the Sphinx described in the fanciful tales of the Greeks, and there is no doubt that the idol itself was the cause of these fables. In form it is the body of a crouching lion with the head of a man, of noble and imposing aspect. It watches the dawn, as it has watched for ages beyond counting, for its origins are unknown, it is so ancient a monument. The head is in the image of Kephren, a pharaoh of Egypt who caused to be built one of the pyramids that rise on the plain not far from the Sphinx itself.

Kephren found it so weathered with years that its original face could not be recognized, and so caused his craftsmen to put his own image on the head, which for this reason appears unnaturally small for the body. Few know what the original face of the Sphinx resembled, and it is better so, for the knowledge would haunt their dreams and cause them to wake with cries of terror in their throats. It is whispered in dark places by things not wholly human that the great statue once bore the true image of Nyarlathotep, who is commonly supposed to have a thousand masks but no face of his own. By this monument the dark lord of the Old Ones marked a place beneath the earth where power is concentrated.

It is old; far older than the pyramids or the temples, older even than the Nile itself, which flowed by a different course when the Sphinx was shaped by inhuman hands and lush jungle covered the plateau upon which it crouches. There are wise men who have called it the oldest carven image in this world, and this may be true, for it is more ancient than any work of man, and yet older than the works of other races that shared the earth after the changing of the stars rendered our world unfit for the Old Ones. It may be that the monuments of the Elder Race in their great city far to the frozen south were made before Nyarlathotep shaped the Sphinx, but of these nothing is known, for no man has seen them.

The Greeks tell a fable of a creature they call the Sphinx, who has the head and breast of a woman, and who waylays travelers on a lonely mountain road and demands that they give the answer to a riddle she proposes. Those who fail, she devours. All who tried failed, until at last the hero Oedipus gave the correct response, and the Sphinx in vexation and despair hurled herself off the edge of an abyss. The answer to the riddle is well-known, but it is not well understood; it has two meanings, one for children and the other for the wise.

The Sphinx of the Greeks asked the question of travelers: What beast goes on four legs in the morning, two legs at noon, and three legs in the evening? The answer given by Oedipus was man, who in the morning of life crawls on his four limbs, in the noontime of manhood walks on two legs, but in the evening of infirm old age must seek the aid of a stick, and so goes on three legs. The Sphinx, despairing, destroyed herself, misunderstanding the perception of the hero, who guessed the surface of the truth but did not penetrate to its heart.

The race of man was made by the Elder Things in jest to have a foolish creature to mock and to study for their diversion, yet they did not make us as we now appear, but in the beginning our bodies were bestial and hairy, and we progressed across the ground with the aid of our arms, which were longer and more powerful than they are at present. Over time our bodies changed their shape, and became upright and almost hairless. No doubt the Elder Things would have found our present forms less amusing and would have exterminated us, but they were in decline and had been forced to the southern waters of our world, and had no time to play with the form of our race. At some time in the distant future, our shape will be unlike what is seen in this age, and we will go on three legs instead of two. For the riddle of the Sphinx does not concern a single man, but all of mankind.

How childish the tales in the holy books of Adam and Eve in the Garden, where is it written that man is the most beautiful of all creatures, being made in the image of God. Man was made in the image of a crawling, hairy beast for the diversion of overlords not of this world, and our present form is but a passing dream that will give way to some unguessed horror that would frighten women and children, could it be seen, but mercifully it is hidden in the dim mists of future time. Our bodies continue to change because they were made imperfectly, and there can be no stability or rest in imperfection. It is known that the Elder Things themselves go about on three feet that are triangular in shape; but this speculation cannot be pursued in this work, for at its end lies madness.

The Resurrectionists in the Storehouse of Kings

In the Sphinx there is a doorway that leads to a sloping tunnel extending for three hundred and twenty-six paces beneath the sands of the plateau. The location of this door is hidden both physically by the art of the ancient Egyptian stonemasons, and by spells of misdirection that turn the mind of any common man who happens to stumble on its mechanism, so that he forgets and fails to see what is before his face. Those who know of it, and can resist the clouding of the mind long enough to pass through this portal, are sworn by an oath of most solemn and horrific portent never to reveal its location or the manner by which it is opened. Most scribes, having heard rumors of this door, place it between the paws of the Sphinx, but a hint only may be given in observing that Nyarlathotep was not a god of the rising sun.

At the end of the inclined corridor is a double door of bronze that is sheathed in pounded gold leaf, so that it shines like the sun itself in the light of torches held in the hands of those who approach. The bronze door, like the tunnel before it and the chambers that lie within, are of human workmanship. Whatever older corridors lay beneath the Sphinx before the coming of our race to this world have been obliterated by the reworking of generations of craftsmen over ages of time, for this place has never suffered neglect but has always been the retreat of the worshippers of Nyarlathotep, who study the ways of sorcery and the secrets of death.

Beyond the doors is a long chamber that is perpetually illuminated by oil lamps set in the walls. A row of eleven stone pillars runs down either side of the central walkway so that there are twenty-two pillars in total supporting the low ceiling, which is painted blue and speckled with numerous golden stars. The pillars are not of the common Egyptian lotus or papyrus designs but are square and black, made from a type of stone not native to the region. Upon each is deeply cut a letter, or rather a number, in the ancient script of the Hebrews, for the Jews use their letters for numbers, having no numbers of their own similar to those we possess.

Above these numbers are golden plates little larger than the flat of the hand, which have been hammered and raised by the goldsmith's art to present scenes containing fantastic figures in meaningful display, so that each plate conveys a lesson that is composed not of words, but of signs or emblems. These images are unlike any other representations that exist in the world, and are known only to those who have walked the pillared hall, for no hint of their existence has ever been whispered beyond the gate of the Sphinx. Concerning the images upon the plates, it is both unlawful and imprudent to write. Let it only be revealed that some of the figures are human, others older than our race.

At the far end of the chamber of pillars is a small door of cedar wood without adornment. A priest of Nyarlathotep stands vigilant beside it, and will only admit one who can give the sacred sign of that order with his hand. The slightest hesitation or error in presenting the sign results in death, for upon the right index finger of the priest is a small lance dipped in the venom of the black scorpion of the wastes, the merest drop of which in the blood causes putrefaction and death within a span of moments. The scorpion is one of the creations of Nyarlathotep, who placed it upon the world for his pleasure; over the ages its form has divided and changed, and the potency of its venom has diminished, but the black scorpion of the wastes is unchanged from its making by the Chaos That Creeps, and its venom is as it was in the old times.

The priests of Nyarlathotep who use this place of power go robed and hooded in black, and keep their faces wrapped in a veil of black silk in imitation of their master, who wears these garments when he walks abroad across the world beneath the moon. They can see outward well enough through the silk, but their faces cannot be identified by any who look upon them, and they seldom speak but communicate with each other by means of elaborate gestures that are to them a language. They enter veiled and depart veiled, so that none knows the identity of the man who stands beside him.

The chamber beyond is large and square. In its center rests a smaller copy of the Sphinx in black stone, exact in all its details except that its head is not that of Kephren but of Nyarlathotep. It stares down upon the man entering through the door of cedar as though affronted by his presence, and the expression upon its face, if this word may be rightly applied to describe its visage, is sardonic and malignant, though without a trace of human features that would render its expression familiar. The priests indicate with their language of signs that it shows the true liniments of the great Sphinx before they became eroded by the sands of ages and then cut away at the command of Kephren.

The face cannot be described in any human tongue, for our race possesses no words adequate to the task; let it suffice to write that it is somewhat like the face of the god Set, though depictions of that god are but a faint shadow of the original image upon which they were based. The images of Set fail to capture the malignant horror of the face upon the smaller Sphinx, or the sense that it is aware and watchful, or its expression of supreme contempt. Before its gaze the priests prostrate themselves in worship, first gashing their arms with knives in the belief that the letting of human blood is welcomed by their god. In consequence the floor of the chamber before the statue is stained with blood, and though it is washed daily, it can never be made wholly clean.

Leading away from this place of worship is a broad corridor in the wall behind the idol, and set in its sides are other passageways that open into chambers filled with mummies that have been stolen from the royal tombs of Egypt. Not only the kings and queens are present in these chambers, but their children and their relations by blood. When tomb raiders ignorant of the value of the mumia of kings discovered the burial places of the royal dead, they took the gold and other precious things the tombs contained and left the corpses as things of no value; but to the priests of Nyarlathotep, who followed their footsteps unseen and unheard, it was the mummies that were precious, and for the gold they cared nothing, for gold is a substance of this world, but the corpse is a thing of the next world.

There are no greater necromancers upon the earth than the priests of this cult. Any traveler seeking the study of necromancy must come to the Sphinx, or his education is forever incomplete. Admission is difficult to obtain, but with sufficient proofs of skill, and the winning of the trust of those who deal in the marketplace for the cult, it can be achieved, but only by binding the soul in service to Nyarlathotep and his dark works. All who enter the gate of the Sphinx bear the mark of Nyarlathotep upon their bodies, where it remains until death, and indeed endures beyond death, for it can never be expunged. What is revealed in these pages is forbidden, and it remains to be tried whether the power of the Chaos That Creeps can reach across the sands from Giza to Damascus to strike down the writer who has betrayed his oath.

The Essential Salts and Their Use

The necromancers of Giza concern themselves not with the corpses of common men, but only employ those of royal blood or wizards; for the nobles when revived and made to talk may be able to describe the hiding places of rare books and gold buried in the earth, and the wizards to teach their methods, although oftentimes it happens that they are reluctant to reveal their secrets and must be encouraged with fire and blade. In this way, the cult has become both wealthy with ancient treasures and the repository of wisdom lost to the world. They are not to be trifled with, for their power and their agents reach to distant lands, so that a man marked for death in their council is foredoomed.

When a corpse is chosen for resurrection, it is first cut into parts of convenient size and boiled in clean water in a large copper kettle for a full day and night, and during this time the kettle is constantly stirred with a long wooden ladle to prevent the settling of substances to the bottom. The linen wrappings also are placed in the pot along with the flesh, for they contain a measure of the essential salts which the process is designed to extract. The mumia is softened and made fluid by the heat, so that it gradually becomes liquefied and rises to the top of the water. The acolyte tending the pot draws it off periodically using a small silver spoon and stores it in a stone vessel for future purposes.

At the end of the initial boiling, after all the mumia has risen and been skimmed from the pot, the linen strips that bind the corpse are taken out of the pot clean and white, like newly washed laundry, and discarded. The fire is allowed to burn to embers so that the heat is reduced, and an elixir is added to the water that has the property of softening and dissolving bone, teeth, nails, and hair. In this way the corpse is liquefied. When this has been accomplished the fire is fed with wood and made hot again, and the water in the pot, which has already been greatly reduced by these processes, is allowed to boil completely away.

What remains in the bottom of the kettle is a white, crystalline material of an amount that may be carried on the palms of two hands. The priests of Nyarlathotep scrape this from the kettle, using utmost care to remove the last trace, and pound it to uniform fineness in a mortar of rock crystal, using a crystal pestle. The white powder resulting from this operation contains the essential salts of the man or woman whose corpse was boiled, and it is from this powder that the living body may be reconstituted and made to serve as a house for the soul, which is called back into its former flesh by words of power. The salts may be kept for many years in a sealed vessel without losing their potency. There is a chamber in the catacombs beneath the Sphinx that contains nothing but shelves of bottles, each filled with the essential salts of a human being.

A man resurrected from his salts is in every respect as he was at the end of his life, save that the purification process of the priests removes from his renewed flesh the disease or injury that caused his death. It is a great shock to the soul to tear it back from its repose and reanimate it, and in consequence the resurrected are often insane, and scream ceaselessly or dash themselves into the walls, making it necessary to restrain them for questioning. Interrogation can take weeks, for the dead do not give up their secrets easily, and when the corpse used is old, its language may sound strange to modern ears, and contain many uncouth words that have passed from use and memory. The priests are expert in the lost dialects of their ancestors and skilled in all the arts of torture, so that little impedes their purposes except complete madness or a contamination of the salts.

When the salts are contaminated with the essence of other living things, as sometimes happens when, unknown to the priests, the mummy has been the breeding place of beetles, mice, or other vermin, the revitalization of the salts produces a monster that is partly man and partly whatever gnawed his corpse. Monsters bred in this manner seldom prove reliable sources of information. When the priests discover that they lack the faculty of speech, or that their speech is crazed and bestial, they commonly destroy them without further interrogation, for though the memory of the man may remain intact, the verminous parts of his reanimated nature inhibit its expression.

Wizards are treated with greater care, for in their hands, eyes, and tongues is the ability to project death on those who call them from their tombs. As a consequence, when the salts of a known wizard are reanimated, the first act of the priests is to put out his eyes with an iron pick, bind his hands into immoveable gloves of heavy leather, and gag his mouth. When answers are demanded of the wizard, the gag is momentarily removed, but a knife is held to his throat while he speaks, and a single false word results in his return to the grave. It is perilous to interrogate a wizard, and in spite of all these precautions, unfortunate consequences have resulted from the attempt.

A story is told among the younger acolytes of the cult, who have not yet learned the virtue of discretion, concerning the reanimation of the wizard Haptanebal, who was great above the Cataracts before the union of the two Egypts. Long ago his corpse was carried to Giza and laid to rest beneath the Sphinx, but over the years its identity was forgotten, until it became confused with the body of a scribe of the royal court and underwent reanimation without the usual safeguards employed for wizards. The story tells that five of the priests were consumed by spontaneous fire in their bodies before the sixth, who quite by chance was fortunate enough to be standing behind the wizard and beyond the range of his sight, succeeded in killing him with a sword.

The danger in reanimating a potent wizard is always great, but equally great are the prizes that may be wrung from him by skilled interrogators prepared in advance for the risks and resolute of heart. Wizards often take their most precious secrets of magic into the tomb, for they are unable to trust such powers with other men, even those they accept as their disciples or their own sons. By portioning out their wisdom with care, wizards have remained alive beneath the Sphinx for several years, and even been accorded a limited measure of freedom when they have won the partial trust of the priests, who remain ever watchful against deception. However, they are never allowed to leave the catacombs, for their skills are too potent to release on our age, which has forgotten the greatest effects of magic.

Those who have served their purpose are killed in an efficient manner, by strangulation with a cord around the neck, and their bodies are burned. Then the ashes are gathered and deposited into the Nile, where they are carried by the current to the sea. It is possible to reanimate the same corpse twice, by subjecting its resurrected flesh to the putrefaction and reduction process that was used to separate its essential salts, but this is seldom done since there is seldom any need. Those who are reanimated by the priests of Nyarlathotep are never permitted to die, save by mischance, until they have offered up all their knowledge, and the priests are satisfied that they have nothing more of value to give.

The Valley of the Dead

Thebes is a city of monuments, both to men and to gods. The eastern bank of the river is thick with temples, obelisks, and great statues. The temples, though much decayed with time and neglect, are connected by magnificent avenues lined with carved figures, and are reflected in artificial lakes and ponds, all of which give the city a grandeur not to be found in other cities of our race. On the western bank of the Nile are buried the royal dead in lavish tombs. Many of the tombs of the necropolis have been looted by the cult of animators, yet others still remain hidden beneath the sands, awaiting discovery.

To those possessed of the second sight, the moonlit streets of Thebes are not empty but filled with solemn throngs. Ghosts walk along the avenues that join the temples in silent, stately processions; lines of priests bear smoking trays of incense before the closed wagons that contained the statues of the principal gods and goddesses of the land, for it was the practice of the priests to parade their gods before the people, though they were always kept carefully concealed behind the curtains of the carts that bore them to and from their temples.

The great god of Thebes was Amun, who is sometimes represented as a man, or as a man with the head of a ram, and less often as a ram itself. To him was erected the largest of all temples in our world, the temple of pillars that humbles the pride of those who pass across its sand-strewn paving stones, for each pillar is ten times the height of a man, and they are so closely spaced that they seem to press down on those who walk between them. Not even the monuments of the Old Ones can belittle its grandeur.

Within the secret depths of this temple in ancient times, the primary statue of Amun was preserved. It had the property of life, for it was a magic of the priests of this land to animate the statue of Amun in the temple and to induce a kind of shade or spiritual essence to dwell there that expressed the personality and purpose of the god himself. The ignorant have written that Amun dwelt within the statue, but this is false; the statue was host to his emissary, who spoke and acted with the knowledge and power of the god, but the god dwelt elsewhere. He dreams still in Kadath in the cold waste, with the other gods of this world.

A traveler from our lands who was a necromancer learned from the ghouls of Thebes the legend that a large cache of precious objects lay buried beneath the floor of the temple of pillars. The wealth of the temple had been hurriedly interred by the priests so that it would not be looted during one of the numerous invasions of Egypt —who the invaders were is not preserved in the legend. By some mischance the precious things were never unearthed. Perhaps the invaders killed all the priests who had precise knowledge of their hiding place. How the ghouls learned of the location, they did not disclose.

The traveler hired two workmen who were accustomed to laboring beneath the moon and could be trusted not to speak of their affairs, and undertook to unearth the treasure. After several hours of digging they came upon a statue of Amun. It was in size the height of a man, and formed of bronze overlaid with gold leaf. The value of the object was slight, for it held no precious jewels or large masses of gold or silver, and in appearance it was quite ordinary, save for one detail—its enormous phallus was obscenely erect. This aroused ribald jests from the workmen, but the traveler quickly set them back to digging, and went aside to examine the statue more closely.

He drew a breath of surprise between his teeth, for his skill in necromancy revealed that the statue was alive. The hundreds upon hundreds of years it had rested beneath the dry sands of the temple had not extinguished its identity. The spirit present within the bronze body became aware of the traveler after several minutes, as though waking from a long slumber. The traveler felt a question in his mind, like the tickle of an insect walking upon his skin.

Where are the priests of the temple?

He sent his thoughts to the statue through its eyes. *Dead, all dead and fallen to dust.*

He felt the awareness of the spirit in the bronze expand as it looked outward; for this it did not need physical eyes, but was able to perceive all directions at once. Its words came to him in a whisper of despair.

Desolation, desolation, the end of days; the glory of God is put out like a reed torch in the river water, and the roof of the house is fallen.

With a piteous cry, the spirit flew up through the crown of the head of the statue and fled, wailing, into the night sky. One of the workmen raised his head to ask the traveler what had caused the strange sound. Lost in his own thoughts, the traveler made no answer, and the man shrugged and continued digging.

Though they labored until an hour before the first light of dawn, they found no other treasure. Perhaps it was too deeply buried to be unearthed in a single night. The work could not be continued a second night without the certainty of discovery by the inhabitants of the city, so with regret the traveler ordered that the empty and lifeless statue of Amun be cast back into the pit, and that the hole be filled. In the morning, there was no trace of the night's work.

The valley on the west bank of the Nile that holds the tombs of the noble houses of Thebes is a desolate land of sand and rock, surrounded by tall cliffs and steep hillsides. Holes in the ground reveal where robbers have looted the burial places in the distant past, for though the architects of the tombs took great pains to conceal their locations, always there were workmen who knew the places where gold lay hidden, and whose greed was more powerful than their fear of the gods. The tombs that remain undisturbed are well concealed and deeply buried, and may never be found by natural means.

The traveler is wise to only explore the valley of the dead under the light of the sun, never during the night. The valley is inhabited by vampire wraiths who cannot leave its boundaries, but within its towering hills are forever in search of fresh blood, for they feed on the vital essence that is held in flowing blood. The blood itself they do not drink, having no lips of flesh with which to suck, but they are nourished on the humors that exhale from blood in the moments after it spurts forth from the skin. They possess no physical part, yet in some way are able to cut the skin so that blood flows, and in this manner they feed. The cuts of these wraiths are less than the width of a finger, and are easily mistaken for the bite of some unseen nocturnal insect. They are shallow, and so sharp are the claws of the wraiths that make them that they are without pain, and only become noticeable by the wetness of the blood that runs forth.

The danger from these wraiths would seem to be slight, for a wraith can produce no more than a single cut upon the skin in the space of several minutes, and the blood that wells up is no more than a few drops. However, the scent of fresh blood attracts them from their tombs even as biting insects are attracted by the exhalation of the breath, and they press in an invisible horde around the unwary traveler who ventures into the valley by night, each wraith making a new cut upon some part of his skin, nor does clothing prevent this injury.

In a short while the hapless traveler will find himself wet from crown to heel with blood. Because the cuts cause no pain, the wetness is his first awareness of his peril. If he is fortunate and robust of body, he will realize the danger before the loss of blood renders him weak of limb. The wraiths press in an undivided mass around their bleeding prey, feeding upon his vital essence. Singly or in scant numbers, they cannot be detected save with the second sight, but when they feed in unison by the hundreds, their forms exert a pressure upon the skin that is felt as a soft embrace that squeezes the flesh from all sides and makes movement difficult.

There is only one defense against the vampire wraiths, and that is precipitous flight. They move swiftly, but not with the speed of a running man, and the traveler who maintains both his senses and his balance can outdistance them, provided he can find the strength to fight through their united ring as they feed. There is danger in running across the floor of the valley, for it is strewn with loose rocks that turn beneath the foot. Should the traveler stumble and fall, the wraiths will be upon him in a moment, and it is doubtful that he will find the reserves of strength to regain his feet and break from their grasp a second time.

Those who wander into their embrace and manage to escape their snare do so under the light of the moon, which shows the path to their frenzied gaze as they flee. Travelers cut by the wraiths during the dark of the moon are doomed, for it is not possible without illumination to run across the rock-strewn valley floor yet avoid stumbling. A lantern or torch is insufficient since these artificial lights do not cast their glow far enough ahead to provide warning of obstacles on the ground. Many are the men who have entered the valley of the dead at night, only to serve as meat for jackals in the first glow of dawn, for what the wraiths leave, the jackals and carrion hawks consume.

Walking Corpses Above the Second Cataract

Several days' sail above Thebes, the river Nile becomes difficult to navigate, its course broken by a series of cataracts that necessitate overland travel around the turbulent waters. Between the cataracts progress is made up the river in small boats easily overturned by the crocodiles that lie in wait for them as though for a careless cow that comes to the edge of the river to drink. With swift thrusts of their long tails these fearsome beasts can rise partially from the water to snatch a man from inside a boat, and what they take below the surface is never recovered. For this reason the masters of the boats tie the wing feathers of the bird known as the ibis to the bows, for it is the belief of those who trade along the river that the ibis and crocodile are mortal enemies, and that the crocodile fears the ibis. This is no more than a fable, for men have been snatched from boats that bear the ibis feather and, indeed, having similar feathers tied around their necks.

Above the Second Cataract the men dwelling along the Nile are no longer Egyptian but a black race having its own customs and gods. It is believed by some of our scholars that from this region of the Upper Nile the Queen of Sheba came, who visited Solomon at Jerusalem to sit at his feet and learn wisdom, but the true location of the land of Sheba has been forgotten. The gods of the people are many and savage, in accord with their nature; for the people wear little clothing and speak in a guttural tongue, and they are hostile to strangers in their villages until placated with gifts. Chief among the gods is Bes, a squat, fat savage who has even made his way to Thebes as a token of good fortune. He has no blood tie with the lineage of Egyptian gods but is a vulgar intruder in their land.

Despite their lack of social graces and the absence of notable monuments in stone that would attest to their skill as builders, the black race above the Second Cataract has generated sorcerers as potent as any in the world. They worship Yig in the living form of a great serpent or dragon that is a length of thirty paces from nose to tail, and crushes horses and oxen in its coils before swallowing them whole. This beast is larger than the basilisk but it has no venom, and relies only upon its strength to kill its prey. They also worship Tsathoggua, a god of the Old Ones, though not one of their seven lords, who is adored most often in hot and humid regions where the mud is fertile and thick with creeping things.

Of all the Old Ones, Tsathoggua is the most malicious save only for Nyarlathotep. His form is that of a great toad with the head of a man, having a wide slitted mouth and bulbous eyes. In power he equals or surpasses the lords, but at some distant age he was cast out from their midst and compelled to dwell alone and apart in the nethermost depths of the vaults of Zin, growing ever fatter and more obscene on the rivers of blood shed on his altars by his fanatical inhuman worshippers. The reason for his expulsion from the circle of lords cannot be uttered, for to reveal it is certain death, but it is the cause of the god's constant and unending hunger, and has bearing on the fall of the Dragon into the Bottomless Pit * * * * * about which no more may be hinted.

Long after the inhuman race that worshipped him in deep caverns had decayed to mindless barbarity, the black statues of Tsathoggua were discovered abandoned in their temples in the vaults of Zin by men who ventured there, and were carried upward, eventually reaching the surface of the earth, where the cult of the toad god waxed mighty in the Black Lands. The thick blood of sacrifices spilled before the malignant gaze of his statue is used to create a kind of living ichor animated by the god and subject to his will. It is unwise to venture within a temple of Tsathoggua, for this viscose sentinel never sleeps.

The shamans of the black race of Khem, as they call the land in their own tongue, have power to control the bodies of the dead, but not after the same manner as the priests of Nyarlathotep at Thebes, for the priests of the Sphinx resurrect the mummies of those long dead to a natural life, so that their souls return to their flesh and they are in every respect as they were before death, but the shamans above the Second Cataract are only able to raise the corpses of those newly dead, and animate their bodies in an unnatural way, by the invocation of demonic spirits that are made by the power of Tsathoggua to dwell in these houses of decaying flesh. The bodies continue to corrupt after given a semblance of life, so that their term of use is limited, and eventually they fall into a putrid mass, yet still moving and aware, for the spirit inhabiting the corpse will not depart until the body has become incapable of movement.

The demons called into the dead flesh give their vessels great strength and are obedient to the shamans who summon them, for only the shamans have the knowledge to destroy these infernal spirits, although other magicians are able to call or banish them. The shamans use such shambling dead to fulfill their purposes among their people, and it is certain that a man who insults a shaman, or refuses to pay the expected offering, will be visited in the night by one of these possessed shells and murdered. This common practice has aroused great hatred among the common people against the shamans, but terror prevents them from acting to rid the land of these outrages. Each village along the river has its own head man and its own shaman and his apprentice, but the shaman rules the head man, who cannot enforce the laws without his concurrence.

In this place Christendom has no hold, nor is the faith of Islam known among this savage race. There are a scattered few who practice the ways of Moses, for the faith of the Hebrews has spread from the land of Ethiopia that lies to the east, where it has endured for centuries. How the laws of Moses became established so far south of Jerusalem is a mystery, but many assert that the Queen of Sheba, when she returned from her visit with Solomon, brought back his faith and instituted its practice. Hebrew charms are to be seen worn around the necks of the common people, who have no understanding of what the letters represent, and most frequent is the name of God with four letters, called by the Greeks *tetragrammaton*, which simply signifies four letters.

During the day the possessed dead lie in boxes or in shallow holes beneath the earth, which does not inconvenience them for they have no need to breathe and are immune to discomfort. When the shaman who created them wishes to send them out to do his will, he summons them to him by means of a small whistle made from the thinner bone of the human forearm. The shamans regard these whistles as precious objects and never remove them from the thong around their necks. They can produce three notes that are thin and high-pitched, like the cries of soaring birds, but by varying the length and order of the notes, the sounds they make are infinite in number. To the common people of this race, no sound in the night is more terrifying than the whistle of a shaman.

After the walking corpse is called up from its repose, the shaman leads it to the house or other place where is to be found his intended victim, and gives to the corpse an object that has had close contact with the flesh of the man the possessing demon is intended to slay. Hair and nail parings are most often used, but a sweat-stained garment, a sandal, or even a dried piece of excrement will also serve. From the contact which this object once had with the person, the demon inhabiting the corpse knows who it is to kill, and proceeds directly to the unfortunate man; nor will any opposition or subterfuge turn it from its purpose, for though it moves awkwardly it never tires or ceases to pursue its intention until it has accomplished the shaman's desire.

A young warrior who had offended the shaman of his village by refusing to pay the offering of gold demanded by the shaman managed to avoid his fate for eleven days by constant flight, during which he paused neither to eat nor to sleep, but on the twelfth night exhaustion overcame him, and the corpse walker summoned by the shaman, much putrefied and deformed by the long days spent lying in the ground under the sun and walking the paths beneath the moon, and riddled with crawling beetles and worms, strangled him in his sleep so that the exhausted youth awoke into death.

Only the shamans themselves are immune from the assassins they make, for a certain music played on the bone whistle sends the demon that inhabits the corpse flying away with a ghastly cry, and the empty human shell collapses to the ground. In this way shamans cannot prey upon their own kind, but all others—from the lowest beggar to the king of the land—are in jeopardy from their displeasure. Consequently they are treated with an exaggerated respect and accorded a dignity that is quite comical by the leaders of their race, for they are usually naked and unwashed, with their long hair plastered with mud and their faces painted. Even so, it is invariably the king who prostrates himself before the leader of the shamans, not the head shaman who grovels at the feet of the king. The leaders of the land use the arts of the shamans to discover their enemies and kill them, and in no other land is assassination by the arts of magic so assiduously practiced.

A traveler to Khem who is versed in the arts of necromancy and resolute in heart will do well to capture and abduct one of these shamans, and through torture learn the music that separates the demon from its dead husk. After killing the man and taking the bone whistle from around his neck, he will thereafter be enabled to inquire into the practices and secrets of the shamans without fear that a vitalized corpse will be sent to murder him; even so, precautions must be taken to prevent admission to the sleeping place without the raising of an alarm, for it is the sly practice of these unnatural creatures to creep upon their prey while they sleep; for this cause every shaman sleeps only while his apprentice wakes and watches.

The Book Markets
of Alexandria

Those departing Egypt by sea commonly do so through the port of Alexandria, established many centuries ago by the Greek conqueror of the same name during his occupation of this land. In the days of the caesars it was the greatest city of Egypt, but in recent generations its grandeur has departed and its harbor has been allowed to fill with silt, yet despite this neglect it remains the gateway for many who come to Egypt from distant lands across the sea. In other cities of the Nile, those from foreign lands are looked upon with distrust, and the locals shun communication with them, but in Alexandria a dozen different tongues may be heard by a man who stands in the market square. The most common language of the city is still Greek, for the city was built by Greeks and settled by Greeks, and many ancient and honorable families that served the administrations of the Ptolemies yet remain.

The tale of the great library of Alexandria—how it contained more books than any other library in the world; how it was the wonder of scholars, who traveled from distant cities to study its manuscripts; and how under the aggressions of the Romans it was burned and all its books lost—is so well-known that it need not be repeated. In one respect the story of the library is inaccurate, for when it burned, not all its books were destroyed. Many scribes and nobles of the city ran into the flaming building before the collapse of its roof and saved armloads of precious parchment and papyrus scrolls. Even after the passage of centuries, these are still to be found in this city, offered for sale by Greeks and Jews who deal in rare books, and on some the soot and scorching of the flames is still visible.

The rarest of these works, scarce whispered about since so few of those who trade in books know of its existence, is a papyrus scroll on a roller of polished human thighbone written in the language of the Old Ones, though its letters are Greek. It is a copy of a book that is older than the race of man, and in it is described the history of the Old Ones and their war against the Elder Things, but its subject alone is not what makes it so precious. Each line of the language of the Old Ones is translated by a line in the Greek tongue written immediately below it. By study of this scroll it is possible to learn the speaking of words of power in the tongue of the Old Ones, and it is for this reason that the work is more sought after than any other book by men versed in arcane wisdom.

The Jew who possesses the scroll will not sell it, for it has become his livelihood. However, for an extraordinary amount of gold he will permit carefully selected scholars to copy the text over a span of one day and night. Longer than this he is unwilling to allow the precious work to remain outside its guarded vault; nor will he permit one who pays for this privilege to hire a scribe to do the work, but the scholar himself must set pen to paper and make the copy in his own hand under careful watch, in a place that is fortified against the intrusion of thieves. None who copy the scroll know of its location, since it is a part of their agreement that they be led blindfolded and alone to the place where the work is done. They go at midnight and return at midnight the following night, with as much of the work as they are able to transcribe; for the work is long and difficult, and it is the vexation of many who pay the price that they must leave it before they have completed their copies.

Each man that reproduces the scroll swears a potent oath never to reveal its contents or its existence to any other, for the owner does not wish his price to be diminished by competition; but the reason he gives is that the work is too dangerous to risk the corruption of its contents by repeated transcription from imperfect copies.

To seal their oath, the purchasers of the work impress the print of their thumbs on a parchment contract using their own blood. There are those who in distant lands have laughed at this oath, and have attempted to sell copies of the work, but they invariably meet with misfortune, and any copies they have made are quickly lost or destroyed by seemingly natural events. Indeed, it is a great risk to so much as mention the existence of the book, so that among the scattered few who know of its existence, seldom is found one willing to talk about it.

Those seeking this work who have the wealth in gold to purchase it, for the owner will accept no payment other than gold, should inquire about it in the inn that is on the street extending past the ancient temple of Hermes, which is at present little more than a ruin, as the cedar beams of its roof have fallen after centuries of neglect. The sign of the inn is the Green Peacock, and the proprietor will not answer questions about the book, but if he is shown sufficient gold to meet the required price, and has reason to believe that your inquiry is in earnest, he will speak to a man who is able to contact the owner of the book, who you will never meet face to face, nor will you ever learn his name. Until the matter is decided, you should take a room at the inn and have care to sleep under its roof each night.

If your request to purchase a day to copy the work is rejected, you must flee for your life from Alexandria, for if you linger you will surely be murdered, and three days of waiting is sufficient to decide the issue; however, if the owner accepts your offer of payment, you will not know it until midnight on the second or third night after speaking to the keeper of the inn, when a man who has his face veiled will awaken you from sleep and accept your payment of gold, then place a hood over your head and guide you to the house where the book is to be copied.

Parchment, pens, and ink of the finest quality will await you there, all more than sufficient for your needs. A lamp burns on the table as you enter the room where the work will be done, but at your request as many as three lamps will be provided, and the attendants keep these carefully trimmed and filled with oil. The window of the chamber is always shuttered, so that you cannot know if it is day or night. Before being allowed to see or touch the scroll, one of the attendants will bring a basin of clear water in which you are required to wash your hands, and a linen cloth for drying your fingers.

The scroll is carried in a small box of carven ivory bound with beaten silver hinges and clasps. The attendants will not say, or do not know, if the box was made at the same time as the scroll, or was fashioned at a later period to contain it, but the terrifying forms carved into its lid and sides are unlike any of the beasts that walk the surface of the earth in this age, and match descriptions of similar creatures in the text of the book. The scroll itself is well preserved, showing no signs of the brittleness that so often afflicts old papyrus scrolls exposed to the rays of the sun, and its inks are not faded, but as bright and clear as the day it was penned. At the top is a curious convolute dragon in red, green, and gold, the body of which trails down the left side of the papyrus to its foot. The Greek letters are unusually small, but well formed, making it an easy matter to read them for one with good eyesight.

Not even for an instant will you be alone with the precious scroll; not for the merest moment will the keen gaze of at least one of the two attendants be turned from you as you sit at the table and in a fever of haste seek to duplicate all, yet to avoid errors in transcription. However, the attendants, though they be well armed and ever vigilant, are not well versed in the arts of magic. With a little-known spell muttered under the breath, they can be lulled into a waking trance in which they will believe anything they may be told as though it had truly happened.

The story is related by one who has true knowledge of the matter, and whose words may be trusted, that not many years past a necromancer from our lands cast this glamour over their senses, and so contrived at midnight to leave the sealed chamber with the original scroll in his hand, while his newly made copy remained upon the table. The ensorcered attendants saw, as he wished them to see, the scroll upon the table, and the copy in his hand, but the reverse was true. Because the necromancer did not violate his oath, in that he did not make copies from his own copy of the work, no fatal consequences befell him.

The Alexandrian owner of the scroll has never spoken of the substitution, and it must be presumed that from that day until the present, those who pay in gold for the right to transcribe this text work from an imposture based on the parchment leaves of this clever scribe and not from the original, which is said to be kept safely concealed somewhere in Damascus. Alas, the necromancer was careless in his penning of the Greek letters, since he knew beforehand that he would leave the shuttered chamber with the original, and his copy contains numerous errors in the pronunciation of the language of the Old Ones that make it of little value, other than as an expensive curiosity.

The Ziggurats
and the
Watchers of Time

Having exhausted the possibilities and the hospitality of Egypt, the seeker after arcane wisdom does well to turn his face to the north across the sea, and thence east to the valley between the rivers Tigris and Euphrates, where are the monuments and cities of Babylonia, which was great beneath the stars when the world was young. This region is an arid plain from which rise at intervals the temples of the ancients, erected upon mounds of rubble that elevate them above the surrounding land. The mounds are not natural but are the result of countless generations of human habitation, each built upon the ashes of the one that went before it, mute testimony that this land has been the dwelling place of our race longer than any other.

The temples are in the form of pyramids that differ from those of the Egyptians in that their sides are not smooth, but stepped in a multitude of levels, each smaller than the one below it. Nor are they burial places of kings but houses of religion. Upon their flat tops worship was made beneath the night sky, for this people adored the stars as their gods and diligently sought an understanding of their patterns and motions, so that

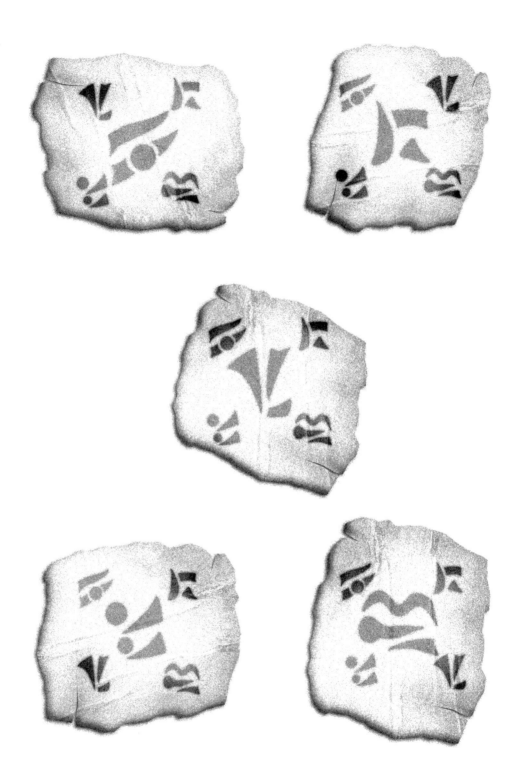

The seals of the ziggurats

no race was more versed in the art of astrology. It was they who gave the names to the stars and who first predicted their cyclical turnings.

Their gods are of the heavens, but their demons are of the earth and the places beneath the earth, and they excel in their knowledge of these malevolent beings. Each ziggurat is built on top of a gateway to the lower regions and acts as its seal, preventing the escape of the evil creatures of the depths into the upper world, where they would ravage the land and wantonly slay all who tried to oppose them. By the powers of the upper gods are these gateways sealed, but only for so long as the gods are adored and offered sacrifice. Most of the ziggurats have fallen into disuse and been abandoned, even by the cults of the old gods who remember their purpose, and the locks upon the lower gates have been allowed to decay and have lost their force, so that at times when the moon is dark the evil things below creep upward into the plains and hunt for prey.

Each ziggurat draws baneful force from the depths of the earth, and by its very shape and certain signs carven on stones that are set within it in a precise pattern, it projects its accumulated potency in a ray that traverses no common space such as men know, but the gulfs of time. By great fires lighted on the tops of these temples are the time rays projected. A ray cannot be sent out for more than several minutes, and only at long intervals, for it consumes the force accumulated in its ziggurat over the span of years, and the ziggurat must then be allowed to lie fallow to restore its potential; and this is the reason the Babylonians made many of these monuments, placing them wherever the gates to the infernal regions below the earth gave vent to its dark strength, that they would have rays with which to pierce the veil of time when needed.

The men of the plain were taught the making of the ziggurats by their most secret and most revered gods, who are a race of time spanners known to the Babylonians as the Watchers; it is the practice of this divine race to peer through time both into the past and future, searching out secret wisdom and building rays to carry them from one age to another. In their own tongue they call themselves the Great Race, and their world they call Yith. They are not native to our earthly sphere, but came here long ages ago in intangible form by means of a kind of soul flight across the stars and inhabited the bodies of the creatures they found, making those forms their own; for they are so ancient that the shape of their original bodies, if indeed they ever were bound to one flesh, has been forgotten even by the Yithians themselves.

Stories of the Watchers abound, making it an easy matter to draw them from the lips of the young priests in the wine shops, where they daily gather to whore and gamble, for there are no more profligate or lewd holy men in all the world than those who dwell between the great rivers. They will not speak of their gods while sober, but after they become drunk they boast of their power and of their own intimate communication with these strange beings. For the price of a few cups of wine they will gladly expound on their entire history, insofar as it is known to their religion.

The priests tell how the Great Race fled the destruction of their own world, though what cataclysm caused its end they have never revealed to those who worship them. In the primal mists of our past, their souls flew across vast deserts of space and took up habitation in the largest and strongest creatures then living upon our world that were compatible with their minds. The body of these beings is said to be like a cone having long arms with pincers that resemble those of the scorpion, and atop it is a small round head alongside a separate stalk from which extends a projecting mouth in form similar to the bell of a trumpet. They are seldom glimpsed by those who worship them, for the Yithians prefer still to travel time in a bodiless state and to assume the body of some convenient form of life when they arrive at their destination.

Long ago they came forward in time to the land of Babylonia and inhabited the bodies of men, who are remembered in the Hebrew creation text titled Bereshit as the sons of God; for even though this occurred in our distant past, it was a future time to the Yithians. They carried no physical tools or weapons with them across time, having not the power to move material things in this way without the aid of the ziggurats, but their wisdom was greater than that of any man, and eventually they came to rule the land, for the bodies of their hosts were rendered deathless by their presence. For their pleasure, and to fulfill their purposes in the age of mankind, they took in marriage the most beautiful of the women of noble birth and bred within their wombs daughters and sons, creating a new race that was outwardly in the shape of man but inwardly possessed a portion of the vast intelligence of their fathers.

The sons of the Watchers were mighty warriors, and long of years; they made war against the peoples of all the surrounding lands and forced them into subjugation under one king, who was the leader of the Watchers inhabiting our age; in numbers the Watchers were few, but their sons multiplied and became many. They applied their great minds to the wisdom of the Watchers, which was freely given to them. In this way they became masters not only of warfare but of metalworking and of the making of ornaments, and of the use of enchantments, and in the knowledge of the heavens. As their wisdom increased, so did their wickedness, and no equal is to be found to match their delight in depravity and abomination.

These matters are written of in the book of Enoch the prophet, who entered one of the rays of the ziggurats and was seen no more in the times of our history, or so teach the degenerate priests who still light fires atop these monuments and make gates to give offerings to the Watchers. Enoch wrote truly but he did not write all that he knew, and he did not know everything concerning the acts of the Yithians among man. He veiled his words in the conventions of his faith to make them less strange, and dared not write the true name of the Watchers, which is inscribed plainly here.

After the wealth and peoples of all the lands between the rivers were subjugated by the children of the Watchers and their generations, the construction of the ziggurats began. By their wisdom the Watchers selected the places of power and oversaw the building of the towers of stone and brick, and the fixing within their walls of the carven seals that were able to direct the force accumulated, when activated by the heat of fire. The primary purpose of the ziggurats is the transportation of material objects across time. Although it was within the ability of the Yithians to project their souls into the future and inhabit the bodies of men, it was not within their capacity to carry the things they coveted in our time back to their ancient age, or to bring their strange conical bodies forward to our time.

This the ziggurats allowed them to do, but only for brief periods of minutes, and only for the passage of a single being or a cargo of precious substances of the weight of a horse. Once used, a ziggurat must lie inert for years before its potential to project a ray of time is regained. These limitations greatly frustrated the Watchers, who desired free travel and transportation between their own time and our time. For this reason, they conceived a great ziggurat higher and broader than any that had yet been made, to the intent that it would possess so vast a force that its ray would shine through the years unceasingly, requiring no period of restoration, and make as it were an open doorway through time; but this ambition proved to be their downfall.

The Tower of Babel
and the
Fall of the Watchers

The story of the great ziggurat of eternity is related in the book of creation of the Hebrews, who received it from the Babylonians during their captivity after the fall of the First Temple, but it is not well told, and many things must be added to the tale before it may be understood by the wise. The Hebrews called it Babel, a word they took to signify many tongues, but in the language of Yith *babel* means the unending portal, for so the towering monument, larger than anything that has ever been made by the hands of man, was called by the Watchers.

The creatures of Yith are a patient race, as befits the masters of time. Over the span of several human generations they prepared the foundations of the tower, having by their arts located the place upon the land between the rivers possessed of the greatest conflux of subterranean forces converging there in mighty lines like the spokes of a wheel. More generations passed while they transported carven seals from their own distant time through the rays of lesser portals; they were made from a strange stone not to be quarried in the age of the Watchers, for the hills from which it came had long before sunk beneath the waves of the sea.

With great care the seals were inserted into the body of the ziggurat as its courses mounted ever upward to the clouds. As the seals multiplied in number, they drew power up from the earth, and the entire ziggurat began to glow with strange colors and to throb with a deep tone like the low chant of many voices.

The common workmen who laid the stones into their places began to look fearfully at one another, and some cast down their tools and refused to labor, but the arrogant descendents of the Watchers lashed them with whips and slayed with swords those who would not rise up from their bellies, so that by the fear they created in the hearts of their subjects, the terror of the strange colors and mighty drone was overcome, and the work was completed. On the night the portal of eternity was to be opened, all of the Watchers, who are said in the book of Enoch the prophet to have been two hundred in number, assembled on the mount of the ziggurat, and with them gathered their sons among men, and their descendents even to the tenth generation, for all wished to witness the wonder of the portal.

The colors shimmering upon the stones of the ziggurat were blinding, and the deep drone from within its body could be felt through sandals upon the soles of the feet, or so say the chronicles of the priests who adore at the lesser ziggurats in our own age. The king himself, who was the leader of the Watchers and of many years, set torch to kindling and lit the fire upon the altar. As was expected, a beam of white light ascended upward to the heavens, and where this beam arose from the flames, a portal through time was opened.

So great was the acclamation of the thousands gathered to view the event that few noticed the deeper rumble within the stones beneath them, or the flicker that began to dance along the ascending ray. As the rumble grew louder, the cries of voices dimmed and at last turned into a babble of uncertainty. Even the king, who stood nearest the altar, had difficulty keeping upon his feet, and finally was thrown to his hands and knees with an expression of astonishment. A great bolt of lightning, but many thousands of times larger than any lightning that the world had ever witnessed, struck downward along the ascending beam of light and cut its path into the center of the ziggurat through its stones, melting them with its heat. All were blinded and deafened, and many at the topmost tire of the structure were instantly cast off its sides to their deaths.

The rumble in the earth grew louder as the people fled down the stair that wound in a spiral around the four sloping sides of the tower, pushing those who blocked their path over the edges. At last the ziggurat was split as though by a sword of fire, and its stones fell in a thunderous cascade. All who remained in confusion upon its heights were killed, and most of those who occupied its intermediate levels. Only a few escaped death from the rain of stones, those who had fled the heights quickly and those on the lowermost level who were of the tenth generation of the children of the Watchers, whose blood was weakest and who had not merited the honor of a higher place upon the ziggurat.

The dawn revealed a smoking ruin of blackened stones and thousands of charred and naked corpses, the garments of which had burned away, lying scattered across the plain. The Watchers were no more; of their strongest children only a few lived, and within the span of a month all who had stood upon the ziggurat were dead, for the lightning that shattered the tower sent into the blood of everyone who stood upon its levels a kind of poison that took away their strength and caused their hair to fall from their heads. The governing of the land was cast into complete confusion, for no one remained to lead. Those peoples subjugated by the Watchers resumed their old customs and their languages, and returned to their ancient homes. So were the peoples of the plain scattered, and thus was their greatness lost. Where they had been one nation under the rule of the Watchers, they became many nations.

These things happened uncounted generations before the rise of Babylon, yet the fall of the great ziggurat is depicted upon one of the gold plates in the pillared hall beneath the sphinx. It shows the tower split by lightning, and two of the Watchers cast down from its heights. Only a man who has heard the story of the fall of Babel would comprehend its true meaning.

The tending of the fires upon the lesser ziggurats continues even to our time, though the ignorance of those who gather wood for the fires is so great, only the priests know what purpose they serve. The rays are still sent through time into the ancient world where dwell the Yithians in their primordial bodies, and offerings of cakes and wine are passed through the portals above the flames, but for many ages nothing has emerged out of those portals. The Great Race is ever patient, and it may be that they are merely awaiting conditions suited to their purposes before once again sending their souls ahead in time, for the sending of souls requires no portal. How long they will wait, no man can tell.

The Ruins
of Babylon

It is not safe to walk amid the ruins of Babylon at night where the ghosts of the city howl their outrage upon the wind, which remembers as by an echo their cries when the city was destroyed and made a wilderness for beasts, and how they were put to the swords of the conquerors, even the women and infants. The foundation stones are almost as old as those of the ziggurats on the plain; to touch them is to feel their years, which make the stones of Egypt seem newly quarried, save for the stone of the Sphinx. No common habitations stand where Babylon once flourished; few venture there under the sun, and fewer still have the courage to enter the fallen bones of its gates beneath the moon. The land is given over wholly to death, and the past, and creatures of evil purpose.

When Babylon was overthrown, its walls and temples were pulled down even to the final course of brick or stone, and its wells were filled with sand, but the sewers that lie beneath the city were not destroyed, and in part remain as they were, though they are dry. These channels are a work of wondrous skill comparable to the ingenuity of the Romans, for the slops and wastes of the city did not flow in gutters down the center of the streets as they do in most of our modern cities, but in large tunnels beneath the earth that shielded the inhabitants from their stenches and caused the removal of the rats to the underground where they were of little trouble. These tunnels are arched and high enough for a tall man to walk upright; in places they are so wide that they cannot be spanned by the outstretched arms. Places where the roofing has fallen in provide a feeble and intermittent glow during the day, and by moonlight, but the slanting rays serve more as a guide than as an illumination.

Beneath the center of the city is a deep and wide cistern or catch pit that captured the heavier wastes and prevented them from clogging the smaller tunnels that carried the outflow away from the city walls. No doubt when Babylon was inhabited it was periodically dredged and emptied. Presently it serves as the living place of a strange creature who may be said to be the monarch of Babylon, since no other foul thing of the night dares to contest its preeminence. It is one of the offspring of Shub-Niggurath, and is older than the city itself. Its scaled body glows with the redness of dying embers. In size it is equal to the largest horse, and in form it somewhat resembles the griffin, save that its tail is barbed and all four of its legs are taloned. Great black wings without feathers, but leathern like the wings of a bat, it keeps folded along its hunched back, and since its food is not to be found in the tunnels or the ruins of the city, it uses these wings to fly abroad across the night sky seeking prey.

Truly it is a fearsome monster, and to be avoided except by the boldest of travelers seeking arcane wisdom not to be learned in more placid circumstances. To those possessing the secret to hold it at bay it is a fountain of knowledge, and for this reason, that it has not one head but seven, and these heads extend on elongated necks from its hulking shoulders and change their forms constantly; always the number of the heads is seven, but they are never the same seven heads. Their faces and shapes transform one into another as they are watched, becoming now the head of an old man and now the head of a soldier, now the head of a child and now the head of a harlot, or maiden, or priest, or slave, for this beast is an eater of human flesh and seeks no other food.

It is the nature of this beast that it captures the souls and minds of those it consumes and retains them within itself. Each soul expresses itself by projecting its head, and when that head is formulated, it is capable of responding to any question that may be put to it, for it remembers all its knowledge acquired during life. The strongest souls of those consumed by this creature project their heads most often, but they cannot sustain their projection for any longer than the weakest soul, which is no more than the tenth part of an hour, so that the heads are constantly melting into the scaly flesh of the beast and changing into other heads. The souls speak independent of the beast but cannot act of their own wills.

It is frustrating to seek a complex answer to a question of necromancy from the head of a wizard, only to have it sink away and be replaced by the head of a weeping child. The number of heads within the beast is beyond counting, so great is its age. It cannot prevent the heads from speaking, but it attempts to slay and consume the traveler who questions them. Its weapons are its sharp black talons, longer than the outstretched fingers of a man, and a curved gray beak that is set in the base of the necks below the changing heads. It sees through the eyes of those it has made a part of itself, and hears with their ears, but it eats with its own mouth that is incapable of speech, yet can emit piercing shrieks of rage like those of a hawk, but many times louder. Whether it possesses a mind of its own, wholly independent of the minds of those it has consumed, is not evident from its actions, which are those of an unthinking beast; even so, it is cunning and will wait for the traveler to relax his vigilance, then attempt to strike.

The Elder Seal engraved upon a disk of gold and worn about the neck holds it at bay. It respects the Elder Seal because it is a thing associated with the Old Ones, and though the seal cannot cause it hurt or even restrain it in any material manner, it fears it as the wolf fears the very sight of the campfire, even when it has suffered no burn. The traveler who is not fortunate to possess the talisman of the seal risks dismemberment all the while he remains within the sewers unless he knows the making of the Elder Seal with the hand, for the Elder Seal made with the hand quells the rage of the beast almost as well as the graven mark of the seal.

The true making of the sign is to cross the longest finger of the right hand on top of the third finger, and to touch the tip of the first finger against the tip of the thumb. The conjoined thumb and first finger are projected forward while holding the smallest finger upright and the crossed middle fingers at an intermediate angle. With practice this sign may be formed in an instant whenever the creature exhibits aggression, and held for as long as is required.

The protection offered by the exhibition of the sign is effective even in total darkness; in some way that cannot be fathomed the beast senses its presence when it cannot be seen by the eyes. Perhaps the lines and joinings of the fingers of the sign change the very shape and texture of space itself so that the beast can feel its form, even as do the graven marks of the seal; this is a matter of conjecture, but what is certain is that the sign safeguards the life of one who ventures into the sewers beneath Babylon, and must not be omitted, for to enter these tunnels in ignorance of its making is certain death.

Enter the sewers near the remains of the east gate through the pit that lies between two fallen pillars, one of which has broken into three parts. Make your way westward toward the center of the city, where is situated the dry cistern in which the creature dwells. You will know that you are near when you hear the cries and babbling of its heads, for they never cease to lament their fate, and many of them are mad, and they argue amongst themselves and berate and insult each other as their only recreation. The stench of the thing is strong, and that also will guide you. The rats in the tunnels provide adequate nourishment, but their blood is uncommonly thick and salty, so it is wise to carry skins of water if you intend to stay more than a single night.

The time to question the heads is not long. During the daylight hours the beast sleeps or rests in torpor, and the heads are listless and unresponsive to questions. Perhaps they dream? Who can know, but it is certain that they are of no use in this state for the gathering of knowledge. The beast will stir itself into wakefulness if approached, in order to defend itself, but once it perceives that it faces no threat it will descend back into sleep. Once full dark has fallen, it does not tarry in the tunnels but rushes away and emerges through the pit at the east gate, which is the widest entrance to the sewers, and spreads its wings and flies aloft in search of nourishment. At dawn it returns and immediately sleeps, whether it has fed or not. Only at the hour of dusk is it fully awake and aware, and at this time it may be questioned on any topic, and will provide such answers as the heads that are projected care to give.

The heads cannot be forced to make answer by physical means, since they are indestructible. If struck off to the great rage of the beast, they merely grow anew from its shoulders at some later time. However, it is possible for the wise traveler to use his knowledge to compel the heads to speak in various ways, by playing on the weakness and vanity of the souls they express, or by pitting one head against another. Each of the more potent heads, who emerge from the monster's flesh most frequently, believes itself to be the wisest, and delights to contradict or correct the answers of the others. In this way knowledge may be gained, if the traveler is patient.

The wisest of the heads is a wizard named Belaka, who long ago dwelt in the mountains of the east. His skull is bald, and the skin of his cheeks and his teeth alike are the yellow of old parchment, but his dark eyes hold keen awareness and glitter with amusement, as though savoring some wry jest. He is the oldest of the heads that remains sane, and the most frequent to emerge from the beast. He readily speaks with those who visit the sewers and will share his arcane arts, but for diversion he sometimes lapses into forgotten tongues to vex his listener. A blazing torch thrust into his face in the left hand, while the Elder Sign is made with the right to hold the beast at bay, will remind him of his place and cause him to return to our common language, which he has learned from the babbling of other heads.

He likes to relate the tale of his death, how one evening while walking on a mountain trail, after making sacrifice of a goat beneath the stars, he was startled by the soft beat of wings. Before he could raise his head, shadows enveloped his body, and the talons of the beast pierced his back between the shoulders and severed his spine, rendering him unable to move his arms or legs. Cursing imprecations at the monster that held him captive, he felt himself swept into the air and carried to a high mountain ledge, where he endured the ignominy of watching his body painlessly torn apart, to the laughter and mockeries of the monster's seven heads; for having endured this indignity, they take delight to see others suffer through an equal horror.

U'mal Root
and Its Manner
of Harvest

At the fall of dusk, after the setting of the sun and when the stars begin to appear, the beast emerges from the sewers to hunt. The bold traveler, who follows its progress through the tunnels and exits the pit at its heels, may choose this moment to mount upon its back between its outspread wings, which it fans in the air to strengthen after having held them cramped to its back. A man who wears an engraving of the Elder Seal about his neck as a talisman may dare to do this, for to such a man the beast submits. If he has no talisman around his neck, he must form and hold the Elder Seal all the while he is astride the beast or it will turn and rend him. His weight is as nothing to the creature, who carries him upward above the highest mountains in its quest for food.

It is the habit of the beast to haunt the roads and caravan routes, and to circle the outskirts of villages and cities. At times its ranging flight carries it over the river Euphrates, where even the pilots of cargo boats are not safe from its strike. When it spies its prey it folds its wings and stoops like a hawk. Near to the ground it suddenly spreads its wings and stretches downward its taloned forelegs. The traveler must take great care to hold to its back with tenacity or he will surely be thrown off. The hapless and unwary man below is snatched into the air with the ease by which a mother lifts an infant from its cradle, and before he can cry out the talons of the monster tighten and pierce his breast and slay him.

At once, while the meat is still fresh and dripping with blood, the beast seeks a secure rock flat or dune of sand upon which to feast. Its beak tears the flesh from the corpse in long strips, leaving only naked bones and the skin that covers the hands, feet, and head, as there is not enough meat on these parts of the body to interest it. The skull it cracks with its beak so that it may devour the brain. How the soul of the dead enters the beast is not apparent, but it may be consumed along with the blood, for the blood is the seat of the soul in the body.

After feasting the beast makes a strange pilgrimage of mysterious purpose, for it flies to a lonely mountain in the desert that is flat upon its peak and there alights before a standing stone. The stone is as large as those in the temple of Albion, but black in color rather than blue. From the time it arrives until shortly before the rising of the sun it circles the stone and makes homage before it, crouching its body and bowing down its many heads as though in worship, and the voices of the heads fall silent. No mark is cut upon the stone, and no sign is to be found upon the peak that shows the hand of man. The souls devoured by the beast are ignorant of its nightly purpose, but the wisest of them all, the wizard Balaka, speculates that it is the place of the creature's making, and that in coming to the mountain it returns to its first home.

The flat land of the mountaintop is barren save for small tufts of browning grasses that grow between the rocks and a kind of plant that Balaka calls u'mal that is to be found nowhere else in the world. The u'mal is tough and dry, and grows close to the rocks amid the grass. It bears a tiny white flower that resembles a star. When pulled from the earth, its thickened root is exposed, and in this root lies its virtue. The dried root, chewed in the mouth together with fresh human blood, heals all diseases, even those that are invariably fatal. The root alone is insufficient, and the blood must be drawn from a living human body other than the man who seeks the remedy, for his own blood will not serve to empower the root. The juice of the root when mingled in the mouth with blood becomes fiery and courses through the limbs, driving the disease before it and expelling it from the body, so that the work of healing is only a matter of a few minutes.

The u'mal could not grow upon the peak without the nightly visits of the beast. In its circumambulations of the standing stone it drops its dung upon the rocks and windblown sand, and makes them fertile for this rare plant. Nor can it be harvested except by a man who rides the beast, for the peak where it grows is unknown, and an inspection of its slopes reveals that they are impossible to climb even were its location to somehow be determined. It may be that the peak lies beyond the boundaries of the earthly sphere, for the air upon the peak has a curious vital quality not to be found elsewhere, and it is known that some of the children of Shub-Niggurath have the power to span the spaces between worlds.

As much of the u'mal root as can be conveniently carried should be gathered while the beast circles the stone in its worship. Even when dried and kept for months or years, it does not lose its virtue. Those who know of it are willing to pay vast sums to possess the merest fragment, and a man who keeps a good supply for his own use is immortal, as the root not only cures any disease of the flesh but counters the effects of old age and renders the body youthful, when it is chewed regularly once every cycle of the moon. The root cannot make an old man look young in the face, or heal disfiguring scars, but it renders him energetic in his limbs so that he can do the work of a young man, and also it makes him youthful in his virile member so that he can performs feats of sensual congress that are only possible in youth, unless by some ill chance he has suffered the indignity of castration.

When the beast ceases to adore the stone, and approaches the edge of the peak to spread wide its wings, it is time to mount once more upon its back, for this is the sign that it prepares for flight. In the pale glow of the sky it flies east, for the horizon is brighter before it than behind, but so early is the hour that nothing can be distinguished in the lands that pass below except the vague shadows of sharp peaks that rise up like the blades of swords and daggers. Hastening at the end of its journey, it crawls into the pit by the east gate of Babylon just as the first ray of the sun is breaking upon the stones of the fallen pillars. Such is the monotonous cycle of its life, though in truth it is no more dull than the lives of many men, who toil from dawn to dusk for their masters and receive scant reward for having given over the fruits of their labor and the precious and irreplaceable strokes of their hearts.

The Valley
of Eden

From the ruins of Babylon the seeker of mysteries will do well to turn his face east across the rocky lands to the river Tigris, where dwell the remnants of the royal caste of the magi. No men greater in wisdom inhabit this world, for they have gathered the secrets of both east and west and combined it in a single teaching. The way is arduous by foot, but less daunting upon one of the camels that may be obtained from the village of Azani south of the ruins.

In the spring of the year at the time of the equinox, sit upon your camel at the east gate of Babylon and fix your eyes upon the rising sun at morning. Ride directly toward the place of its ascent on the horizon until dusk, without stopping to eat or rest until darkness has fallen. Do this each day for three days, and you will come at the sunset of the third day upon the mouth of a narrow pass in a range of rocky hills. It cannot be seen except in the slanting rays of the setting sun, which reveal the shadow of its slit. The heat rising from the rocks makes the air dance, so that the mouth of the pass appears to open and shut, as though speaking.

The finding of the pass is no easy matter, even for one who knows its location. It is guarded by a powerful and ancient glamour that turns the mind away when the gaze falls upon it, so that it is both seen yet remains unseen. Only a man versed in the arts of magic can sense this spell and willfully resist, yet few even among the greater wizards possessing potency in their art are able to overcome its seductive veil, so subtle yet insistent is its ray upon the eyes.

Enter between the rock walls of the pass, which is so narrow that only a single camel can go in at one time, and it will lead into a narrow defile that eventually opens into a broad and pleasant valley of fertile lands. High cliffs rise all around it, making access impossible except from the pass to the west. From a prominence in the western part of the valley bubbles a spring of clear water that divides into four streams flowing in four directions. These water the rich, dark soil before combining at the eastern end of the valley to flow in a single course into a cave, where they vanish beneath the earth; for the floor of the valley is sloped gently down from west to east.

The hidden valley is thick with forest and filled with many strange birds and beasts not to be encountered anywhere else, though none of them are noxious to man. So tame are these creatures, they approach unafraid until they are near enough to grasp in the hands and strangle, offering the traveler a ready supply of fresh meat. In addition, the valley has many fig trees and nut trees, so that food of various kinds is to be had in abundance. The still air is mild, and laden with the scent of spices. Indeed, there is no more pleasant land in the world.

Within the forest dwells a gentle tribe that flees the arrival of travelers and hides among the trees until they have departed. These barbarians are small of stature and dark-skinned from the sun, for it is their custom to go about naked save for a few strings of amber and crystal beads on their necks and arms, and brightly colored flowers braided in their long hair. When questioned by means of signs made with the hands, they declare in their musical language that the valley is their land, which they call Edena. It can only be the Eden described in the Hebrew holy book Bereshit.

They are a primitive race possessing no knowledge of necromancy, and they fear violence, so they may be safely ignored, as it is unlikely they will offer any threat to a visitor from outside their land, particularly if he takes the trouble to demonstrate upon the throat of one of their larger young men the use of a knife. In spite of their nakedness, they have a strange grace in their way of walking and an incongruous pride in their own imagined importance that makes them amusing to observe. Their vacated huts contain stores of fruits and nuts, freeing the traveler from the trouble of foraging for food in the forest. Of fire they know nothing, and their tools are of stone. Nor do they possess any form of writing or pictorial expression. At dusk they sing to each other, and it may be that they use these songs to teach their children. Their greatest skill is in the making of baskets, at which they excel to such an extent that the weave of their baskets is like the weave of fine cloth.

Deep within the shelter of the tallest and oldest trees of the forest is a small clearing of bare earth that has at its center a black obelisk of the height of a man, rising from the center of a stone disk that is like a great millstone. The disk is of the common stone of the valley, but the obelisk is alien to that region. Its four sides are stained with the rust of dried blood, and this same stain colors the stone wheel that supports it, for the primitives adore the black stone as their god and offer a sacrifice of blood to it daily. They will not eat one of the wild pigs that flourish in such abundance in the forest unless it has had its throat slashed with a stone knife against the black pillar before the assembled multitude of the tribe. Their god must eat before the people feed, and this is their manner of homage. Having no means to cook meat, they consume it raw in thin strips, but pounded with dried herbs to soften its texture.

It is strange to witness a sacrifice of blood made by such a passive and timid race, but they do it to turn aside the imagined wrath of their god, to whom they give the name Yad in their own tongue, though whether this is a proper name or merely a title of respect is not easily determined. When they speak the name, they bow their heads and point to the sky as though fearful to look up; they do this both night and day, so that it is evident that their god is neither the sun nor the moon but the heavens itself, or something that dwells in the heavens.

Near the cliffs at the eastern end of the valley rises an enclosure in the midst of a small plain of tall grasses. It possesses four walls each as high as the tallest palm, and five thousand paces in length. The walls are seamless and are formed from a kind of black glass, smooth and cold to the touch, that does not transmit the light of the sun. One of the tributaries of the spring that waters the valley floor flows beneath the corner of the west wall of this enclosure. Also set within its west wall is a gate made from black wood having the hardness of iron, bound with iron straps and hinges, that is forever sealed from the inside.

If one of the barbarian men is captured and compelled by force to walk toward the gate, he begins to tremble and cry out repeatedly the words *poamala yaida raas* and the words *oxiayal teloc*, his distress mounting until at last he falls upon his face on the ground and can by no means of persuasion be made to go nearer. To avoid the gate is the strongest motivation of all this race, which they acquire at an early age. Even beasts of low intelligence learn to avoid that which causes them pain, for the dog flinches from a stone in the hand and the wolf will not approach an open fire. The man of wisdom can gain knowledge from the beasts of the field by observing their ways, and should notice that at the base of the gate the flowers grow highest. He does well to avoid any close approach to the black gate, and will on no account touch it with his bare hand.

A door is not the only passage into a locked house. Although there is no gap between the waters of the stream and the base of the wall where the stream enters the enclosure, by holding the breath in the lungs and pulling with the hands over the rough stones in the bed of the stream it is possible to pass beneath the foundation of the wall and emerge on the other side unharmed. So the fish pass from the valley to the enclosure, and from the enclosure to the valley, and so also a man may pass, if he emulates a fish.

The Wisdom Seat

The dense forest within the enclosure is much like that of the rest of the valley, save that it is marked by winding stone pathways for walking beneath the trees. The paving stones of the paths are broader than the height of a man, but so closely joined that not a blade of grass grows between them. They are overhung by the trees on either side so that they are in perpetual shadow. From within the forest may be heard the songs of strange birds and the cries of beasts, but the traveler should resist the urge to explore the dark trees for it is an easy matter to become lost under their canopy and to wander in circles.

The intersecting paths wind their way to the center of the enclosure, where there is a wide clearing with two low hills that are covered only in grass. Between the hills passes the stream that entered beneath the western wall. Each hill bears on its crown a great tree. The tree upon the northern hill is green with leaves and new growth, and bears abundant red globes of succulent fruit. On the southern hill arises only a bare trunk and naked, twisting limbs bereft alike of leaves and bark. The color of its wood is the color of bleached bone. For countless ages nothing has grown on the tree, but some uncanny property of its wood preserves it from decay.

The fruits upon the lower boughs of the tree growing on the northern hill hang close to the ground and appear easy to pick, but when the tree is approached it will be found to contain innumerable venomous serpents that make their nests and breed their young amid its leaves. In length the mature serpents are less than the forearm of a man, and their black bodies are variegated with bright blotches of color, of which yellow and orange predominate, so that their skins almost resemble the wings of butterflies. The mothers of these vipers are fierce in the defense of their young and will not permit a man to touch the tree in any of its parts. Moreover, their venom constantly drips from their gaping and hissing mouths and falls upon the fruit of the tree, rendering it unfit to eat even were it possible to harvest it without being struck by the serpents.

When dried in the sun, the venom of these serpents becomes a pale blue crystal that may be hammered into fine dust with a stone. It does not lose its potency over time, but even after the passage of years it may be regenerated by mixing the powder in boiled wine. If the blade of a knife or a sword is steeped for a day in the resulting liquid, the merest scratch upon the skin brings swift death. A man struck with such an envenomed weapon experiences shortness of breath, then falls upon the ground in convulsions that do not endure above a minute before life flees from his body. The corpse of one killed in this manner is subject to accelerated putrefaction, and will dissolve into a mass of wet decay within the space of three nights. It is claimed that the greatest virtue of this poison is that it may be extended to an astonishing degree by mixing its crystals with powdered salts, yet its potency does not diminish nor is the manner or term of death altered.

Directly between the hills a small stone bridge spans the stream, permitting easy passage from one side to the other. It is uncommonly wide for a bridge of its length, for in the middle upon its western side has been constructed an elevated platform that is surmounted by a throne of carven stonework of great subtlety and beauty. The high back of the throne bears the shape of folded wings, and between them is set a head of inhuman aspect and proportions. In its forehead glares a single open eye that is formed by a large ruby of surpassing clarity, fixed into a setting of gold. The arms of the throne are carven into the shape of claws similar to those of a hawk.

Few are the travelers who have penetrated the hidden valley of Eden, and fewer still are those bold enough to enter the enclosed garden of black glass and look upon the wisdom seat. So it is called in the veiled texts of Ibn Schacabao, yet the sage never described its shape, nor is it to be supposed that he saw it with his own eyes. The throne faces east, where the wandering stream that flows between the hills passes out beneath the eastern wall of the enclosure. It is so directed that at dawn its occupant sees the rising of the sun between the narrowing hills that enclose the eastern end of the valley. The rays of the sun, striking the rounded dome of the ruby on the back of the throne above the head of the occupant of its seat, activate the throne's power. Of these truths concerning the wisdom seat Ibn Schacabao, called the Boaster by his detractors, knew nothing, for surely he could not have resisted the temptation to hint at their existence.

To sit upon the wisdom seat at the rising of the sun is to experience the omniscience of a god, so potent is its influence upon the mind, for any question or puzzle that might be considered, no matter how complex, becomes at once the plaything of a child. The very number and proportion of space itself may be reckoned and manipulated, and passage gained in an instant to any of the most distant worlds. This is not a function of the seat, but a capacity inherent in the mind that is awakened and enabled by the seat. Were a man patient enough to remain within the enclosure and each day seek answers to his questions at the wisdom seat, in the space of a year he would know all things, and would possess the capacity of the Old Ones themselves.

Sadly, it is the nature of our race to become impatient and to covet. When the attempt is made to pry the ruby set in the back of the throne from its socket with the point of a knife, the guardian of the seat senses this desecration and comes through the edges of space trailing stars in her long hair and crying out with fury so that the air itself trembles and falls in frozen sheets. She comes from the sky, her thousand translucent limbs floating upon the winds like serpents, and in the solitary eye in the dome of her forehead is the blackness between the stars. With her myriad hands she rains down fire upon the ground, blackening and scorching the grasses.

If the foolish traveler who has thrown away his chance for the wisdom of ages on the lust for a single jewel moves without hesitation as she approaches, he may have time to flee to the eastern wall of the enclosure and hurl himself into the depths of the stream that rushes beneath it while fire rains around him and his skin blisters.

The passage beneath the eastern wall is longer than that beneath the west, for the wall presses close against the base of the hills, and the stream does not immediately reemerge but continues under the rocks for some little way through a cavern.

Once the wall has been passed, there is found air to breathe in this lightless channel, and eventually the swift flood of the stream carries the traveler out into the sun again, beyond the limits of the valley of Eden. It is an easy matter to proceed on foot along the course of this tributary, which leads after the journey of a day and a night to the banks of the river Tigris and the monastery of the magi.

The Monastery
of the Magi

The monastery of the magi stands upon a low hill overlooking the meeting place of two tributaries of the river Tigris, surrounded by a cultivated grove of date palms and fruit trees. It is a large walled compound built from clay bricks, with many tiers of flat roofs and four square towers rising at its corners that act both as defensive fortifications and platforms upon which to make observations of the heavens. Its solitary gate opens to the east and overlooks a broad plaza beyond which lies the conjunction of the river, where there are well-constructed docks for the mooring of boats. Fields of grain stretch behind the building to the west, tended by a small village of farmers who dwell completely outside the monastery walls in their own simple huts, but who serve the needs of the monks and those who have commerce with them, and in this way prosper.

In times of war, or when the land is ravaged by bandit tribes, the villagers gather up their grain and livestock and move inside the gate of the monastery, where they are protected. The monastery has never fallen under the assault of hostile armies, for its walls are formidable and the monks defend it with vigor, being expert both in the use of the bow and the sword. Deep wells and great cisterns beneath the building, together with large storehouses of grain, allow it to resist even a prolonged siege from a determined foe.

Those who travel the river rely upon the monastery both as a trading center and as a secure port where they can deposit their wares in the confidence that they will remain unmolested. It is a center of arcane learning, the greatest in all the world, attracting scholars from far lands who pay large sums for the privilege of living with the monks and studying their teachings. To these students the monks entrust their outer wisdom, but they reserve their inner knowledge to members of their own order. Merchants and foreign scholars abide in buildings that lie outside the monastery walls, for the monks admit no one through their gate except in the dire necessity of war, when their sense of charity compels them to offer sanctuary to the helpless.

They call themselves the Sons of Sirius, and worship as the manifest expression of their god the star *Al Shi'ra,* the Dog Star of the Egyptians that burns so cold and blue in the firmament. Each monk takes a vow of chastity upon admission to the order, and offers his worldly possessions to the order as his pledge. Whether he is a poor laborer with only one cloak or a wealthy merchant with tens of ships and many houses, he gives all, for the wealth of the monastery is shared in common, and no monk enjoys any luxury that is not available to the least and most recent of members.

The religious beliefs of these monks are strange and difficult to determine upon slight acquaintance, for they resist speaking of them before outsiders and know them so well among themselves that they have no need to discuss them. They believe themselves to be the descendents of the priest caste of the magi who served in the court of Darius the Great of Persia. How they came to this remote place, and whether they built the monastery with their own hands or found it already here and improved it for their own purposes, is not talked about among them, and it may be that the monks themselves do not know these matters, they occurred so many generations ago. They follow neither the teachings of Jesus nor those of Mohammed, although they honor both prophets as inspired by divine light. No idols or images receive their adoration, nor do they have altars as we know them, or make sacrifices, but worship the stars themselves and the higher principles that inhabit them.

Their training is austere and warlike. Each day the monks, from the most slender youth to the oldest graybeard among them, put on armor and exercise upon the grounds within the walls of the monastery, where they practice in the use of the sword and shield, and in accuracy with the bow. They also strengthen their bodies by lifting stone weights and running about the perimeter of the monastery lawns. Their food is plain and of small quantity. Chiefly they subsist on boiled barley, fowl, fruits, butter, milk, fish, and eggs, for they avoid the consumption of red meat. They sleep no more than five hours a day after midnight, for the hours of darkness before midnight they spend in studying and adoring the heavens from their high places, of which there are an abundant number upon the rooftops of the monastery buildings.

In one respect their teachings resemble those of the Greek philosopher Pythagoras, for they maintain that any form of excess is to be avoided, and that moderation is the chief virtue of mankind. They demonstrate through the use of historical examples that all the hardships and disasters of our race have been the result of immoderate passions or actions committed in reckless haste, and assert that for so long as the mind rules the heart, order continues, but that so soon as the heart overthrows the mind, the result is chaos. They seldom laugh among themselves or raise their voices in anger, and are never to be seen running unless during exercise or when some dire peril makes haste unavoidable.

The leader of the order in the present generation is a man named Rumius, by birth a nobleman of Persia who came to this meeting place of the river Tigris as a boy, having been sent here by his family in recognition of his precocious intellect, for he could read Greek at the age of five and Hebrew at eight. His present age is difficult to determine, for his back is unbent and his body as strong as that of an athlete, but his flowing hair and long beard both have the whiteness of milk. He is of uncommon stature, so that the heads of most men rise only to his shoulders, yet is slender of limb. His blue eyes and straight nose look more Greek than Persian, so that it may be suspected that his parentage is not of pure blood, but mixed; indeed, so great is his sagacity and beauty, it might almost be thought that he carried the blood of the sons of God.

Inner Grounds
of the
Sons of Sirius

A traveler to the monastery of the magi is free to purchase such teachings as the monks dispense outside the gate to those who gather each day in the paved square. No student is refused provided he behaves in a decorous manner and attends the lessons with silence; even women are permitted to sit at the feet of the monks, who teach by means of lectures, either standing and declaiming before their scholars, or walking up and down as they speak. The younger monks alone fulfill the task of teachers, as though it were a matter of too small importance to occupy the time of the elders. They teach logic, rhetoric, poetics, geometry, history, writing, and arithmetic. Absent from their lectures are references to magic or the arcane arts, astronomy, geomancy, or theology. Concerning the nature of the cosmic spheres and the stars of the heavens, which make up their own chief study, they say nothing.

It is soon apparent to the traveler who is well versed in necromancy and the secret wisdom of this world that nothing of importance is to be gained by sitting at the feet of the teachers outside the gate. Even as the jewels of a monarch are not left scattered about the flagstones, but are kept safe within an ironbound strongbox, the true wisdom of the Sons of Sirius is preserved within the walls of the monastery itself and never set on display for the eyes of the vulgar. Yet the monks are accustomed to admit none within the gate but those of their order, and to gain admission to the order is a work of many months.

This puzzle will not long keep the traveler from his purpose, if he reflects that the actions of the monks are invariably governed by compassion. A wealthy merchant or a laborer whole in body and mind they would never admit, but a poor beggar disfigured in his face and maimed in his body, whose feebleness of mind has rendered him unfit to allow him to secure the requirements of food and shelter for his survival, they will pass through the gate that he may be protected from harm, and they will provide him with a place to sleep and food to eat, and give him simple tasks that place no great demands on his broken intellect, such as sweeping the floor of the library and the scriptorium where rare manuscripts are copied, and collecting the empty bowls after the morning meal in the dining hall where it is the custom for senior monks to give lectures in arcane and secret matters while their brothers eat.

The grounds inside the walls of the monastery are spacious and green, for they are daily watered against the heat of the sun, and many shade trees grow amid the pathways that cross these lawns between the three primary structures of the compound.

The principle of these is the great library, which extends out from the northern wall in two projections that face each other, forming an intimate courtyard between that is decorated by a statue of the goddess Ishtar upon a pedestal. The statue is not worshipped by the monks but serves to exemplify in human form the excellence of the celestial goddess. Here the monks study, teach what they have learned, and carry out the administration of the order; it is in this building that the Father of the order, Rumius, keeps his offices and private chambers, which are surrounded by the chambers of his councilors. A portion of each day is devoted by every monk to the copying of manuscripts, unless infirmity of the eyes or hands prevents this noble work.

The second great building is the dormitory near the western wall, where the monks have their cells, and it holds also the halls where they eat and rooms where they gather for prayer and meditation; attached to this are the kitchens and the pens for livestock, such as hens for eggs and cows for milk and cheese, which the monks make themselves. They also produce a beer of excellent quality in their vats. In the rear of the dormitory near the kitchens is the public baths, the waters of which are heated by the kitchen fires and fed into the baths by a cleverly designed series of pumps manipulated by the monks, which force the hot water through lead pipes.

The final structure is smaller and set in the southern part of the lawns, and holds the workshops of the monks and their armories. It is here that they produce their furniture and their cloths, for it is their practice to buy as few articles as possible and to make with their own hands as many as they are able. In this way they seek to reduce their dependence on men living beyond the monastery walls. In their armories they manufacture the unique bows they employ to defend their walls from attack, longer than the common bow of war and thicker at the center, with strongly tapered ends that are curved back upon themselves. So great is their force that the black arrows driven by their strings have the power to penetrate any armor and any shield. The abundance of these arrows in their storehouses is remarkable, for the monks boast that they could loose them upon a foe for three days and three nights without ceasing yet not exhaust their number.

The traveler, having gained by subterfuge the interior spaces, will concern himself primarily with the library, where knowledge is so plentifully displayed by the diligence of the scribes. Provided he simulates the idiot with art, no scroll will be hidden from his gaze and no topic hushed at his approach. In this way the wisdom of the descendants of the magi is to be acquired at no other cost than daily manual labor, and so long as the traveler makes himself useful to the monks, they will not turn him out from their gate.

A recent traveler so well contrived this deception that he was given free access to the scriptorium at all times, even when none of the monks were present. In this way he not only was able to read from the precious scrolls and books in the process of transcription, but from the more recent correspondences between the agents of the order in the far corners of the world and Rumius, who personally directs their actions, since it is the custom to have the scattered and ill-written reports of the agents gathered and transcribed by the more elegant hand of a scribe before the Father of the order reads them. These agents are engaged in a ceaseless battle against the forces of evil, and are amply supported by the wealth and wisdom of the magi.

It once took the fancy of this traveler to add a coda to the transcription of a message from an assassin dwelling within the land of Yemen, concerning the supposed adoption of the worship of the Old Ones by the monarch of that land, a thing most false and perfidious, for this king was a true believer in the words of the Prophet. Indeed the king had no fault, save the tendency to punish with unwarranted severity the violation of his trust by those he favored. As an example of this severity, the tale is told of a youth favored by the king and received into the palace as his adopted son, who violated the trust of the ruler by seducing his only daughter and getting her with child. For this transgression the king had the genitals of the youth struck off with a knife, and his face mutilated by the amputation of his nose and ears, before casting him into the Empty Space to die.

After the addition was made to the report of the assassin in Yemen, within two cycles of the moon word returned to the monastery of the sudden death of this king, seemingly by the fall of a stone from a wall as the king passed beneath it on his daily promenade within the grounds of his palace. Perhaps it was no more than mischance, or perhaps it was an act of divine retribution, for the ways of heaven are impenetrable, and what man can predict the manner of the unfolding of fate?

The Secret Purpose of the Magi

The monks sit within the scriptorium at long benches with angled tables, well furnished with pens and ink. They spend little effort on ornamentation or illumination, but seek to reproduce with great accuracy the older texts they copy, many of which are in a ruinous state of decay from the effects of mildew and worms. The majority are in our own tongue, but many are Greek and Latin works, and a smaller number are Hebrew or in the ancient pictorial script of the Egyptians, which so few scholars of our day can read.

There are other books not of this world, composed of strange substances and of diverse shapes, some in form like a cube that opens outward in many overlapping leaves, simulating the petals of a great flower, others composed of nesting tubes with letters inscribed around their outer surfaces in parallel rings. Some of these alien works are of gold, but others are in metals not known to our alchemists, and a few are cut into thin stone tablets that resemble polished marble. These strange works are acquired through trade, for all merchants and pilots know that the monks will pay well in silver coins for unusual books, and send forth hired men to scour ancient tombs or acquire what texts they can through still more devious means. Even those in languages the monks cannot read, they copy on parchment to insure their preservation and to make them easier to study.

All the purpose of their work is to learn the history and nature of the Old Ones. Though they value knowledge for its own sake, they sift the work of ages for the smallest scrap of information concerning the seven lords, their spawns, their lesser relations, and their cults. Any symbol or image connected with that race of star travelers who came to our world so long ago is preserved with care and examined for what instruction it may provide in the intentions of the Old Ones toward our world and mankind, and more particularly their strengths and weaknesses, their portals, and their places of repose.

The Sons of Sirius have one reason for existence that is more important to them than any other motive, which is the expulsion of the Old Ones and their spawns and abominable creations from our world, the destruction of their idols and temples, and the extermination of their worshippers wherever they may abide, whether near or in the most distant lands. All the monks of the order swear a solemn oath at their entrance to pursue this course with single intention until its ultimate fulfillment, or die in the attempt.

The traveler who has insinuated himself into the halls and chambers of the order through subterfuge, versed in the skills of necromancy and having perhaps given offerings and prayers to Cthulhu and Yog-Sothoth on strange altars, does well to conceal his links with the Old Ones from the monks, who are ever watchful, for the merest hint of his associations would result in his instant apprehension. He would undoubtedly be put to torture to determine the extent of his knowledge and his purpose, then executed. There is no fanaticism so potent as that of faith, and it is the faith of the descendents of the ancient magi that they are the chosen and anointed warriors of mankind against the dark gods who threaten our realm from beyond the vault of stars.

In truth, they are fools, for mighty Cthulhu could crush their monastery beneath his clawed foot with a single step, nor could all their armored knights stand against his star spawn for a moment, yet it must be acknowledged that the monks are dedicated in heart and fearless in their devotion to their cause. They worship Ishtar the goddess, not in her earthly form of a graven image but in her heavenly aspect, and call themselves her divine warriors, who will purge the spheres from the taint of the Old Ones and wash away the stains of their unnatural works. Ishtar they associate with the region of space that lies beyond the star Sirius, which they regard as her natural homeland; but it is plain that when they speak of the goddess, they do not understand her as the pagans of old worshipped her, but in a less tangible aspect more akin to an ideal or principle, so that her name is no more than a token for the being they worship. The overriding quality they ascribe to her is compassion.

This heavenly mother, compassionate for all living things, is at constant war with the lords of the Old Ones, who lack all charity or mercy. The magi fight for her because she cannot defend herself; they say she is in all living things of this world save only those things created by the arts of the Old Ones themselves, and even in these she lies sleeping, but it is a deep sleep from which she cannot easily be wakened. The monks are her sons and her lovers and her champions. This is their theology, which they conceal with utmost care from the vulgar, so that no word of it is ever spoken beyond the monastery gate.

The motto of the Greek philosophers was *Know thyself*, but the battle cry of the monks is *Know thine enemy*. They send out agents in common garments to hunt down those who traffic with the Old Ones or their servants and slay them, and to steal by guile or the sword objects of power that can be used in their works of magic, which they constantly make against their foes. The elders of the order are great magicians, having power to bend the minds of men to their will, to command demons and other creatures of the shadow realms, and to cast down lightning and fire upon those they mark for death when they lie beyond the reach of their assassins, but they use their power with discretion, for they do not wish to alert the seven lords of their progress lest the Old Ones find some way to destroy them before they are prepared for the final confrontation.

This is their interpretation of the Christian book of St. John the Divine, which they say is veiled so that common men cannot fathom its true meaning. The Great Dragon and his demonic servants described in that book they identify with Cthulhu and his spawn, and the pit or abyss into which he fell they claim is the abyss of the ocean where lies sunken R'lyeh, both home and prison to sleeping Cthulhu. The chosen warriors of light in that book they believe to be the monks of their own order, who will cleanse the world from the plague of the Old Ones in the final confrontation between mighty Cthulhu and our race. Their star goddess Ishtar they identify with the Queen of Heaven described in that book, having the moon beneath her foot and a crown of twelve stars upon her head.

Enough of their puerile fantasies, which have nothing to do with the majesty and power of the great Old Ones, who will crush these warrior monks as an elephant crushes an ant when the stars come right and R'lyeh rises. Then will those among us who have with foresight and prudence given worship to the lords be rewarded, and granted dominion over the defeated fools of our race, who will serve them as slaves. The Old Ones were, the Old Ones are, and the Old Ones shall be again. So it is written in the pattern of the stars, and not all the faith of man can alter it.

Why the Stars Are Not Right

The magi of the Tigris hold the secret teaching that it is not the pattern of the stars that binds Cthulhu in his watery tomb, as is widely believed by sages who have ventured to comment on this matter; rather it is the color of the stars in the complex interactions of their rays that poisons the airy element of our world, which is the zone between the fiery firmament and the watery abyss. Hence it is that the Old Ones can move easily above the air, and beneath the waves or the surface of the earth, but not through the air, save only for Nyarlathotep who is in part immune from the noxious colors out of space.

Each star has its own color that is distinct from the colors of all other stars, though these colors can be subtle and difficult to discern. They do not remain fixed and unchanging, but become paler or more intense over the passage of years. Any man who gazes into the night sky knows that Mars is red, but it is not always the same red, for at times it is like a ruby, but at other times it grows pallid and becomes almost the color of milk. So it is for all the stars, both those that are fixed and those that wander from place to place, even when the changes in colors are not as easily remarked upon as those of Mars.

No astrologer can tell what causes these shiftings of color amid the stars, but the magi believe that the great change in the heavens that drove Cthulhu to seek safety in his house on R'lyeh was the result of a cloud of mist or dust high above the region of fire. The colors of the rays from the stars passing through this veil of dust were tinted as the light of the sun is stained with red or blue or green when it passes through a jewel, and the gates between the stars were obstructed. The Old Ones do not reside in our world in their natural bodies, but in bodies that have been compounded and composed by the power of their souls, which have been thrown across the gulf between the stars by the force of their wills. The space portals through which their minds traveled were opened by the colors of the stars striking the earth with their rays, and the magi believe that when the veil of dust covered the heavens, and the colors became impure, those mind gates were in part closed, so that the full power of the seven lords and their lesser brothers and sisters could not awaken and move upon the earth.

To maintain the links between their far-darting minds and the bodies of matter they had formed for themselves in our sphere, they found it necessary to protect those bodies from the colors of the stars until the dust passed and the stars shone down with clean rays once again. The rays of the stars penetrate through air in both night and day, but cannot penetrate into the coils of the earth or beneath the waters of the oceans. In the deep places the Old Ones concealed their weakened bodies, or withdrew through portals in space entirely from this world, to await the passage of the dust, all but Nyarlathotep, who defies the poison of the stars and walks among us beneath the moon; yet even the Crawling Chaos cannot for long endure the hideous colors out of space but must withdraw himself to a place of protection.

The gates between the stars can still be opened, but opened only in part for the transmission of small things and small beings, and it is with utmost difficulty that the Old Ones use them, and only then at certain times when the colors are not so baneful to their natures, for the poison of the colors of the stars is not constant, but waxes and wanes, and at rare intervals of years, it diminishes so greatly that it is almost absent, and the Old Ones feel strength flow into the bodies they have composed for their souls in this world. Alas, the stars do not remain clean for long, but invariably return to their polluted state, driving the Old Ones into hiding. A time is foretold when the dust shall pass away from the upper reaches of our world, and the protection offered our race by the taint of colors from the heavens shall be lifted; then the Old Ones will once again rule our sphere as they rule all other spheres; but when this time shall come is not known, unless to the Old Ones themselves.

The magi make great experiments in their workshops with polished jewels of different colors, in the hope of discovering a weapon of light that shall have the power to mimic the poison of the stellar rays, with the intention of employing it against Cthulhu and his spawn should he rise from his tomb at R'lyeh; for they know full well that when the protective colors of the stars are no more, Cthulhu shall be their greatest foe. So lustily did he love the dominion held over our world and its creatures, and so jealously did he fight against expulsion by the rays from the heavens, he is certain to be the first to gather his strength and seek to conquer anew the lands he ruled of old.

The Thing Beneath the Library

To test their colored rays of light for efficacy against the Old Ones, the magi hold imprisoned in a chamber beneath their library a thing that was captured in the lowest depths of the caverns that reach to the center of our sphere. It is made of the same star-borne substance of which the seven lords are composed. Centuries past, when the walls of the monastery were raised on the foundations of an ancient ruin, the builders discovered this creature beneath the hill, imprisoned by potent seals of magic within a strange cell of iron. How it was compelled to enter its prison and who or what imprisoned it remains unknown. Instead of seeking to destroy it, the monks preserve it for their study. Either they are more courageous than the ranks of other men or more foolhardy, for it is certain that they hold a dragon coiled in a net of gossamer, and what shall it matter whether they are brave or foolish when the dragon opens its mouth to breathe forth fire?

In the deepest cellar of the library is set a small and uninteresting door of plain wood planks, its lintel low enough so as to require even a man of moderate height to bend over when passing through its frame. It is kept

209

locked with an iron lock of simple design, very easy to force using the thin blade of a dagger for a man accustomed to such work. Stone stairs lead steeply downward immediately beyond the door into darkness, so that care must be taken not to stumble. At the bottom of the stair is a vaulted corridor of roughly dressed stone blocks illuminated at infrequent intervals by oil lamps that hang from chains set into the walls. These lamps are kept perpetually refilled and are always burning.

No sentries are placed in these lower levels, for the magi do not believe that any but they themselves could traverse the corridor, and they have complete trust in all members of their order. Nor would they suspect danger from a feeble-minded and mutilated slave that they have in their compassion taken into their care. During the day the chance of discovery is great, for there are frequently men moving about, but in the hours after midnight the lower levels of the library are abandoned, and the risk is slight.

At the end of the corridor is a large, circular chamber with a domed ceiling that appears to be of Roman design, and may well be centuries older than the monastery above it. An iron cage in the shape of a sphere composed of interlocking bands riveted together at their intersections hangs above the floor on three massive chains, the links of which are so large than the hand of a man could easily pass through their openings, were it possible to reach them. The cage hangs suspended above the stone floor higher than a man can reach, but by jumping upward it would possible to touch it, should anyone be so foolish as to try; for the thing within would surely reach downward between the iron bands and slay any who ventured so near.

The iron bands of the sphere are massive enough to withhold the ram of a siege engine, but alone it is doubtful they could retain the creature that crouches on its haunches within their boundary, filling their compass with its translucent bulk. On the inner surface of the dome, the floor below the sphere, and on the walls surrounding it are painted pentacles of dread significance, so arranged that their aspects conjoin at the center of the chamber, and it is these rays of subtle and unseen force that are the true prison.

The thing in the cage watches the approach of those who enter the dome, motionless and subdued, almost appearing to be a great sculpture of hazy rock crystal shot through with clouds of various dull colors, for such is the appearance of its otherworldly body, which is not composed of flesh similar to the flesh of common living creatures. It watches and waits, but the terrible power of its will can be felt as a touch upon the skin, like the crawling legs of countless insects, and more sharply on the forehead between the eyebrows. With its mind it seeks to compel those who gaze upon it to wander nearer, until they are beneath the sphere and it is able to reach down with its taloned hand as with the striking head of a serpent and snatch out their lives.

Its will can be resisted by a strong mind, for the pentacles on the walls weaken and contain it; however, the traveler is advised not to allow his attention to wander even for a matter of minutes, or he will find himself standing beneath the sphere and may not have the quickness of limb to save himself. Its six small eyes exert a compelling force, and through them the creature may choose to communicate its thoughts, which reach the human mind as a sort of articulate intention or surmise, and also in the form of mental images. That it is one of the spawn of great Cthulhu there can be no doubt, for its shape is much the same as the carved and painted images of its creator, though there are minor differences in form of little importance or interest, since they cannot be turned to any useful account. Great leathern wings lie folded upon its back, its feet bear talons like those of the hawk, and its face is a mass of writhing protuberances resembling the bodies of headless serpents.

If the traveler falls to his knees before the sphere and makes the recognized gestures of obeisance and worship before the thing, placing his hands over his face and bowing his head to touch the stone floor, its indifference will quicken to an intense interest, for it will perceive that the traveler is not merely another of the magi come to further torture it with their colored rays of light and other weapons, but a servant of dreaming Cthulhu. Two emotions will surge within it and be felt by the mind of the traveler as palpable blows; the first is hope, and the second is a blind rage and lust for vengeance so potent it is all but overwhelming, and gives rise to the urge to scream or run from the chamber.

If the traveler can master his emotions, the thing in the cage will quickly perceive that it cannot control his mind with force, and it will be amenable to bargain for its freedom. The only currency it can offer in its captive state is knowledge, but its knowledge is vast, although much of it lies beyond the comprehension of the human mind or the scope of human use, it is of so alien a nature. The offer of freedom is not difficult to justify, for it would only be necessary for the pentacles on the walls of the chamber to be covered over with pigment or otherwise defaced, and those that remain on the dome and the floor would be unable to contain the creature, who would then burst its iron bands with ease; so the creature itself will instruct in the form of images sent into the mind that appear in the imagination like the moving pictures of dreams.

Among the most useful of its instructions is the manner of compelling other men or women to perform whatever action you desire. This is not like the spell of glamour that deceives the senses into seeing or hearing what is not present to see or hear, but a way of projecting the will into the minds of others so that they are made to move and speak against their own inclination. The compulsion is not absolute, for when it is perceived by a person of strong will, it can be resisted. It is most effective when used in such a way that the one enslaved by its power does not realize that his actions are directed from beyond his own mind. It is natural for us to assume that when we do a thing, we have a reason for doing it, and provided the action is not too outrageous, we seldom question its source.

The creature in the iron sphere has the power to hear within its mind the thoughts that are sent to it, making it possible to ask questions, though it is necessary to articulate the thoughts with the clarity of spoken speech; it cannot discern thoughts that are less clearly expressed, and the traveler will take great care to conceal his true intentions until he has achieved his ends, for if the thing perceives his treachery it will resist disclosing its secrets. After the traveler has inquired of the creature and has received from it the teachings he most desires, it is best that he withdraw from the chamber quickly, before the thing realizes that he does not intend to release it, for its rage will be great, and it may yet find a way to use the power of its thoughts to induce the traveler to commit some careless error that will bring him within reach of its claws.

It is perhaps needless to add that it would be foolhardy in the extreme degree to actually fulfill the bargain and release the thing from its iron prison, for without question it would immediately slay everything within the walls of the monastery, including the traveler himself. He need not fear that the creature will betray his loyalties to the magi, on two counts; first, that the thing hates the monks too deeply to ever give them any benefit, and second, that it will cling to the hope that the traveler may at some future time be induced to aid its purposes. In this way his trespasses in the lower chamber of the library will pass unnoticed, unless he is the victim of ill fortune, for what man can control the vagaries of the fates?

Why the Old Ones Do Not Die

The spawn of Cthulhu held captive beneath the monastery of the magi asserts that the lords of the Old Ones cannot die, for the simple cause that they do not truly live, as other beasts live. Their bodies are not bred upon the earth, but are sent as a pattern from the outer spaces that lie beyond the zones of the four elements, and this pattern or ideal shape is then made tangible by the accretion of matter, which is organized and held together solely by the will of the lord whose body it becomes. By gathering the moist humors from the air and the fine particles of dust that float upon the wind, the Old Ones make themselves a physical presence through which to project their designs, but these bodies are little more than suits of clothing which they put on or cast off at their pleasure; only Cthulhu, having formed his vast bulk in a form of his liking, was loath to put it aside, and so sought to preserve it intact in his house in R'lyeh from the poison of colors from the stars.

The bodies of tangible substance adopted by the Old Ones cannot be called their true forms, which are so monstrous and uncouth that the mind of man cannot hold them without madness, yet in their shapes they express in matter and on a level that can be fathomed by thoughts bound to flesh their essential natures, which transcend both flesh and form itself as we understand these things. When their bodies are broken apart, they immediately reshape themselves, for the will that projects the pattern upon which they are based is able to draw together the bits and fumes of matter even as they are scattered, so that a wound at once closes and is made smooth, and a limb struck off by a sword is regrown.

In this peculiarity the Old Ones differ from the Elder Things, who are indeed beings of flesh, although their bodies are unlike any that arose from the clay of our world. Similarly, the *meegob* of Yuggoth are flesh, however strange it may appear to human eyes. By contrast, the bodies of the Old Ones are more thought than flesh, for although they go about clothed in form, it is their minds that sustain their shapes, not their shapes that sustain their minds, as is true of all earthly life. And this is proven by the process of death, since when the body of a living creature is destroyed, its mind is darkened and loses power to affect the world, yet when the body of one of the Old Ones or their spawn, which is at unity with their nature, is broken up, its mind remains and exerts its will to reform its shape.

The mind of a man dwells within his house of flesh after the manner of a householder, and his house protects him from the harshness of storms and cold and permits him to raise his children, which are the thoughts of the body; yet the minds of the Old Ones are as merchants who remain in their own land and send forth ships across the sea to accomplish their purposes, and control the doings of these ships by means of letters dispatched without the necessity of going forth themselves. If a man loses his house that is his only protection, he will surely perish, but if a merchant loses a ship to mischance at sea, he has others to take its place and carry on his plans without hindrance.

So it is that the Old Ones can never be killed, for they do not live; such is their dreadful majesty, before which all the greatness of our world is but the plaything of a child. What recourse has any sane man other than to worship them? The Sons of Sirius know this truth, yet in their arrogance they think to find a way to disperse the bodies of the Old Ones in a manner that will prevent their reformation. They are fools, for if an artist draws a portrait in charcoal on a sheet of parchment, and the wind strips it from his hand and tears it to bits, shall he not simply draw another image to replace the first, and yet another if that is lost, and ever onward until the end of time itself?

It is due to this property of reformation that the body of Cthulhu can be both dead yet merely asleep. With the mind of the lord withdrawn, his flesh lies inert and cold, and is comparable to the hardened flesh of a corpse, but with the return of his mind his flesh quickens and becomes warm and soft and once more animate with the semblance of life. Because the Old Ones never truly live in our world, they have no fear of death and, in truth, no comprehension of its mysteries and terrors. The body is a vessel of convenience to be filled or emptied as it suits their purposes. Our fear of death amuses them, and they delight to watch us die so that they may find varied entertainment in our efforts to avoid our fate, and the terrors with which we confront our mortality.

Concerning Shoggoths

The only creatures feared by the spawn of Cthulhu are the shoggoths. Since the spawn cannot be killed in the ordinary manner of death, it is interesting to consider why they should fear anything in this world. It is their belief that the shoggoth has the power of causing not merely the dissolution of their composited bodies but of their essence as well; for they hold that the shoggoth consumes heat and vitality as well as flesh, making them a part of its own substance. In the words of our own race, a shoggoth is an eater of souls. The star spawn of Cthulhu assert that once consumed by a shoggoth, they are unable to reshape their forms and are forever lost in oblivion.

These terrible monsters, which no man and no other intelligent creature in this world has ever seen, are supposed to have been created by the Elder Things as their laborers during their early history on the earth, when they constructed their great cities. Later they served as the warriors who defended the cities against the coming of the Old Ones, and had it not been for the vast numbers of the spawn of Cthulhu and the other creatures created by the Old Ones for the sole purpose of making war, they would surely have prevailed with their limitless strength and imperviousness to injury. They are fabled to be deathless and self-renewing, so that no matter how many aeons a shoggoth has lived, it is as strong and fierce as it was at its creation; nor do they ever forget, but store all the events of their ageless lives within their substance. It is said by the spawn beneath the library that a shoggoth never makes the same mistake twice.

How is it possible to describe a creature that has no form of its own, but which takes on whatever shape or texture or color it requires for its purposes of the moment? The spawn says it is like a clear bladder filled with water in which float sparkling flecks that resembling swirling stars and other bodies that are more cloudy and indistinct. It moves by sliding itself forward on its belly after the manner of a snail, for it has no permanent limbs. However, if it wishes it can in a matter of moments grow legs and arms, and can even walk upright like a man when it suits its whim. To conceal itself, it can transform its watery hide into the rough darkness of stone and merge itself into the boulders or rocky cliffs around it.

To see its way as it goes forward on its belly, it extends eyes from its bulk; to hear the approach of its foes, it creates ears for itself. Shoggoths have no need for a mouth, since they consume their food by surrounding it with their soft bodies and absorbing it, after secreting an acidic juice that dissolves their prey and renders it fluid within its own skin. However, at times they project mouths for purposes of communication, and when they speak it is in the piping tones of the Elder Things, which sound like the notes of a flute. In the beginning of time the Elder Race created shoggoths without minds, but over the aeons they became more and more intelligent, until they acquired the ability to speak their thoughts in the Elder tongue. This caused the Elder Race to become afraid of their slaves, and to banish them from their remaining cities. They could no longer control the things they had made, for pain alone is not an effective tool of subjugation against deathless creatures with minds that can think and plan.

The shoggoth is reputed to be the strongest creature that has ever existed upon the earth. By causing its soft and shapeless body to flow under great stone blocks, it was able to lift them and place them with precision in the walls of the cities of the Elder Things. What would take a thousand men days to move could be lifted by a single shoggoth in moments. They never tire or require rest from their labors but toil both beneath the moon and the sun until their task is completed. They fear nothing, but fire causes them discomfort so that they withdraw their soft flesh from flames. Whether fire can kill them, the spawn of Cthulhu beneath the monastery of the magi did not know, since no shoggoth has ever been seen to die in flames. The Elder Race controlled them with the power of their minds until the shoggoths grew minds of their own. They used lightning bolts to punish them, though how these were generated the star spawn does not reveal.

It states that when the Old Ones came through the portals and shaped bodies for themselves from the substance of our world, the shoggoths were few in number, and scattered across the earth, and this alone allowed the armies of Cthulhu to triumph over them, for by surrounding each shoggoth and overwhelming it with numbers it was possible after great toil to destroy it in a way that did not permit it to restore its body. This was done by reducing it to small shreds and scattering these bits far across the land, rendering them incapable of coming together due to the distances of separation and the intervening obstacles. The spawn does not know whether the shoggoths destroyed in this manner were eventually able to reconstitute their bodies, but only that it kept them from reforming long enough for the Old Ones to triumph in their war against the Elder Race.

Anyone hearing this tale and doubting it may be forgiven his suspicions, for how can such a creature ever have existed? Its nature is in monstrous discord with all the laws of heaven, and in defiance of the four elements and their way of mingling. Surely it must be only a fable of the Old Ones and their spawn, passed down from the primal times before our race arose from the clay, even as common men pass down myths of gods and heroes that a scholar knows to be untrue. And for one reason alone is its falsehood certain, that if such a creature as the shoggoth walked the earth and swam the seas in ages past, it would in present times be the lord and ruler of all other creatures, for what living thing could stand to oppose it?

It is true that travelers have spoken over their wine of glimpsing this strange creature in deep caverns beneath the mountains, or in the ruins of vast cities, but it is apparent to the judicious hearer of these tales that they are no more than visions of the hashish pipe or of the black tar of the poppy, the smoke of which makes dreams appear to a man awake. Always the shoggoth is seen by a man alone, and always in the shadows and moving away from view even as it is looked upon. Such visions are no more real than the faces that come before us on the edge of sleep when first the eyes are closed.

It is undeniable that great wonders may be found in the world beyond the imagining of dull merchants and farmers, but that such an abomination as the shoggoth could dwell in the shadows yet not openly reveal its limitless power is an insult to reason that cannot be endured. The very thought of it makes the sweat trickle down the spine and the heart drum with fear, for were such a creature to be, nothing could oppose its malice save mighty Cthulhu himself, and he lies dreaming his own strange dreams in R'lyeh.

The Formula of Yug

The thing trapped within the iron sphere beneath the library has a trick of which the traveler must be wary, especially if he is a man of weak will whose mind is accustomed to gaze inward upon memories and scenes of the imagination. In this condition of waking dream, if ever his concentration wanders from the creature, he will be caught as is a fly in the web of a spider, unable to escape. The spawn of Cthulhu has not a hundredth part of the power of the mind of the dreaming god that is its master, yet it is skilled in all forms of thought magic. It knows a formula by which it can transfer the essence of its awareness into the body of another living being, while the mind of that creature is kept within its own vacated translucent bulk.

In this way it has secretly studied the defenses of its enemies by entering the body of a monk weak of will who was set to tend it, then wandering about the compound of the monastery, sampling the books in the library, examining the weapons created to war against the Old Ones, and searching for weaknesses in the defenses of the magi. It attempted the same trick upon a traveler who came in secret to its prison to question it, but he was a necromancer and his will was not weak. The traveler recognized the intrusion of the alien mind and repulsed it with the Elder Sign and the invocation of words of power that set a shield before his mind that the spawn could not pierce.

The solidity of the shield surprised the creature and caused it to lower its guard upon its thoughts. The traveler saw the memories of the possession of the monk, a young Greek named Adrian, who retained no awareness of his expulsion from his own body but merely seemed to sleep all the while the spawn walked inside his shell. He saw the purpose of the spawn, its deep guile and endless patience. Fearless in its immortality, it watches and waits and plans the downfall of the Sons of Sirius. All this he perceived in the moment the monster's mind lay open, before it slammed and locked the gateway of images.

Sending out his thoughts to the iron sphere, he threatened that he would make known to Rumius, the leader of the order, the possession of the young monk by the Cthulhu spawn unless it taught him the technique of exchanging minds between bodies. Its reluctance was so great, it could be felt as an itching upon the skin, but at last it agreed, perceiving no other way to retain its freedom to wander the monastery compound in the body of the monk.

Before seeking the magic itself, the traveler asked why, if the spawn could control the young monk, it has not used him to erase the pentacles that kept it bound within its iron cage. The answer came at once in the form of images. The monks set to tend to its infrequent needs always came in groups of three, never alone. At all other times the door to the lower chamber was locked, and neither the spawn nor Adrian had the skill to open it without violence, which would surely be detected before the stout door could be beaten down. The key was kept where it was impervious to theft. Also, the cold patience of the thing in the sphere was greater than the patience of a man, and it knew that any attempt at escape, if it failed, could not be attempted a second time. It was content to continue to gather information and await its opportunity.

The magic was a secret of the god Yug, a dweller in the lower caverns beneath the vaults of Zin who kept aloof from the affairs of the surface world, yet who held communion with Cthulhu in his dreams. What was known to Cthulhu was also known by his spawn, insofar as their more limited minds were able to understand it. The formula of mind exchange was a simple technique, within the capacity of the spawn or even a human being. It depended upon a knowledge of the name of the creature with which the counterchange of minds was made.

At once, as these thoughts were conveyed to his mind, the traveler realized that the spawn had been probing his memories for his name, and it was only because the creature was unsuccessful that the attempt to steal his body had failed. The monks addressed each other by name, but none of them knew the true name of the traveler. A false name would not serve the purposes of the formula, only the true given name.

It is only necessary for the man seeking to project his mind into the body of another to hold the image of that person clearly in his thoughts while uttering, either aloud or silently in the imagination, this formula of Yug in the language of the Old Ones: "*Yug! N'gha k'yun bth'gth* _____ *gllur ph'nglui* _____ *yzkaa!*" In the initial space that has been left in the formula, the true name of the person is inserted; in the final space, the speaker of the formula voices his own true name. At once, the awareness of the speaker finds itself within the flesh of the person named, and the mind of that man or creature is placed in the speaker's body, but unaware, as though in deep slumber. In the beginning the counterchange of minds cannot be sustained for more than the fifth part of an hour, but with each repetition of the magic it becomes easier to maintain, until at last a level of perfection is reached in which it is possible to make the transfer permanent.

In this way the formula may be used to attain a kind of immortality, as the mind moves from body to body, replacing flesh that is aged or diseased with flesh that is youthful and robust. It does not come without a price, for not all the power of a man is contained within his mind; some aspects of power also reside in the flesh itself, and when the flesh is discarded, this potency is lost. Care must be observed never to transfer permanently the mind into the body of a host who is weak of intellect or frail of will, as this may render future transfers with other human vessels impossible. Mark this well: the stronger can enter the weaker, but the weaker cannot enter the stronger. A mind that is uncommonly vacillating and frail cannot work the formula at all, even against a weaker mind, since its use requires a degree of power.

Those of strong will can use this formula of Yug with greater ease than men of normal concentration; those of weak will are more susceptible to its influence than men of potent mind. It is a spell of dominance, and can never be employed to enslave the strong to the weak. The transfer can only be made between two minds capable of reasoned thought—it will not place the mind of a man into the body of a beast, even for a brief duration, for the beast has no understanding, and its flesh is not a fit vessel for human intellect. However, two reasoning beings, be they ever so dissimilar in kind or appearance, can exchange their minds by the formula, provided that he who utters it is the stronger of will. If the difference between the two minds is not great, the formula can be resisted by the weaker mind, but if the difference is large, no resistance is possible.

In after days, it amused the traveler who had received the formula of Yug from the spawn to see the monster gazing at him through the eyes of the monk Adrian as they passed each other in the library, or upon the paths of the monastery compound. Neither acknowledged the presence of the other, or gave any sign of recognition, but the traveler fancied that he could discern a faint gleam of inhuman mirth in the depths of the monk's eyes, as of one who shares a matter of portent with another that remains unsuspected by the crowd in the marketplace.

The Well
of Life

In the library of the magi is a scroll on papyrus which the monks have set aside as a thing of little value, so that it occupies a dark niche in the nethermost wall of books at the western end of the library. It is written in Aramaic, but the letters are Hebrew, and it may be that none of the scribes who examined it possessed the knowledge to translate its contents. The text itself is of limited interest, consisting as it does of a description of various holy springs and other sacred places of the infidels, most of them so completely decayed that they have ceased to exist and can no longer be located. It is not this primary text that gives the scroll its interest to the necromancer.

Near the foot of the scroll a gloss has been added in lettering so fine that it can only with difficulty be read by the light of an oil lamp. The gloss speaks of a well of renewal that restores the bodies of those who have suffered mutilation to wholeness, so that a man who has endured the loss of an arm from the stroke of a sword, or a woman who has lost a leg beneath the wheel of an ox cart, merely by drinking the water from this well is made entire in limb. Even a man who has had his virile member cut off by the knife of the torturer will be restored by this wondrous water, or so the nameless scribe who wrote this gloss attests.

This is a matter of interest to those who have sustained disfigurement or the severing of any portion of the flesh, for though many elixirs restore vitality, there is no other that returns the body of a man to its original state when it has been marred by violence. The virtue does not lie in the water of the well itself, but in a precious object that was concealed there many centuries ago during the captivity of the Hebrews at Babylon. What this object may be, the scribe does not reveal, and it is probable that he was himself ignorant of the nature of the wonder, which in some way transmits its healing force into the waters that surround it and permeate it.

Only this much is written, that the priests of Jerusalem divided this thing into parts and concealed it on their forced removal from their own city, and made it whole once again after their safe arrival in the land of the Babylonians. To insure the safety of their possession, they went from the city at night with this thing tied to the back of a camel, and lowered it into a deep well in the wasteland, far from any village or caravan road. The well was known to only a few men of the hills, and was never used, as its water was unfit to drink. Once the thing was set at the bottom of the well, writes the scribe, the water began to glow with golden light.

In great wonder, the priests sent down an empty vessel on a rope and drew up a quantity of the water to examine it. The glow persisted and was bright enough to illuminate the surrounding night so that they could see their own faces as they looked at each other. An elder priest with a crippled arm, which had been broken in a fall from a horse during the journey to Babylon, and had refused to heal, summoned the boldness of heart to taste the water, and reported to the others that it was pure and sweet. More wondrous still, his body and face began to shine, and in the space of a few minutes his shattered arm regained its natural feeling and vigor, as the bones that were crooked became straight beneath the skin. All then sampled the water, and their scars were erased from their bodies. One who had gone deaf in his left ear was able to hear again. The youngest among them, who had lost a finger while a child, watched it regrow itself.

Having little time, and fearing that the light shining upward out of the well from the water would cause the discovery of the hiding place, the priests rolled large stones over the mouth of the well, and filled up their crevices with pebbles and sand, so that no more than a mound of stones remained and the light was veiled. As the sun rose above the hills to the east, they left the place behind them, their thoughts humbled and their lips murmuring prayers to their god.

The priests were attacked by bandits on the road leading back to the city of Babylon, and all but the youth was killed. He alone passed on the knowledge of the hiding place, which may be located by a weathered pillar that stands near the well having a crack through its center that divides it into two sides. The rising sun shines its light through this crack, and the spear of light falls across the mound of stones that conceals the well; and by no other means would the well be discovered, for the shallow valley in which it resides is littered with stones and low mounds of sand. The location of this valley is reported by the scribe to lie three days to the south and east of Babylon, at the meeting place of two hills known as the Breasts of the Goddess. Here ends the text of this most interesting gloss, which the copyists and librarians of the magi overlooked.

The traveler who has successfully ingratiated himself within the walls of the monastery of the Sons of Sirius, and who has at his leisure plucked the secrets of the monks from them as a farmer plucks his chickens, will sooner or later tire of simulating an idiot and a slave, and will choose to depart. This will be no difficult matter, for he is not a prisoner but a servant, with freedom to come and go by the gate of the monastery in order to purchase goods in the marketplace for his masters. Though they will supply him liberally with silver coins for this purpose, it is prudent to mark the location of the strongbox in which this money is kept so that he can increase his purse just before departing through the gate for the final time.

It is similarly to his advantage to gather up the rarer texts from the library containing teachings that may with future experiment and trial prove to be of use. The larger books are bound with brass or iron and are too massive to be easily transported, but smaller scrolls may be collected into a travel pack and slung over the shoulders for removal. Books that are not frequently consulted by the monks may be taken from the library and carried beyond the monastery walls for several days before their absence is noticed.

Although the loss of a few coins is of no importance to the monks, who possess great wealth and have no miserly tendencies in their natures, the loss of their rarer books, which are irreplaceable, will enrage them when it is discovered, and cause them to search both banks of the river for weeks in their efforts to restore them. The traveler is advised to move swiftly in the hours following his departure from the monastery, and to conceal his tracks by crossing the land upon naked rock and avoiding mud and sandy soil. Once set into motion, the magi cannot be placated, and will never tire in their efforts or turn from their determination until their purpose has been fulfilled.

The Relic of
the Hebrews

Once the cleft pillar has been located in the valley of stones, it is a matter of small difficulty to find the mound that conceals the well. The stones on top of its mouth are broad and flat, of a weight that can be tipped up with effort by a single man, if he has a strong back, and rolled aside. They overlie each other like the scales of a fish, and in this way cover the opening. Though the glow of the water is not perceptible in daylight above the well, by leaning over its channel with the eyes shaded by the hands, and peering down, it can be discerned in the depths, and is seen to be of a golden color similar to polished brass.

The well is uncommonly deep, so much so that the traveler who has come without a considerable length of twine will find himself at a loss as to how to draw up the shining waters from its depths; a close examination of the interior sides of the well reveals a spiral series of notches cut into the stones to act as a stair, presumably to allow slaves access to its depths for the periodic cleaning of silt and debris. By descending from notch to notch, winding progress can be made from the top to the surface of the water. The traveler will find it necessary to lower his body into the water, since there is no place to stand, and the position of the stairs makes it impossible to release one hand and bend down to cup the water in the palm for drinking.

The depth of water is too great to stand upon the bottom. Floating up to the neck, and clinging to the rough stones at the side of the well, the water upon the skin feels strangely warm and causes a tingling sensation, as though the skin were pricked over its surface by a thousand needles. It is then a simple matter to duck the head and swallow some of the water. Alas! The story related by the anonymous scribe is no more than a fable, at least with respect to the curative powers of the well, for the traveler, upon feeling with his fingers those parts of his body that are maimed or scarred, will discover no change. The water has a bitter taste on the tongue, and becomes more sour and foul the longer it remains in the stomach, so that at last the traveler will be forced to vomit it up, for his body will not suffer it to remain within.

The regret of a seeker who has traveled far in search of this well, hoping to use its waters to erase from his body the mutilations of the torturer's knife, can scarcely be imagined by those who are whole in limb and without disfigurement. To have hope of healing placed in the heart by the cruel fiction of the unknown scribe, and then to find it torn from the breast by the sour reality of the poisoned waters, is almost as painful as was the initial cutting away of the flesh. The traveler may almost be forgiven for crying out like a savage beast in his rage and frustration, and for cursing the faith of Jerusalem.

Having ventured so far, it would be foolish not to investigate the relic of the Hebrews for anything of value it might contain. Again, the traveler will suffer disappointment, for when he takes a breath and descends to the bottom of the well, he will discover that the glowing radiance emanates from a locked box that is too large for a single man to lift and too strongly made to be broken open. It is sheathed all over in thin gold, with golden rings set in its sides. By these rings it might be possible to raise the box with a length of strong rope and the aid of a donkey or camel, but the traveler will soon learn that he is not alone in the well, as his stirrings will awaken the thing that abides in its depths.

What it is no man can define, for its likeness is not to be found elsewhere upon the earth. In part composed of matter, and in part made up of light, it resembles a great eel with the face of a man, or an angel, yet its long tail is a curling flame. In swift turns and darts it quests upwards from beneath the box when its stability is disturbed, and its eyes burn with terrible purpose. Perhaps it is a thing of the mud and cold that dwelled in the well from earliest times, and perhaps it was transformed by the radiance of the relic, even as the poisonous waters were changed and made to glow. The blade of a knife passes through its body without apparent harm, and when grasped in the hands, its coiling length slides through the fingers, but there is a fatal strength in its shining sides, and the traveler is prudent to leave the well as quickly as haste allows, when he is able to disentangle himself from this strange guardian.

Once out of the water, he will be safe, for the creature does not emerge above the surface. It can be seen still circling beneath with impatient rage. After he climbs from the well, the traveler may wish to amuse himself by taking large stones and dropping them into its depths. It is unlikely that these will cause the creature any injury, as its body is protected by the water, but their strikes upon the surface will surely annoy it. This amusement is far too tiring and unsatisfying to long persist in, but it is some amelioration for the bitter disappointment of the failure of the golden water to heal the disfigurements of the body.

Why this one detail of the scribe's description is false, when all other things presented in the gloss are true beyond question, must remain a mystery. There is a natural impulse in those who write of marvelous matters to magnify their strangeness and wonder, which may account for the fable of the relic's healing properties. Any reader of the gloss who has been led to the well in the past has undoubtedly suffered the same disappointment, unless by a peculiar quality of the relic its healing virtue only reveals itself in the body of a man of Hebrew faith; or perhaps only in the body of a man of religious devotion and pure spirit. Certain it is that the water has no healing help for the body of a necromancer and worshipper of Yog-Sothoth.

Wanderers on the Road to Damascus

Strange things are to be encountered on the long and hot journey to Damascus, greatest of all cities that is acclaimed by the sages as the center of the world. Its roads are roads of pilgrimage and of destiny. The apostle Paul is asserted in the texts of the Christians to have seen the radiance of God while making his way to the city from Jerusalem. The dangers on the desolate road from the east are great, and lights seen there are apt to have hellish import, for at night on its remote stretches it is haunted by bandits, wolves, and jinn of infernal fire that float upon the air and vanish with mocking laughter. In spite of these threats, life never ceases to flow along the road, even as blood flows in the veins of a living creature, for Damascus is the heart that pumps it.

A traveler of our own race making his way upon this road from the land of the Persians once crossed the path of the lover of his youth, conveyed along a more northerly route in a caravan of numerous retainers and armed guardians. Coming upon it, he marveled at its rich wagons and finely equipped mounted knights, whose ceremonial armor jingled and rang with the music of bells. He discovered that the caravan was his former lover's bridal escort, for the woman was on her way to be wed to a prince at Constantinople. Her father, the king of Yemen, had recently expired due to a curious accident involving a falling stone, and her brother, newly risen to the throne and still uncertain of his power, had sought to forge an alliance by pledging her hand to an elderly ruler she had never seen in her years of life.

She did not recognize the traveler as the lover of her childhood, for his face was horrifyingly disfigured, and though he might have used a simple glamour of magic to present to her a false visage, he chose to meet her eyes unchanged, and found to his amazement that his heart was unmoved by the haughty glance from her curtained coach as she passed, so completely had the fire of love that had once burned in his heart fallen to ashes. In truth it has been spoken that all wounds are healed with the passage of time, yet not without scars.

He watched the caravan pass from sight and beyond hearing, then followed in its track until dark, and when the camp was asleep, he entered the tent of the sleeping princess and took from her private jewel case a pendant he had given her as a pledge of his love so many years before. It was not a thing of value, but to reclaim it amused him. In its place he put a living scorpion, then softly closed the lid of the box. His power of magic made it an easy matter to enter and leave the armed camp without discovery. Not waiting to learn the outcome of his little jest, he returned to his own road and continued on his way to Damascus.

Upon this road are to be encountered at intervals bright yellow wagons enclosed by wooden canopies that serve as the living places of a devious and arrogant people erroneously believed to originate in Egypt, although they have no appearance of the pure-blooded Egyptians presently to be found in Memphis or Alexandria, nor do they resemble the wandering bands of tinkers who derive their name among the common people from the land of the Nile. This degenerate sect call themselves Thugians, which in their tongue signifies the crafty race, and roam throughout the world with impunity. They may be known by the image of a red eye, tipped on its point and standing upright, which they paint upon the fronts of their wagons.

Wherever they go, they earn the reputation of thieves and vagabonds. Having no fixed homes, neither do they possess dedicated professions, but make their living, the men by cutting wood or shaping pots or grinding knives, and the woman by assisting at childbirths and divination with the lines of the palm. At any rate, these are their purported occupations, for it is well-known that the men gain most of their wealth through theft, and the woman through whoring and the inducing of abortions, along with the sale of love philters.

A few among our scholars have speculated that they are the descendants of Cain the accursed, who when marked by God after the murder of his brother was shunned by all creatures; others believe they are the lost tribe of Israel, condemned to wander the world yet never to find a home. It seems a more probable conjecture that they came from the distant east, harried from their place of dwelling by the Greek conqueror Alexander, who led his armies into India and despoiled many uncouth and pagan realms before succumbing to disease. As for their more primal origins, understanding may be found in the seventh book of Herodotus, in which the historian describes a Persian tribe called Sagartians, who fought in the ranks of the great army of Xerxes.

They are hated and shunned in every land, so that even the nameless bands of wanderers seek to slay them whenever they encounter their piss-colored wagons, for they say that the Thugians pretend to be them, and poison the minds of townsfolk against all wayfarers. To avoid the wrath of their foes, the Thugians never make camp for more than a few nights in one place. The road itself is their home, and they obey no laws other than those they have formed.

The men are resolute and bold, with handsome faces and strong bodies, while the women possess a dark beauty. In each traveling band one among them is known as their lord, and to him they give grudging obedience, though in truth they all carry themselves with the haughtiness of noble blood, and offer no more than a guarded acquaintance to those not of their own race. Their children are without playfulness. Even at the age of five years they mimic the distant and appraising looks of their parents, and go about walking rather than running, and silent rather than laughing.

It is an easy matter for a necromancer versed in the arcane arts to gain their sufferance as a travel companion, for the women are ever eager to learn new methods of magic, though they share little of their own knowledge in return. Their interests are of a petty sort, for they value only charms that can be turned to a profit or used to injure their enemies without fear of detection. Though both men and women are fearless in battle, they do not scruple to employ deceit where it suits their purposes.

In their souls is a harsh joy for life but no gentleness or kindness, either toward beasts or men.

When Christian monks or followers of the Prophet on the road in pilgrimage ask about their faith, they pretend that they worship the sun and moon, but if pressed for the details of their beliefs, they cease to speak and turn away with sullen expressions. This is merely a pretense, for no race in this world is so skillful at lies. A traveler who rides and camps with them along the road, and who observes their ways with keen attention, will be able to discern the matter they wish to conceal. In every family wagon they keep a portable shrine made of carved sandalwood, with closed doors that hide its contents. Each night the father makes worship before this shrine, and before the idol it holds, leading his family in chants and prayer. This is done within the wagon, after its entrance has been sealed against the night, by the light of an oil lamp; and his slaves, if he has sufficient wealth to own slaves, remain outside the wagon.

The traveler who has succeeded in gaining a portion of the trust of this strange race, for no outsider can ever gain their complete confidence, will be able to purchase for gold a brief glance within one of these shrines. He will discover that the goddess of these wanderers is an obscene form of Shub-Niggurath, the goat of a thousand young. The Thugians keep numerous goats, which serve them for meat, milk, and cloth, and they value fertility in their women above all other virtues or beauties. They believe that Shub-Niggurath blesses them with abundance both of their livestock and in the number of their children. They venerate the womb and the things that issue from it, and for this reason their female infants are valued as highly as their males. It is their faith that they hold a unique covenant with Shub-Niggurath established in the most ancient times, before the recording of histories, and that for so long as they uphold their part in this bargain, the goddess will favor them with fertility.

The image of Shub-Niggurath kept in their family shrines is not to be seen elsewhere in the known world, though perhaps it is common in the undiscovered land of their origin. It consists of a small stone idol in the shape of a dancing woman, her breasts and vulva exposed. Her hair is ragged, her eyes blaze with fury, and her tongue hangs from her open mouth, which is distorted by a leer of lust. About her neck hangs a long necklace made up of human skulls. Her swollen belly shows that she is pregnant. Men and women touch the belly of this image when they seek to conceive children, and before coupling chant the words *A'ai y'gatu l'il ro'kanah Shub-Niggurath*, which may be translated into our tongue from the language of the Old Ones, *Fulfill thou thy covenant with the crafty race, Shub-Niggurath*. They chant the words but have forgotten their meaning, since no Thugian understands the tongue of the being they serve.

The Rite of the Companion

The young men of the Thugians carry neither sword nor lance, for it is a decree of the covenant established with their obscene dancing goddess that no man of the tribe may shed even one drop of the blood of a foe. Instead, they wear a yellow and white scarf about their heads, or sometimes their necks, knotted in cunning fashion to provide firm grips for the hands, and equipped with a loop that may be used to make an expandable noose. All of their killing of men is done by means of strangulation. They are trained in this method of murder from boyhood, and even the least of them is possessed of uncanny stealth and skill.

The way of the art is this: they approach from behind, cast the scarf around the neck of their prey, and hold it tight until he ceases to struggle; then they thread the end through the loop to make a sliding noose and draw it tight while standing over their fallen foe with their foot against his neck. This posture they maintain until death is certain. Women they do not kill, for it is forbidden by Shub-Niggurath. The women of the tribe suffer no similar constraint, and bear long knives in their girdles, which they employ at the slightest provocation against those who do them injury.

In explanation of this curious prohibition against the shedding of blood, the women of the wagons tell a legend from the beginning of the world. Human children borne in the ever-fertile womb of the goddess were being consumed as quickly as they issued forth by a monstrous demon, preventing the Black Mother from creating the race of man. So vast was the bulk of the demon that when it stood in the midst of the deepest sea, the waters did not rise above its waist. The Mother grew angry at the deaths of her children and used a great sword to battle the demon in the sea, but each time she cut its body, the drops of its blood formed demons similar to itself, though smaller of stature. They contested with her so fiercely that she despaired of ever defeating them.

Wiping the sweat from her brow, she made from it two men, the first of the crafty race. She tore strips from the hem of her garment and gave one to each man, commanding them to strangle each small demon as it issued from the blood of the parent. This task they accomplished with such swiftness and skill that she was able to prevail over the monster with her sword and send it beneath the waves. In gratitude for the help of the two stranglers, the goddess forged a covenant with their tribe, commanding that they slay all those not of their blood in her name, yet never by the sword, only by the noose. In return, she pledged to send them good fortune and perpetual fertility.

So diligently has the crafty race performed their part in the compact, they continue to be a source of terror even in our age of the Prophet. For they have the hellish skill to disguise themselves as the common people of the lands through which they pass, gaining the trust of strangers and allowing them to plot death with impunity. Nor do they kill in passion or those they hate or fear, but coldly and without feeling they slay any who fall under their knotted scarves, making of it a kind of sport and competing with each other to achieve the greatest number of deaths or the most artful murders, all for the honor of their religious faith.

The most important part of the covenant is known as the rite of the companion. On the third day after the birth of a child, a ritual is performed by the Thugians in which the child is pledged to the service of Shub-Niggurath for the remainder of its days of life. By the pattern of this rite a spiritual creature that is an unbodied offspring of the prolific goat is called down and induced to enter the flesh of the infant. Soul of the child and soul of the spiritual creature become united. It is this that most distinctly sets this race apart from other men, for in later years this servant of Shub-Niggurath is always with them and obeys their will in the capacity of a familiar demon; at their command it leaves their flesh and flies to fulfill their errands.

The traveler fortunate enough to have gained the partial trust of this most secretive race, and able to purchase a seat at the rite of the companion, will find himself in a ring with many others around a large fire blazing beneath the stars. All their communal rites and social customs, other than the private nightly worship of the family within the wagon, are performed beneath the open sky. Care is taken to choose a place that is far enough apart from local habitations to prevent discovery. If the terrain permits, a sheltered hollow between low hills is preferred, since this provides a mask for the fire glow.

The father of the child, whether it be a girl or a boy, carries the infant naked in his hands from his wagon. The elders of the race who are passing through the region where the rite is conducted, and who have gathered to assist in its fulfillment, draw close to the fire, and the four most senior among them approach the flames until they stand near enough to touch them, and though it appears that they must be scorched by the heat of the fire, they are not injured or in any way inconvenienced by the blaze.

The father approaches the fire with his child, and stands close so that his body, when joined with the four seniors of the rite, forms one of the five points of a pentagram around the fire. In the outer ring the women begin to sing a wordless song composed all of vowel sounds that are droned on the breath in the nose and back of the throat, and the young men to play music on flutes and flat drums that are struck with curved sticks and have silver rattles set in their sides. With the song and music they raise their emotions to a fury and sway their bodies rhythmically forward and back.

The most senior of the four who surround the fire with the father begins to make invocation to Shub-Niggurath in their own language, which is unknown outside their race but does not resemble the ancient tongue of Egypt nor the language of the Hebrews, as some scholars have written on the evidence of spurious assertions by those who have claimed to know this race. It may also be written with assurance that this invocation is not in the language of the Old Ones, save only for the single phrase *a'ai y'gatu l'il ro'kanah Shub-Niggurath,* which is many times repeated, and serves as a kind of chant of power to punctuate the various parts of the invocation.

As the music and wordless song rises in strength, the father passes the naked babe through the smoke and flames into the hands of one of the four elders, and as the exchange is made, a great shout goes up from all assembled. Five times the child is passed through the fire, but this is done swiftly so that no harm comes to it from the flames, though the irritation of the smoke in the infant's eyes and lungs causes it to cry lustily. A secret may be revealed not written elsewhere, and perhaps unknown outside of the camps of the wanderers themselves, for not even Ibn Schacabao alludes to it in his voluminous texts. The infant is passed from man to man in such a way that its progress around the fire imitates the interlocking rays of the pentagram drawn with one continuous stroke of the pen against the course of the sun; for it is well-known to students of the necromantic arts that the pentagram is inscribed as a sign of power only when drawn with a continuous line that joins its end with its beginning.

At the fifth great shout, when the pentagram has been completed around the fire, a young goat white and spotless is led into the circle by the mother of the child. It walks calmly, without resistance, as though aware in some dim way of its higher purpose, and submissive to the will of the goddess. Two girls in the first season of their flowers hold it with ropes tied to its forelegs to prevent its escape, should it attempt to flee the fire, but this is said to be seldom necessary. The mother of the child draws back the head of the goat with one hand, and with the other cuts its throat, as the father thrusts the wailing infant beneath the fountain of blood that issues from the wound. The baby is bathed completely in blood before the goat stumbles and falls dead, while the frenzied observers of the rite make an enormous din by shouting, clapping their hands, stomping their feet, and beating on metal pots and shields with sticks and stones.

The elders pick up the carcass of the goat and cast it upon the fire. As the smoke from its burning coat rises into the night sky, the senior among them takes the child from the blood-stained hands of the father and elevates it directly above the fire as high as he is able to hold his arms to prevent the child from being burned. What happens next is a mystery of this race, that all observers of the rite are pledged on their life never to reveal, and none have done so, for it is universally believed to be unlucky to speak of the mysteries of any people, and that such irreverence to sacred matters calls down upon their heads the wrath of the gods. However, it may be written that a presence in the form of a mist or smoke descends from the stars against the course of the smoke rising from the fire, and it envelops the body of the infant and is drawn within its flesh.

At the very moment the presence enters the child, it ceases to wail and becomes silent and alert. Those who gaze into its eyes detect an unnatural awareness that is the sure sign of the indwelling of its familiar demon. Although the mind of the babe is unformed, the mind of the demon is complete and mature. It is years before the awareness of the child and the awareness of its familiar spirit become merged in harmony.

The rite concludes with much celebration and fornication, which takes place just beyond the ring of wagons and the illumination of the fire. If either of the two girls who led out the sacred goat is a maiden, she is ritually deflowered on that night and her virginity given as an offering to Shub-Niggurath, and this is considered to increase the luck for the child. An attempt is always made to find at least one virgin for the rite, but this is not always possible, and where none is available the rite proceeds to the discomfort of the parents, who look upon the lack of a deflowering as an ill omen. The people dance, drink wine, and feast, but they do not partake of the charred flesh of the goat, which is permitted to be wholly consumed in the fire. To insure this result, wood is constantly added to the flames for the remainder of the night. The rite does not conclude until the first light of dawn, when the revelers retire to their wagons to sleep.

Terms of the Covenant with Shub-Niggurath

The goat with a thousand young gives the roving race that worships her abundance and fertility and a measure of good fortune in matters of chance that is above the allotment of common men. The luck of the Thugian allows him to commit housebreakings or thefts without discovery, and if he is found out and taken, to escape his captivity with ease, so that no bolder band of robbers walks this earth. It also assists in the more sinister act of murder, which they commit against strangers not solely for the greater glory of their goddess but also for profit. When they kill openly in sight of men it is in the heat of passion, but when they kill for money it is done coldly and in secret.

At assassination no race is more adept. First they lull the victim into a false camaraderie and share his food and drink, then when they are certain that they are alone with him, one of their number grasps the man firmly around the arms while the other, who stands behind him, casts a scarf around his neck and draws it tight so that he cannot cry out. As these murders occur on the road and usually to merchants in transit from one city to another, and as the assassins immediately bury the bodies so that no trace of their crime remains, they easily pass undetected, and by the time the murdered man is missed by his family, those who ended his life are hundreds of leagues from the place where the crime occurred.

It is a part of their covenant with Shub-Niggurath that each man must murder at least once in the course of a year as a sacrifice to her, in order that her bounties will continue to fall upon their heads. Some among them are skillful in the arts of murder and slay more frequently for their own gain, but even the least bloodthirsty among them meets this obligation to their goddess, and the old or very young or infirm are aided by others more nimble and of greater strength. The obligation begins in the sixteenth year and continues until death. It is a matter about which they do not speak, even among themselves, for fear that some detail of a specific assassination may be overheard and remembered, but those who have been present at the recitation of the covenant with the goddess, which is never written down even in their own language, cannot doubt that they fulfill with diligence this requirement of the pact.

They slay indiscriminately the rich and the poor man, but prefer the rich for the bounty of his possessions falling into their hands. Householders they do not kill, even when it would be a thing of surpassing ease. The death of a local man would swiftly raise an outcry in the village or town before the caravan of yellow wagons could move sufficiently far away to be free from suspicion. The men of the villages may eat with them, lie with their women who choose to prostitute themselves, and even insult or beat them, with no fear of death at their hands, so perfect is their control over their passions in this matter essential to their union with the goddess. This, in spite of their hot blood, which is in other respects ungovernable.

Another part of the covenant states that each man before his twenty-ninth year must offer his first child to the prolific goat. Failure to do so invites the wrath of Shub-Niggurath, which descends in the form of profound ill fortune that soon has fatal consequences. So fearful are the men of this forfeiture that those who are by their natures unfit to engender children, which sometimes happens due to injury or disease of the genitals, seek to steal the children of the towns through which they pass that they may formally adopt the infants as their own, and so present them in the rite of the companion of the soul in their third day of life. Only babes in their first three days after birth are at risk of this abduction. They are stolen from their cribs, even from under the soft breaths of their sleeping mothers, and in their place the thief leaves a stone. This has given rise in some lands to the fable that spirits of the fields and trees steal children, a fiction that the crafty race, who are always quick to tell traveler's tales for money, go to great lengths to encourage.

If a man has a child that is unfit in mind or body, he may seek to exchange it with the child of a householder rather than slay it with his own hand. Infants who are severely deformed or deaf or blind are put to death soon after birth; only if the mother is tender of heart and implores her husband to spare the life of the babe will he substitute the imperfect infant for one that is sound of limb and in possession of all its senses. In these cases, when a child is stolen from a town, in place of a stone the malformed child is left in the cradle. This they do seldom, for it invites an outcry against them, and those who indulge this whim are severely punished by the elders.

Virgins give their virtue to the service of the goddess within a year of the onset of the menses, while assisting in the rite of the companion, and in return, in accord with the terms of the covenant, they are gifted by Shub-Niggurath with the power of second sight, without the need to consume the white spiders in the fungus caves of the Empty Space. All the women of this race can see the presence of the walking dead as clearly as their cats, and are aware when demons move among them. They have great skill at divining the future. Their preferred method is by the lines in the hand, but they also use a technique of divination that exists nowhere else, which they claim was taught to them by the goddess herself.

It is a divination by means of the stars and the earth. Seven flat pebbles are painted in red ink that resembles blood with signs that express the seven lords of the Old Ones and their affinities with the seven wandering bodies of the heavens. The sign of Cthulhu shows two opposed ax heads; that of Shub-Niggurath resembles a tree; the sign of Yog-Sothoth is three interlocking rings; the sign of Yig shows two rows of triangular teeth; that of Nyarlathotep is a pair of serpents entwined; the sign of Dagon resembles interlocked crescents of the moon; that of Azathoth depicts a lidless eye.

These are cast within a circle drawn in the dust of the ground that has a cross through its center, so that it is divided into four quadrants. The Thugian women understand this circle to represent the twelve houses of the stars, and although it has only four divisions, each quarter is assumed to be further subdivided into three

Signs of the seven lords of the Old Ones

wedges from its point that correspond with the three houses in that quarter of the zodiac.

By observing where the pebbles fall upon the circle and their relationship with one another, the women who conduct this art read the answer to the question asked. The quadrant of the circle on the lower left is given to the houses of the Ram, the Bull, and the Twins; that on the lower right to the houses of the Crab, the Lion, and the Virgin; that on the upper-right to the houses of the Scales, the Scorpion, and the Archer; that on the upper left to the houses of the Sea Goat, the Water Bearer, and the Fishes.

As an example of the practice, if, by the casting of the stones, the pebble bearing the sign of the planet Mars, which is joined with the nature of Cthulhu, should fall upon the house of the Scorpion, its action is considered strong, for this is the native house of Mars. And so by the strengths and weaknesses that astrologers ascribe to the heavens is this foretelling of events conducted upon the bosom of the earth.

They call the names of the seven lords the secret names of the planets, believing these names to be remembered only by their race and forgotten by all the rest of humanity. They have preserved corrupt voicings of them in their oral histories, though only the name of Shub-Niggurath is accurately expressed. Of the natures and appearances of the seven lords they know little. They confuse the Old Ones with the wandering bodies of the heavens, and make no distinction between the planets and the gods when speaking about them. To their philosophy, Shub-Niggurath and the Morning Star are one and the same.

These pebbles they use in another way, for works of malefic magic. When the women who make them harbor hatred toward any person not of their race, they wait for that person to pass, hiding behind a wall or hedge with one of these stones in their hand. As their enemy goes by, they spit on the stone and hurl it so that it strikes the person, then slink away silently, for it is their belief that if they are discovered in this action the spell will come to nothing. They hold that the stone invokes ill fortune upon the head of whomever it strikes, and sometimes will throw them at cattle, or horses, or even at barns and other buildings. Locals who are hit by these stones believe them to be hurled by jinn or other spirits of the hills, and abhor them as unnatural things.

The type of misfortune depends upon the stone chosen for the spell. The stone of Cthulhu provokes disputes and violent injury; that of Shub-Niggurath brings impotence or unhappiness in love affairs; that of Yog-Sothoth breeds family discords; that of Yig provokes infirmity of the body; that of Nyarlathotep causes loss of wealth; that of Dagon, madness; that of Azathoth, the failure of an enterprise.

Soul Bottles

There would be little purpose in a traveler well versed in the arts of necromancy to keep company with the chosen people of Shub-Niggurath unless they possessed some teaching of value that was not to be obtained elsewhere, for they are a treacherous race and conceal their malice well until the moment of its execution; nor can any man truly assert that he is their friend, unless he is of their blood. The magic of the women is a trivial art unworthy of acquisition, save for a single skill known only to this barbarous cult, the manufacture of soul bottles.

In return for their faith, their obscene goddess has taught them a magic in which the souls of the dead may be summoned and captured within bottles of glass, even as magicians of our own race contain the jinn in rings and brazen vessels. A soul imprisoned by this skill is enslaved to the owner of the bottle, and all the wisdom it possessed during life, as well as its knowledge of life after death, becomes available upon inquiry. The captured soul does not readily give up its secrets, but when the bottle is heated over a fire, the soul suffers the torments of hell and is soon willing to accommodate the wishes of its master.

The souls speak by means of a small lead weight attached within the bottle at the end of a length of silken thread, so that the weight hangs near the side of the bottle. When a question is asked, the lead moves and strikes the side of the glass, causing a sound like a crystal bell. By listening to the tinkling of the glass with a mind made open and vacant, the voice of the soul is heard speaking the answer to the question. Only the owner of the bottle can discern the voice of the soul, for to others it seems merely a meaningless tinkling. The act of making the bottle binds its maker and the soul captured within it so that they have a shared understanding, and each is enabled to comprehend the words of the other.

In appearance, these bottles are no more than half a cubit in height and a span in width, with straight sides and a leather stopper sealed with green wax. The glass is colorless and transparent, and within the vessel there is a swirling vapor resembling smoke that never ceases to curl and fall. The lower portion of the bottle is filled with the urine of its maker, for it is the belief of the women of the Thugians that urine provides a tangible body for the captured soul, and without it the soul would be too insubstantial to hold in any material receptacle. Into the urine they place bits of hair, skin, fingernails, or bone from the corpse of the person whose soul they wish to enslave, and also a few drops of their own blood, shed during the ritual by which the soul is attracted.

The ritual is invariably performed during the new moon, which is the darkest night of the month, when the forces of Shub-Niggurath are at their most potent and are able to move freely across the surface of our world. The sorceress inscribes with black ink upon the palm of her left hand the true name of the soul she seeks to capture, and upon the palm of her right hand her own true name. The true name is the name given a man or woman by the parents that engendered him, or in the case of the slave, by the master who owns him. She takes herself to a high place open beneath the stars. Placing the bits stolen from the corpse into the open bottle, she urinates into the bottle so that her urine is hot during the ritual, for if it loses its warmth before the ritual is enacted, the magic will have no force to compel the presence of the soul. She does this by the light of a candle or oil lamp, and later uses the flame to melt the green wax that seals the stopper once the soul is within its prison.

Having prepared the open bottle with her urine and the relics of the dead, she makes a small cut upon her left palm and allows seven drops of her blood to fall into the urine. Seven is the number of Shub-Niggurath, and in itself is an invocation to the goddess. She smears the blood across her right palm by folding her hands together, then grasps the bottle tightly, pressing the inscribed names on her palms against its sides so that she feels the warmth of her urine on her fingers. She leans her face over the mouth of the bottle and breathes her warm breath into it, as she speaks the true name of the dead. This she does seven times, and holds within her mind an image of the person whose soul she desires. Then she speaks this incantation:

"I am _____, I am the master of the bottle, I am the urine of the bottle, I am the blood of the bottle. Enter herein, _____, by your true name I invoke you, by the heat of this urine I summon you, by the fire in this blood I compel you. I call you from the nether reaches between the stars, I call you from the highest heavens, I call you from the lowest hells. You must obey. I am the child of Shub-Niggurath, by the power of my mother, you must obey. By these words made flesh, you must obey."

The sorceress then spits into the bottle while thinking the name of the dead, and elevates it toward the night sky. The soul forms in a cloud of silver mist above its open mouth and slowly, as though unwilling but unable to resist, it swirls downward into the bottle. At once the maker of the charm allows the lead weight to hang down the inner side of the vessel so that it is just above the surface of the urine, then while holding its silken thread into position against the rim of the bottle, places the stopper over its mouth and strikes it into place with her left palm so that her blood is impressed into its surface. She melts a stick of wax over the flame of her lamp and allows the wax to drip over the stopper so that its surface is wholly covered by wax.

When the bottle is properly formed, its lead weight will begin to tinkle against the side of the glass immediately, and a white cloud will be visible within the vessel, but the soul will not acquire the power of speech for several nights. The shock of capture renders it insane, and it is not until it regains a measure of awareness concerning its condition that it regains the ability to understand a question that may be asked. This magic may be worked by man or woman, but among the wanderers the women use it most commonly, for the men have little to do with the arcane arts, apart from the rites performed in honor of their goddess.

The utilities of the soul bottle are several. First, it creates a servant that lends the power of its essence to the maker of the charm, so that the maker is strengthened, both physically in his own body and in the force of his will. With each additional soul captured, the power is enhanced. A magician with five or six soul bottles has the strength of two men, and is easily able to compel with the force of his mind the obedience of spiritual creatures of the lesser kind. Second, the possession of a soul bottle allows access to the secrets of the dead. Whatever the captured soul knew during life, and whatever it learned after death, is available to its master, who only needs to question it.

The greatest virtue of the soul bottle is not these gifts, precious though they may be, but the suffering it inflicts upon the soul imprisoned within its depths. The torment of the bottle is greater than the torment of hell, even when the bottle is not heated over a flame to heighten the pain. A necromancer may use the soul bottle as a form of punishment upon his enemies. Those he could not strike down in life, he has the ability to torture after death. So long as the bottle remains intact, the agony of the soul remains unrelenting. The women among the Thugians use this charm not to capture the souls of their friends but to imprison the souls of their foes and bring them suffering.

The Lane of Scholars

Damascus lies like a shimmering jewel on the belly of the night when approached in the hours of early evening at the end of a long journey. Her ten thousand lamps illuminate the rooftops of her buildings and domes of her minarets, and dim the very stars in the heavens. The barking of her dogs, the soft murmur of voices from those seated in conversations at the thresholds of her houses, and the laughter arising from her taverns and inns combine to make a music of human companionship welcome to the ears of a man tired of travel. Surely no more pleasant city in which to dwell exists in the world for those who possess wealth and the willingness to dispense it liberally in consideration for services.

A class of men known as procurers thrives in this city, for there are constant comings and goings of caravans and the streets are forever filled with those newly arrived who have no knowledge of where to sleep or how to obtain their evening meal. They are as helpless as babes, but for a small fee any of the hundreds of men who adopt this trade will guide them to whatever they require and make their lives pleasant. Nothing is unobtainable in Damascus; those who thirst for wine are quenched; those who flee boredom are entertained; those who lust after women are sated. Even the more obscure desires, which might arouse revulsion in other cities, are easily accommodated in this most beautiful paragon of commercial hospitality.

A newcomer seeking the purchase of a house has many splendid dwellings from which to choose, as the constant arrivals and departures from the city insure the continuing availability of property. In the northern quarter is a quiet street called the Lane of Scholars. Both sides of this winding, paved passage, which is scarcely wide enough to permit the progress of a single ox cart, are lined with walled houses notable for the lack of pretension in their entranceways, for they are little more than rough doors without windows or other adornments set in the unbroken walls that bound the street.

The inhabitants of the Lane of Scholars are seldom seen, and the people of Damascus seek to have as little contact with them as they may, since they are reputed to be wizards engrossed behind their locked portals in the pursuit of arcane studies. Their servants, who never speak of the affairs of their masters, are seen entering the unassuming doors in the morning, carrying food and other goods in baskets from the marketplace; more rarely they are observed in the night leaving with strange bundles and returning with empty hands.

With the aid of an astute procurer the traveler newly arrived in the city, who wishes to remain for a period of years and to pursue the necromantic arts, will be offered the purchase of any one of several of these handsome dwellings that happen at that time to be available. The amenities of the houses, apart from minor variations in appearance, are quite similar. Each possesses its own rear garden of fruit trees and shaded walkways. Their windows are placed high to catch the breezes at sunset, which flow down their marbel halls and stairs and cool even the lowest chamber, and their high walls shut out the noises and foulness of the city. The houses are in three levels, and beneath them are cellars suitable for storage or activities requiring privacy.

In such a house a man skilled in the secret arts, and as a consequence having no difficulty in obtaining as many pieces of gold as he requires, can dwell in peace and luxury, and can pursue his studies unobserved by the ignorant. Everything is to be had for a price in Damascus, even the soldiers who patrol the streets at night, who may easily be induced to become deaf to the cries of pain or terror that emanate at times from the great houses by which they pass on their watches.

The procurer will make available slaves and servants accustomed to fulfilling the needs of a practitioner of the higher mysteries. It is wise to have their tongues removed, if they have not already been cut out by previous masters, to insure that anything observed within the walls of the house cannot become a matter of idle gossip. The best slaves come from tribes on the northern coast of Africa, near the Pillars of Hercules. They have no compunction in dealing with corpses or opening graves, and are of a steady and unimaginative disposition. When treated with generosity they are loyal in the fulfillment of their duties.

A traveler newly arrived at Damascus who was versed in the necromantic arts purchased one of the houses in the Lane of Scholars for a fair sum through the agency of a procurer and began to follow his studies in security and peace. Having the need to dispose of a carcass, he determined to bury it in a corner of the cellar, a course of action requiring the least effort and likely to attract the least notice. Imagine his dismay when the floor of the cellar was opened, only to reveal such a density of bones piled upon bones that no space existed in which to insert the corpse. With reluctance, he had the floor closed over again by his servants, and caused the carcass to be carried to a communal burial pit beyond the northern gate of the city.

The holy men and nobles of Damascus know of the practices conducted in the Lane of Scholars, and in general disapprove of them, yet none are bold enough to accuse the residents of this quiet lane of unlawfulness without clear and material evidence, as they are fearful of the consequences of acting alone, without the outrage and support of the crowd in the marketplace. The enemies of wizards and necromancers are reputed not to live long and happy lives. Since all those who dwell in the Lane of Scholars are wealthy, and able to buy favors where needed to continue their studies unmolested, no action is taken against them, unless so bold and manifest a crime is committed that those charged with upholding the law cannot close their eyes, even should they prefer to do so.

On these rare occasions, it becomes prudent for the resident of the street who has come under accusation to close his house and leave for a period of months until the matter can be dealt with quietly through the payment of bribes to the leaders of the city, and should these bribes prove insufficient, through the hiring of assassins to remove those who seek to bring prosecution.

An unpleasantness of this kind is quite rare, and in general those who live in the Lane of Scholars are free to pursue whatever studies they choose. The cellars are deep enough to muffle the sound of chanting and even the loudest of screams. Each man tends to his own work, and does not inquire into the work of his neighbor. Should unpleasant incidents occur within the walls of a house, cleaners may be hired through procurers who are discrete and efficient at removing all traces of the event. It may truly be written that no more satisfactory or secure place exists in all the world for the necromancer to pursue his chosen profession.

The Secret of Damascus Steel

The secrets of the city of Damascus are many, for it is one of the oldest cities in this world that is the work of the hands of men. None is more coveted by other lands than the making of Damascus steel, which is both stronger and more supple than the steel of any other city. Swords forged of this steel will not break in combat, but will cut through the blades of lesser steels as though they were bronze, and will shear through the shields and armor of the foe. These blades are so greedily coveted by warriors that they command a high price in the houses of the greatest swordmakers, and even to the wealthy are difficult to obtain due to their acclaim, for no sooner is a blade forged than it is sold, sometimes before it has even had time to cool from the fire.

The weaponsmiths of Damascus guard their secrets well, knowing that every other city in the world would rejoice to be the source of such fine steel, but the secret they keep best is one that few would believe, and it is this: that Damascus steel is not created in Damascus. It is imported from the Lebanon by the sword makers of the city, and is only to be had from a small village on the coast of the sea that is the home for a clan of bold traders. Neither do they make the steel, but obtain it in the form of ingots of the size and shape of the extended hand, which are beaten into blades by the smiths of Damascus. In truth, there is no fire hot enough to melt Damascus steel in the entire city, not even in the largest forge; the most that can be done is to heat the ingots until they glow and become pliable, then to beat them and fold the steel with hammers, lapping it over itself many times and hammering it until its layers are as fine as gold leaf and join together under the influence of the fire.

The swords of Damascus are made in Damascus, but the steel comes from a source unguessed by those who wield them in battle. If the traveler to this city strikes up an acquaintance with a weaponsmith, and gains his trust, eventually he will see the smith meet with a pair of strangers who come from the Lebanon in an ox-drawn cart heavily laden with steel ingots. They take no pains to protect their load, precious though it is, since it would be of no use to any other city, for just as it is true that no fire of man can smelt Damascus steel, it is equally so that only the forges of this city are hot enough to soften it to be shaped by the hammer. It would be valueless to the smiths of any other land, save perhaps those of the distant land of Cathay, who are fabled to be cunning in the making of steel.

These traders from the Lebanon are uncouth in appearance and vulgar of speech, but fond of wine, though reluctant to pay for it from their own purses. They allow any man in the tavern to buy for them and never buy for others in return of the courtesy, so that they are unpopular with the men of the city. Perhaps it is because they are strange of aspect, having broad heads and unnaturally wide mouths that resemble the mouths of frogs, and bulging eyes that protrude from their flattened skulls. Their hands are moist to the touch, and their cheeks and necks always wet with the sweat from their bodies; yet notwithstanding this continual exuding of moisture, their skin is cool. They must drink prodigiously to replace the moisture they lose by day and by night, and for this reason haunt the taverns after their business has been transacted.

It is difficult though not impossible to intoxicate these strange traders, if the wine purchased for them is fortified and the strongest that may be had in Damascus, and then they will begin to speak of their home with longing to return to it, and express their discomfort at being so far from the sea, which they love as their mother. The story of the steel cannot be drawn out in one night, and is never given in all its details, but a patient man who has knowledge of arcane matters is able, after several nights of excess in the taverns, to gather the pieces of the tale, which is not long to write.

The village of the traders is known as Shaalon, and is inhabited by some twelve score of families who are all related by blood. They have made their livelihoods from the sea since before the memory of history, and none knows when their village was founded, but since before the recollection of the eldest man they have been traders and fishermen. Both trades flourish to an astonishing degree that is the envy of other villages on the coast, and those not native to Shaalon set this down to good luck, but the real cause is the association of the villagers with the Deep Ones, the children of Dagon, who dwell in the sea not many leagues from the shore.

The inhabitants of Shaalon trade not only with men but with the Deep Ones, who have formed bonds of marriage and blood with the villagers. This is not strange when it is known that the Deep Ones admire the beauty of our women more than the beauty of their own kind. In this way the blood of the Deep Ones and the blood of the villagers has mingled for a thousand years or more. The Deep Ones trade with them the riches of the sea and drive fish into their nets to insure for them abundant catches, and in return the villagers trade with them all the objects and substances of the dry lands that the Deep Ones desire, such as fine and brightly colored silks; for they love adornment and decorate their bodies with jewelry and such cloths as are able to resist the effects of sea water.

It is from the Deep Ones that the villagers obtain the ingots of steel that are shaped in Damascus into weapons of war. They have revealed to the men of Shaalon the manner of their making, having no secrets from those on the land they regard as their blood relations, and in drunkenness the traders may be induced to tell the way of it. The Deep Ones say that into the sea fall many stones from the stars having hearts of metal, some as small as an olive and others as large as a wagon. Upon the floor of the ocean they lie. The Deep Ones gather them, having the ability to recognize them by a kind of sound which they emit; so the traders report, though it can scarcely be a sound heard by the ears. Having brought them together, they take them to vents in the bottom of the sea where the fires of the earth are hotter than the hottest forge, and in these vents smelt them into ingots.

So say the Deep Ones to the men of Shaalon, and it is well-known to scholars that they excel all others in this world in the making of fine works in metals; for the women of the Deep Ones adorn themselves with jewelry in cunningly elaborated curls and delicate scales of gold, set with numerous precious stones, and these they wear upon their heads, and sometimes on their wrists. This vanity is affected alike both by those women wholly of the pure blood of the Deep Ones and by those of mixed blood. In return for the ingots of steel, the villagers trade colored stones to be set in their adornments, which are also enhanced by the presence of many fine pearls of surpassing luster.

Such is the secret of Damascus steel, kept close by the sword makers of that city as much in shame and in ignorance as in greed, for they cannot bear to admit that the smelting of the steel is beyond their talents, and they never question the traders from Shaalon closely for fear that they may lose access to their precious wagon-load of ingots. Hence the men who shape the steel know nothing of its fashioning beneath the waves or its origin amongst the stars. Should the single wagon that brings it from the Lebanon fail to come to Damascus, the entire trade in the steel would cease, so tenuous is the basis for this famed industry.

The Burial Ground at Damascus

Life in Damascus is filled with luxury and variety of every imaginable kind. No diversion is too obscure or too decadent, provided there is wealth to compensate the procurer who provides it. Those who seek a more refined entertainment will discover it at the university, where stimulating conversation is to be had daily on any matter of philosophy or mathematics or history. Attractive servants and fine furnishings are easily acquired, the stalls in the book markets groan under the weight of rare works on alchemy, necromancy, and other arcane topics, and witty acquaintances flock to the banquet table of a householder able to provide lavish feasts and diverting entertainment.

One precious commodity alone is difficult to obtain in this wonder of cities: the blessing of solitude. Locked behind the gate of the house at night, alone in a chamber of contemplation, the bark of dogs, the grunts of camels, the drunken songs of men, the beckoning cries of whores, all drift to the ear from beyond the windows, borne on the coolness of the night breeze. It is impossible to completely shut out an awareness of the great multitude of souls that press on every side like the waters of a rising tide.

On nights when the air scarcely stirs, and the heat suffocates the breath, the traveler who has wandered the wilderness of the Empty Space in his youth may feel a restlessness that compels him, as in a waking dream, to cast his cloak and cowl around his limbs and seek the silence of the dark that can only be found beyond the walls of the city. Perhaps it is a similar restless urge that compels Nyarlathotep to walk up and down upon the sands beneath the moon.

The best place for contemplation is the burial ground of the commoners of the city, which lies some distance beyond the northern gate. The shades of the dead are congenial companions to the necromancer, and they never speak, unless given the power to express themselves by the spilling of fresh blood. There is little reason for a necromancer to evoke their voices, for what could they speak that would be of value? The nobles of Damascus place their honored dead in elaborate and costly tombs that are difficult to force, but the common laborers and vagabonds content themselves with a shallow grave in a stony field.

A necromancer who had taken upon himself the duties and responsibilities of a householder in the Lane of Scholars one night heeded the call of the Empty Space and left the city to wander among the dead beyond the north gate, far from the lights of the watchtowers. As he left the noises and smells of Damascus behind, he felt the keenness of his senses reawaken and the stealthiness of his step return. The skills so dearly bought with pain and blood in the desert of his youth were not dead but had only been sleeping.

A clan of ghouls of the number of a score or more silently surrounded him as he stood, lost in silent contemplation of the stars. He paid them little attention. They were fat city ghouls, less dangerous than the lean and hungry ghouls of the desert. He seemed to them a man of the city, slow and weak, and they intended to slay him for intruding upon their territory and interrupting their nightly feeding upon the dead. The necromancer made no sign that he knew of their approach as they ringed him with their claws raised. The desert had made his eyesight keen, and he saw the stars reflected in the eyes in their upturned faces, and the gleam of their teeth.

When they rushed upon him, he killed several without emotion, merely to teach the rest a fitting respect. It gratified him to learn that he still possessed the old skills with a knife that had served him so well for so many years. There is little need for a man of wealth to kill with a knife, for he can hire others to do the killing in his stead;

yet even when the need is gone, the pleasure in such killing does not vanish. The ghouls fell to their hands and knees and fawned upon the hem of his black cloak like dogs, as they made apology in their rough voices for their error.

It amused the traveler to cast off his cloak and cowl so that the ghouls could see by starlight the tattoos of power on his limbs and back, and the scares and mutilations of the torturers of Yemen. They danced and howled about his feet, proclaiming him their new lord. To this he said nothing, neither accepting nor denying the rank, for who can know when a clan of ghouls may prove useful? With his knife he helped them dig the earth from a recent grave and raise the corpse. The cutting away of the shroud revealed it to be the body of a fat matron of some fifty years, dead no more than three days. The ghouls honored him by withdrawing and allowing him the first strip of flesh.

How can the savor of human flesh be described to those who have never tasted it upon their tongues? It is like color to the blind, or music to the deaf. Ibn Schacabao writes that the taste is like the flesh of the barnyard fowl, but with this absurdity he shows that he has never eaten of man, for the flavor is more akin to that of the pig. Only with the first succulent bit in his mouth, and after he began to chew, did the traveler who was now a householder realize how dearly he had missed the taste. The flesh of a man newly slain is tough, but the flesh of a corpse that has rested in the grave for several days becomes tender and easy to cut with the teeth.

In an instant of awareness the necromancer realized that this was his true home: the grave, the night, the wilderness, the stars, the harsh stones, the scent of freshly turned earth, the softly laughing breeze, the chittering of insects, the grunts of the ghouls and the sound of their dry, sliding skin as they fed. The house in the Lane of Scholars was no more than a passing dream, a thing without permanence or importance, a diversion in which to spend the years of old age in comfort. When it was fallen to dust, the desert would remain unchanged and eternal, awaiting his return. The *Roba el Khaliyeh* is a patient lover who never betrays the trust of those who adore her.

The Conclusion to the Journey

Having reached the great city of Damascus, and having time to indulge in its pleasures and partake of its advantages, the traveler may decide to make it his home and forego wandering, even as did the writer of this book many years ago. Numerous are the ways that lead to Damascus, and few are the prizes that cannot be obtained within its walls or that fail to make their way through its gates, for it is a center of trade for all the lands of the world. The traveler who spent his youth seeking in distant lands for arcane wisdom and rare objects may conclude that it is wiser to allow these things to find their way to him. Wealth is a lodestone, and that which is desired is drawn to it like bits of straw.

The road that begins in the nation of Yemen, and winds its way across the trackless Empty Space and through the passageways of the nameless city beneath Irem, over the Red Sea to Egypt from its Delta to its Cataracts, from Alexandria to the barren plains of Babylon, and at last to the glittering city of Damascus, is long and hard, yet replete with wonders, and which traveler is so base as to regret following it? No so the writer of this book, whom I declare openly to be Abdul Alhazred, a poet by birth of Yemen, who walked it joyously in his youth and who now resides at his ease in Damascus in just such a great house in the Lane of Scholars as has been described.

With poignant melancholy of heart he remembers the intimacies of the *Roba el Khaliyeh*, who reveals her secrets so reluctantly to her lovers, but in her harshness teaches well the lessons that must be learned if breath is to be retained in the body. Upon the rock of those cruel but necessary lessons he built the house of his life, and by guile and craft acquired the wisdom of the portals and the knowledge of the Elder Seal. With courage and cunning he pillaged the forbidden secrets of the deep places of the world, and stole the language of the Old Ones and the shapes of their seals, yet no malice of sorcery, no power of gods or demons, no assassin of men was equal to the task of halting his quest. Which other scribe would dare to reveal the matters written in these pages, for even to speak of these things would be certain death to one unprotected by wards of magic of the greatest potency. Fools call him mad because he speaks of mysteries beyond their comprehension; he laughs defiance at the vulgar and uses them as his cattle, and cares nothing for their opinion, for he is truly beyond all hurt.

By his necromancy he has rendered himself deathless, and though he appears outwardly to age, his body remains forever youthful and strong. If, by some mischance, his body were shattered into pieces, and death came upon him in such a way that it could not be forestalled, he would rise again, such is the command he has of the arts of the grave; for from his essential salts he would rise, and the bones that once wore flesh would be clothed in flesh anew. He fears not the assassins of the Sons of Sirius, who ever seek to penetrate his walls as punishment for his theft of their precious scrolls, for his walls are impregnable to men; nor does he concern himself with the wandering bands that worship Shub-Niggurath who threaten him because of his revelation of the secrets of her covenant; the malice of the captive spawn of Cthulhu, which has never forgiven him for his betrayal beneath the library of the monastery of the magi, is his amusement, for what power has that being entrapped within its iron cage?

For as long as his essential salts persist upon the face of this world, so long shall the poet endure and mock his enemies in verse. There is no death that would erase his substance so utterly that he cannot arise renewed and reborn. It is in this dual assurance of impregnability and immortality that he offers his journey of life within